The AS/400

&

Microsoft® Office

Integration Handbook

The AS/400

&

Microsoft® Office

Integration Handbook

Brian Singleton

with Colleen Garton

First Edition
Second Printing—September 1999

Technical Editor Joe Hertvik

© 1998 Midrange Computing
ISBN: 1-883884-49-7

Midrange Computing
5650 El Camino Real, Suite 225
Carlsbad, CA 92008
www.midrangecomputing.com

V4R2
Microsoft Office 97

To my brother Devin, the funniest guy I know. . .

—Brian Singleton

For Mum, for everything.

—Colleen Garton

Contents

Acknowledgments

The following people have helped immensely in the creation of this book. Without them, it would not have been possible.

Colleen Garton

Steven Bolt

Joe Hertvik

Merrikay Lee

David Uptmor

Introduction

Welcome to *The AS/400 & Microsoft® Office Integration Handbook*. This book describes some of the techniques you can use to unite applications in the Microsoft Office 97 product suite with data from your AS/400. If you've been around the AS/400 world for awhile, you'll recognize that it always hasn't been easy to retrieve data from the AS/400 for use with other systems. PC support, IBM's old solution to PC connectivity, was often cumbersome to use and not very flexible. Furthermore, productivity applications, such as word processors and spreadsheets, weren't designed to offer a great amount of flexibility for interfacing with external data.

Luckily, all of that has changed. IBM's Client Access for Windows 95/NT is a very capable tool that provides you with seamless integration between Windows desktops and AS/400 information.

COMBINING CAPABILITIES

Combining the presentation capabilities of Microsoft Office with the database capabilities of the AS/400 provides the best of both worlds. For example—using the Microsoft Access report writer—you can create reports that use live AS/400 data in a fraction of the time that it would take you to create them on the AS/400. And they look better to boot. You're reading the right book if you've ever:

❖ Looked at an AS/400's output and thought to yourself, "Gee, I wish I could use my PC data formatting tools on this AS/400 data."

❖ Wondered about an easier way to make nice-looking reports with AS/400 data.

❖ Wanted to use visual query tools to point and click the creation of sophisticated information output.

ABOUT THIS BOOK

The first section of this book introduces you to the various methods you can use to retrieve data from the AS/400 using IBM's Client Access. Some of these methods are easier or better than others for retrieving data. You can decide which one works best in your situation.

Chapter 1 looks at using Client Access to integrate AS/400 data with Microsoft Office applications. This chapter provides a brief overview of some of the issues you should be aware of when installing and configuring Client Access to retrieve data from your AS/400.

Chapters 2 through 8 describe individual methods used to move data between the AS/400 and your PC and Microsoft Office. While the main focus is on ODBC, which provides the most seamless method of AS/400 integration with Microsoft Office, other methods covered include the data transfer function and the network drive functionality of Client Access.

We'll take a look at the Client Access Data Transfer Function, which is a component of Client Access that allows you to retrieve data from your AS/400 and store it in PC files. Also included is information on how TCP/IP's FTP file transfer function can be used to bring data to your PC.

For each of the Office applications that easily can use AS/400 data, there's a specific chapter devoted to showing you how the two can be used together. For example, Microsoft Word easily can be used to create mailing labels, form letters, and envelopes from data on your AS/400. With Microsoft Excel, you can bring data into spreadsheets, perform calculations on the data, and even refresh the data to retrieve updated information with just a mouse click.

Microsoft Query, included with Office, is a helper application that provides sophisticated querying and data-retrieval capabilities. While Query can be used as a stand-alone application, when combined with another Office application such as Word or Excel, its capabilities really start to shine.

Access is a veritable Swiss army knife when it comes to managing data. Its many features include the capability to query AS/400 data and to create beautiful, sophisticated reports. Wizards even lead you through the process.

Outlook is the e-mail client and personal-information manager included with the Office suite. A very powerful tool, Outlook's many uses include retrieving e-mail from the AS/400 when the AS/400 is set up as an e-mail server.

As you will see, the combination of the AS/400 and Microsoft Office gives you a powerful set of useful tools that can be leveraged in many different ways to make your job of delivering information easier. Without further ado, let's dive right in!

1

Client Access Overview

Before you can grab data from your AS/400 using Client Access and place it into the Office applications, you must have a correct installation of Client Access (or another third-party AS/400 connectivity package). You also must have an AS/400 connection configured. It pays to take a few minutes to get to know what options are available to you and what you can do to maximize convenience and productivity when exchanging data between Microsoft Office and the AS/400.

First, consider the options available when you install Client Access. You might be surprised to know that—even if you didn't pay for Client Access—a lot of its functionality is available. For example, you can use ODBC, a Client Access component that doesn't require a license, to retrieve data from the AS/400.

CLIENT ACCESS COMPONENTS

Client Access is a collection of tools that perform different functions to help PCs and AS/400s interact. Several of these components are useful for moving data between an AS/400 and a PC. Take a look at some of the more prominent Client Access components. I have ranked them in what I think is the order of importance in connecting to Microsoft Office applications:

❖ **ODBC**. As shown in Figure 1-1, ODBC is part of the base support of Client Access, and it is one of the primary methods used by the Microsoft Office applications to retrieve data from external data sources such as the AS/400. ODBC is covered throughout this book. See chapter 2 for detailed information on ODBC.

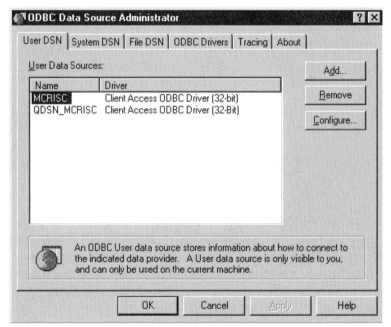

Figure 1-1: ODBC is part of the Client Access base support.

❖ **Data-Transfer Function**. The data-transfer function (Figure 1-2), formerly known as the file-transfer function, is another useful method for retrieving data from the AS/400 for Office applications. While not quite as flexible as ODBC, it is a solution that stands by itself; no additional programs are required to bring AS/400 data to your PC. It also easily can be automated, and it has a specific function for bringing data into Microsoft Excel. See chapter 9 for more information on the data-transfer function.

❖ **Network Drives**. The Client Access network-drive function (Figure 1-3), a replacement for PC Support's old shared folders, allows you to access your AS/400 system as if it were just another server on your network. While it might not be the speediest solution, it has a lot to offer in terms of convenience. See chapter 8 for more information on the network-drive function.

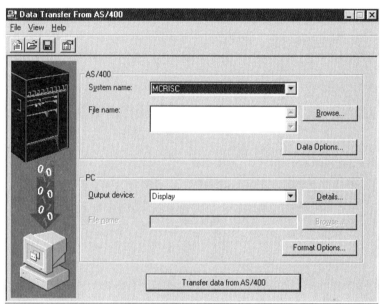

Figure 1-2: The data-transfer function

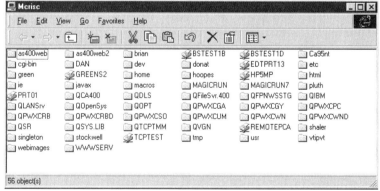

Figure 1-3: The Client Access network drive function.

Network drives, data-transfer function, and ODBC are the three main Client Access components for actually transferring data between the AS/400 and a PC. Some additional components—useful in other circumstances, such as performing configuration operations—are:

❖ **The Operations Navigator.**The Operations Navigator (Figure 1-4) is an excellent tool for managing your AS/400 in many different aspects. It gives the AS/400 a graphical user interface and can greatly ease such common tasks as managing users, setting system and resource security, and configuring system options

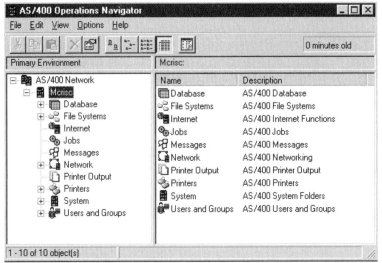

Figure 1-4: The Operations Navigator.

❖ **PC5250**. The terminal emulator (Figure 1-5) included with Client Access is called PC5250. It is the portal to the familiar AS/400 green screen. As such, it is probably the most frequently used component of Client Access.

CLIENT ACCESS LICENSES

As of V3R7, IBM provides—as part of the base OS/400 operating system—some of the Client Access functionality without requiring the purchase of a Client Access license. This can have a great effect on the tools you use to retrieve data from Microsoft Office applications. Figure 1-6 shows a dialogue screen displayed during the installation of Client Access.

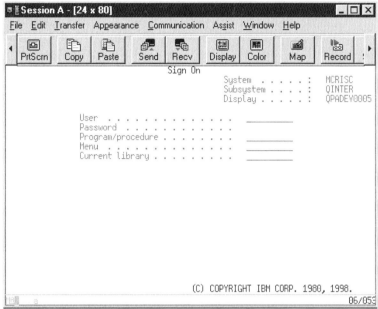

Figure 1-5: The terminal emulator included with Client Access.

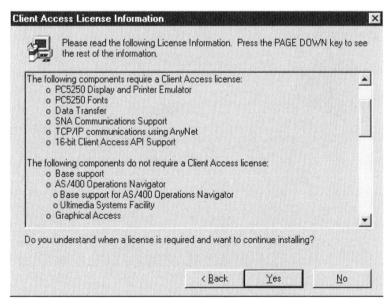

Figure 1-6: The Client Access license requirements dialog.

The screen details which components require a license and which don't.

The main Client Access component used for AS/400 and Microsoft Office data integration is ODBC. Fortunately, ODBC is one of the no-charge Client Access options. Unless IBM's license agreements have changed since this book was published, you should be able to install and use the Client Access ODBC driver without worrying whether or not you are in violation of a license agreement.

Other tools that fall into the "no-license" category are the network-drive function and the Operations Navigator. As mentioned previously, both of these tools are useful when interacting with the AS/400.

Both the network drive function and ODBC are part of Client Access base support, which is always installed when Client Access is installed. The tools in the list (shown in Figure 1-6) that do require a Client Access license are the data-transfer function and the PC5250 terminal emulator.

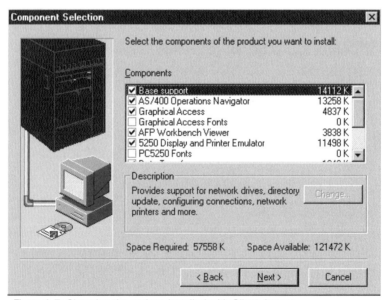

Figure 1-7: Choosing the options installed with Client Access.

INSTALLING MS OFFICE INTEGRATION

Installing Client Access is much like installing any other Windows application. The setup program leads you through several screens to determine which aspects of Client Access you want to install (Figure 1-7).

Before you install Client Access, be aware of the list of components that are included as part of Client Access base support. Base support must be installed when a Client Access installation is performed, and it has some rather potent components included. Here is a partial list of the components:

❖ Network-drive function.

❖ ODBC.

❖ Network printer support.

If you are using only menu-level security on your AS/400, the network-drive function opens up a can of worms for you because it can be used to point and click to delete AS/400 items. Because the network-drive function is always installed when Client Access is installed, and it is integrated immediately with the Windows desktop, you really must be sure that your AS/400's security is adequate. Be sure to read chapter 8 for additional information.

Figure 1-8: Connections are created with the AS/400 CONNECTIONS program.

CONFIGURING MS OFFICE INTEGRATION

Before you can use Client Access to retrieve your AS/400 data, you must create a connection to your AS/400. The place to begin is the AS/400 CONNECTIONS icon in the Client Access program folder (Figure 1-8).

The process for creating the connection is covered in great detail in the *Client Access For Windows 95/NT Setup Guide*. The *Guide* is available from many IBM sources, including the AS/400 Online Library at http://as400bks. rochester. ibm.com/.

When using Client Access to retrieve data for use with Microsoft Office, one configuration item to be aware of is the DEFAULT USER ID parameter that you set during the creation of the connection. If you enter an AS/400 user profile for this parameter, that user profile will be used by default to establish a connection with the AS/400.

The DEFAULT USER ID (Figure 1-9) is important because, under Windows 95, password caching will allow some Client Access functionality to start automatically without requiring

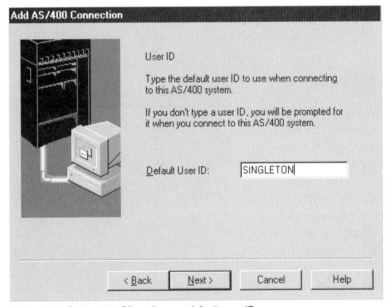

Figure 1-9: Setting the Client Access default user ID.

an explicit AS/400 sign-on. For example, the network drive function of Client Access requires that a user be validated on the AS/400 before the drive function can be accessed in the Network Neighborhood.

If you enter your AS/400 user profile in the Default User ID parameter the first time that a connection is established, Client Access prompts for a password. By default, Windows 95 automatically remembers the password. Therefore, the next time that connection is made, you won't need to enter your password (unless you start the connection from the "AS/400 Connections" screen).

While the default user-identification feature can be turned off, you must be aware that it's on by default. In this case, an added convenience value also can be a security concern.

2

ODBC

You might have heard of ODBC. It is a "glue" that binds various types of databases with various types of clients. Microsoft Office makes extensive use of ODBC to connect to the AS/400 and retrieve data. This chapter shows you how to configure the Client Access for Windows 95/NT ODBC driver for use with Microsoft Office. It also covers the security issues involved with client server technologies like ODBC. And, there are some AS/400-specific ODBC tips as well.

WHAT IS ODBC?

ODBC is an acronym for Open Database Connectivity. It's a data-access standard created by Microsoft and other vendors to allow application programs to access data from any type of database that supports the standard. It's also one of IBM's preferred means of client/server connectivity for the AS/400. Because combined support from industry giants such as IBM and Microsoft ensures that ODBC will be a perennial standard for database access, it is worth your while spending a little time gaining an understanding of how ODBC works.

With step-by-step instructions, this chapter explains how to configure the IBM Client Access for Windows 95/NT ODBC driver. Before you begin those steps, however, you'll need some background information on ODBC.

ARCHITECTURE

ODBC consists of three layers (Figure 2-1) that function together to bring the data to your application. These layers are the:

❖ Driver manager.

❖ ODBC driver.

❖ Data sources.

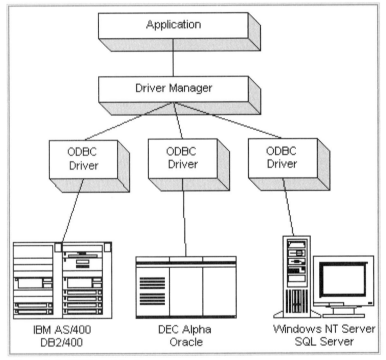

Figure 2-1: ODBC architecture.

The driver manager is a program that manages the individual ODBC drivers installed on your system. It provides the interface between the applications and the drivers, allows for the management of data sources, and handles some of the application programming functionality.

ODBC drivers are the programs that perform the translation between the external data source and the ODBC programming interface. There are specific drivers for many different data sources, including local PC database files and remote databases such as the AS/400.

There are AS/400 ODBC drivers available from—just to name a few product sources—IBM, Wall Data, NetSoft, StarQuest, and HiT Software. Each of these drivers differs slightly in capability, performance, and configuration, but all offer remote database access for ODBC compliant-application programs such as Microsoft Office. You can tell which ODBC drivers you have installed on your system by looking at the list of available drivers in the ODBC administrator program. To do this, click on the ODBC DRIVERS button as shown in Figure 2-2.

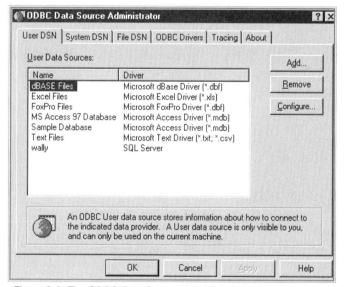

Figure 2-2: The ODBC Data Source Administrator screen.

One term you sometimes hear associated with an ODBC driver is *conformance level*. Conformance level refers to the level of the ODBC specification to which a particular ODBC driver complies, and it determines the capabilities that the ODBC driver provides and the functions that it supports.

Currently, the following ODBC conformance levels are defined: Core, Level 1, and Level 2. ODBC driver conformance levels are inclusive. If a particular driver complies with conformance Level 2, it also provides Core and Level 1 functionality.

Most applications require a driver that is Level 1 compliant or higher. Most of the AS/400 drivers on the market today are at least Level 1 compliant. Therefore, conformance level should not be an issue when connecting ODBC applications to the AS/400. It is, however, something to be aware of when shopping for an ODBC driver.

Another conformance level, called the *SQL conformance level*, indicates what type of SQL-92 grammar support is provided by the driver/database combination. SQL-92 is an industry standard that defines the capabilities and syntax of an SQL implementation. The conformance levels can be Entry (sometimes called Core), FIPS Transitional, Intermediate, or Full.

The final layer of the ODBC architecture is the data source. This is the layer that you deal with most often when retrieving data from the AS/400. Data sources are basically named connections to a database. When they are named, they are given the acronym DSN (Data Source Name).

DSNs are created from ODBC drivers to refer to a specific database or library on the AS/400. ODBC drivers can have many different settings (including default libraries, connection methods, etc.). When you create a DSN with the ODBC administrator program, these settings are stored with that data source. Therefore, the next time you want to access your data, you don't have to again enter the configuration information for the driver.

Under ODBC 3.0, there are three different types of data source names, or DSNs, in the 32-bit ODBC environment. Each type allows different access. The three types of DSNs are:

1. User DSNs.

2. System DSNs.

3. File DSNs.

As shown in Figure 2-2, there is a tab strip at the top of the ODBC driver manager screen that allows you to access the appropriate type. Keep in mind that:

❖ User DSNs are available only to the current user and other users who have authorized access to that user's objects.

❖ System DSNs are available to the operating system and anyone who is using the system.

❖ File DSNs are available to anyone using the system with the proper drivers installed.

For security purposes, user DSNs are helpful, for instance, if you need to create specific DSNs for a specific user and you do not want other users of the machine to be able to see the DSN. In this case, you would create a File DSN because that is the type used by Microsoft Query.

In the older versions of ODBC that ran under the Windows 3.x, 16-bit environments, all only DSN were basically equivalent to file DSNs.

Configuring a Client Access ODBC DSN Under Windows 95/NT

The ultimate goal of configuring ODBC is to create a DSN you can use when communicating between the AS/400 and ODBC-compliant PC applications. There are two steps to making sure that ODBC works to retrieve data from your AS/400. Step 1 is a one-time task that must be done on your AS/400. Step 2 must be done for each different area (AS/400 library or libraries) from which you want to retrieve data.

Step 1: Creating the AS/400 Directory Entry

Before you access your system through the Client Access ODBC driver, be sure you have a relational database directory entry for your local system. Do the following one-time procedure to make sure an entry exists on your system:

1. From an AS/400 command line, type WRKRDBDIRE and press the Enter key. You'll see a screen like the one shown in Figure 2-3.

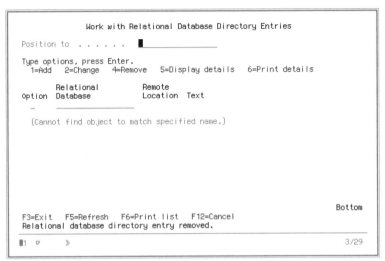

```
                     Work with Relational Database Directory Entries

    Position to  . . . . .  █_____

    Type options, press Enter.
      1=Add    2=Change    4=Remove    5=Display details    6=Print details

             Relational            Remote
    Option   Database              Location   Text

      _      _____

      [Cannot find object to match specified name.]




                                                                      Bottom
    F3=Exit    F5=Refresh    F6=Print list    F12=Cancel
    Relational database directory entry removed.
    _____
    █1   ▽      ≫                                              3/29
```

Figure 2-3: The WRKRDBDIRE command screen.

2. Look for an entry with a remote location of *LOCAL. If a local entry exists, you can skip steps 3 through 6 and continue with the Creating a Data Source section. If a local entry doesn't exist, continue with steps 3 through 6.

3. Determine your system's name. Enter DSPNETA at an AS/400 command line. This will display the screen as shown in Figure 2-4. Note the "current system name".

4. On the WRKRDBDIRE screen (Figure 2-3), put a 1 in the first line of the OPTION column. Type the name of your system in the RELATIONAL DATABASE column, and press the Enter key.

5. For the remote location, enter *LOCAL.

    Note: With OS/400 V4R2, there is a new parameter on this screen named Type. For the *LOCAL relational database directory entry, this parameter should be left blank.

6. Enter a description. The screen should look similar to the example shown in Figure 2-5. Press the Enter key.

That's how you create a directory entry for the local database. This one-time process is necessary for the CA ODBC driver to work correctly.

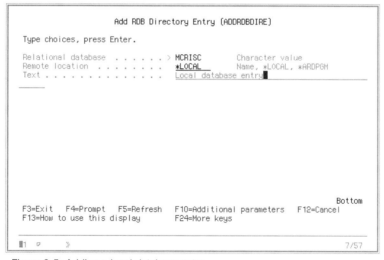

```
                    Display Network Attributes
                                                    System:   MCRISC
 Current system name  . . . . . . . . . . . . . :    MCRISC
   Pending system name  . . . . . . . . . . . . :
 Local network ID . . . . . . . . . . . . . . . :    APPN
 Local control point name . . . . . . . . . . . :    MCRISC
 Default local location . . . . . . . . . . . . :    MCRISC
 Default mode . . . . . . . . . . . . . . . . . :    BLANK
 APPN node type . . . . . . . . . . . . . . . . :    *NETNODE
 Data compression . . . . . . . . . . . . . . . :    *NONE
 Intermediate data compression  . . . . . . . . :    *NONE
 Maximum number of intermediate sessions  . . . :    200
 Route addition resistance  . . . . . . . . . . :    128
 Server network ID/control point name . . . . . :    *LCLNETID    *ANY




                                                    More...
 Press Enter to continue.

 F3=Exit   F12=Cancel

 1    ▽      »                                            1/1
```

Figure 2-4: Retrieving the system name.

```
                 Add RDB Directory Entry (ADDRDBDIRE)

 Type choices, press Enter.

 Relational database  . . . . . . > MCRISC        Character value
 Remote location  . . . . . . . .   *LOCAL        Name, *LOCAL, *ARDPGM
 Text . . . . . . . . . . . . . .   Local database entry




                                                            Bottom
 F3=Exit   F4=Prompt   F5=Refresh   F10=Additional parameters   F12=Cancel
 F13=How to use this display       F24=More keys

 1    ▽      »                                            7/57
```

Figure 2-5: Adding a local database entry.

Step 2: Creating a Data Source

The next step is to confirm that the Client Access ODBC driver is installed on your PC. Because it's automatically installed as part of the base support of Client Access 95/NT, if Client Access 95/NT is installed on your machine, you are ready to go. Otherwise, install the Client Access 95/NT AS/400 ODBC driver by following the instructions provided with Client Access. Once the driver is installed, you create a data source for that driver by using the ODBC administrator program.

> Note: The screens shown in the following steps were captured from version 3 of the ODBC administrator. If you have a different version of the administrator, your screens might vary slightly from those shown. Because the terminology and required steps are still the same, you should be able to follow along.

1. To create a data source that points to your AS/400 database, begin by starting the ODBC administrator program.

   ➪ To start the ODBC administrator, double click on the ODBC ADMINISTRATION icon in the Client Access folder. You also can find the ODBC ADMINISTRATOR in the Windows Control Panel.

2. Click on the FILE DSN tab on the ODBC DATA SOURCE screen.

   ➪ The list box on the left side of the screen contains the names of the file DSNs currently configured on your system. You can configure a specific DSN by selecting it from the list and clicking on the CONFIGURE button. When you configure a DSN, you can change the defaults associated with that data source, including the name of the DSN. You remove a data source by selecting it and clicking on the REMOVE button. You add a data source by clicking on the ADD button.

3. Click the ADD button.

   ➪ Clicking the ADD button will bring up the screen shown in Figure 2-6. On this screen, you select the ODBC river you want this DSN to use. If you do not see the Client Access ODBC driver, that means it has not been installed on your system. Install the driver using the Client Access setup program. Then start again from step 1 to create your data source.

4. Select the CLIENT ACCESS ODBC DRIVER (32-bit) and press the NEXT button.

   ➪ Clicking the NEXT button brings up a screen (Figure 2-7) where you are asked to enter a name for your data source.

5. Enter a name for your data source and click the NEXT button.

   ➪ As mentioned previously, you can enter any name you want, as long as it is a valid filename. Type something meaningful that you can remember.

6. Review the information on the confirmation screen and, if all is correct, click the FINISH button.

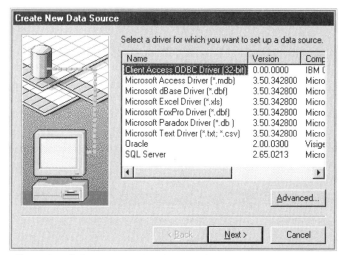

Figure 2-6: Selecting the driver for the DSN.

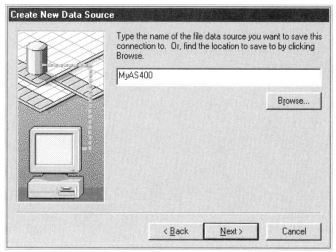

Figure 2-7: Naming a new data source.

Note: Client Access may display an error at this point saying that "The File Data Source was not saved." This error appears to be in error —if you dismiss the error dialog, the DSN will appear and function as normal.

7. Select the new data source from the driver manager and click the CONFIGURE button.

   ⇨ Clicking the FINISH button should bring up the Client Access ODBC driver's configuration screen. If it does not,

   ⇨ On this screen (Figure 2-8), there are many options that can be accessed using the tabs at the top of the screen. In most cases, the default values for most parameters work fine. IBM did a good job of setting the default values so that most users will never have to touch them. However, there are a few parameters that need to be entered.

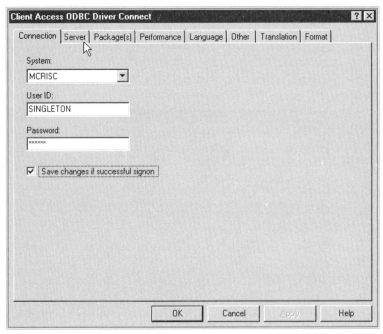

Figure 2-8: The CA ODBC driver configuration screen.

8. In the SYSTEM list box, choose the system to which you want to connect.

   ⇨ The AS/400 systems that are already configured as Client Access connections are found in this list box. If you do not see your system, you can configure a Client Access connection to it. Refer to the chapters 4 and 5 for information on how to do this.

9. In the USER ID field, enter the name of the user ID you want to use to sign on with this DSN.

    ⇨ The user ID can be any valid AS/400 sign-on. If you leave it blank, the user will be prompted for an ID and password at runtime. Keep in mind that the IBM Client Access ODBC driver uses standard AS/400 authorities as defined by this user profile. However, you should be aware of some additional security considerations. See the section in this chapter on ODBC security for more information.

10. In the PASSWORD field, enter the password for the user ID.

11. Check the box to SAVE CHANGES IF SUCCESSFUL SIGNON.

    ⇨ Checking the box saves the user ID and password with the DSN upon a successful sign-on. Otherwise, you could be prompted for this information each time you use this DSN to retrieve data from your AS/400.

12. Click on the SERVER tab to display the server configuration panel.

    ⇨ On this panel, shown in Figure 2-9, you configure the libraries from which you want to retrieve your data.

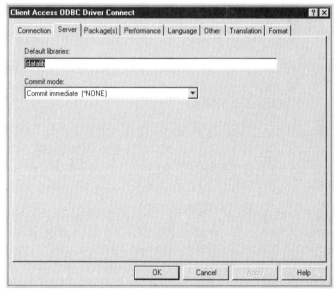

Figure 2-9: Setting the default library.

⇨ You also can change the commit mode of the DSN. Unless you have a specific reason for changing the commit mode, it is recommended that you use a commit mode of *NONE.

There are a few things you should know about specifying libraries on this panel. The Client Access ODBC driver help file says it best:

> The library names can be separated by commas or spaces. The libraries can either be added to your library list or replace the list entirely. To replace the list, specify a list of library names. To add to the existing user library list, add *usrlibl to the list of libraries. All libraries listed before *usrlibl will be added to the front of the user library list. All libraries listed after *usrlibl will be added to the end of the user library list.
>
> For example:
>
> ❏ LIB1, LIB2, LIB3 replaces the server job's library list with the three libraries specified. The default collection will be LIB1.
>
> ❏ LIB1, *USRLIBL, LIB2 adds LIB1 to the front of the server job's library list and adds LIB2 to the end of the list. The default collection will be LIB1.
>
> Notes:
>
> ❏ The last library in the library list will always be qiws. This library is always added by ODBC to include the ODBC server code in the library path.
>
> ❏ Searching all the AS/400 libraries during a query is unnecessary and decreases performance. Specify only the libraries from which you want to access data.

Pay particular attention to the default library explanation. The default library is the library that is used when no library is specified by the PC application. Because this happens quite frequently, it is important to know that the first library specified is the default library.

Note: Keep the list of libraries as short as possible. Many ODBC applications retrieve a catalog of available objects from a data source. If you have a large number of objects, this catalog can take a while for the AS/400 to build. Not only does it take longer to build, but the larger list also takes longer to send to the ODBC application. Keeping this list short ensures optimum performance.

Keep in mind that you can configure as many DSNs as you need for each driver. Therefore, if you want to access separate libraries at different times from your system, you can have a DSN specifically customized for each setup.

12. Enter the library name from which you want to retrieve your data.

⇒ The tables (files) listed by the data source will be from this library, as is the data that is retrieved.

13. Click the ok button.

⇒ There's no need to change any of the defaults on the other tabs. You now have completed all the steps needed to create your data source.

Creating a System DSN

If you need to create a system DSN, the process is much the same. Instead of clicking on the FILE DSN tab (as in Figure 2-2 and in Step 2: Creating a Data Source), simply click the SYSTEM DSN tab instead. The screens for the IBM Client Access ODBC driver data-source configuration are the same, and the same information and parameters apply.

ODBC SECURITY

The security of your data is, of course, very important. You might have heard a lot of talk in the industry press that ODBC is not a secure method to allow users access to mission-crucial data. This is simply not true. According to the *IBM ODBC User's Guide* (SC41-3535-00), "the same security issues have existed since Version 1 of OS/400."

What ODBC brought to the table is an easy method to access AS/400 data. It's true that ODBC can present loopholes in currently used security methods that allow users to update data when you might not want them to, but—with a little caution—these loopholes can be closed. Of course, it is not possible in this book to show you every possible security problem, but some of the major problems can be discussed.

There are two issues for you to consider when it comes to ODBC security. One is the capability to retrieve passwords using ODBC's trace functionality. The other is making sure that authorized users use the appropriate method to update data on the AS/400.

Security and Data Updates

ODBC can be configured to allow the update of AS/400 data from a PC. This allows programs written to communicate through ODBC to modify AS/400 data (which, in many cases, is desirable). For instance, if you have a client/server order-entry program and it needs to save the orders on your AS/400, it will require read/write access to your AS/400 order file. To make this program work, you need a DSN with update capability. One component of the DSN is a sign-on with sufficient AS/400 authority to update the data files.

A DSN with update capability shouldn't cause problems for you and your users if they use the intended program. The problem is that ODBC DSNs are not tied to a specific program.

Because ODBC DSNs work with any ODBC-enabled PC program (such as Microsoft Access), savvy operators could use the DSN to get to your AS/400 data and have full authority to any files designated by the AS/400 profile used to sign-on through ODBC! With Access allowing direct updates to your data, it could spell disaster.

On the AS/400, users can adopt the authority of a program they are running. A typical method of securing access to the database is to give users either no access or read-only access to data files, and then give programs read/write capabilities.

When users run an AS/400 program such as an order-entry program, they adopt the authority of the program's owner. *Adopted authority* allows updates to the data as long as the user does so through the program. The program can contain all the business logic and validations required to keep your data as clean as possible. If a user tries to modify the file when not running the program (i.e., through a file utility), they are denied access. This is a very effective way to ensure that no inappropriate data updates take place.

You have to be careful when granting your users access to the data. They will have the authorities granted by the sign-on used when they sign on through the ODBC driver. This can be an acceptable method to grant users read-only access to the data they want and they will not be able to update the data.

If your users are allowed to modify the data through a client/server program, they will need the capability to update files and, if you grant that authority through ODBC, your users can use any application on the PC to update the data.

What can you do?

If your users do need to update certain data on the AS/400 through client/server programs, you can perform the updates through *stored procedures*. Stored procedures are AS/400 programs that can be executed from ODBC and other places. Stored procedures can use AS/400 adopted authority.

To secure your data and still allow updates, grant users the minimum authority necessary (read-only or no access), and then use adopted authority with stored procedures to facilitate client/server updates. In this way, all updates can go through the business logic present in the stored procedure and, thereby, help ensure the integrity of your data.

But what about exit programs?

Well, exit programs are useful for securing Client Access in many different ways, including ODBC. Exit programs are hooks into the server programs supplied with OS/400.

Each function of Client Access calls the appropriate server programs on the AS/400. For example, there are server programs for processing sign-ons, database requests, and IFS (integrated file system) file transfer requests. These server programs on the AS/400 call user programs defined in what are called *exit points*. There are many exit points for the various servers. Exit programs use parameters to control access to various functionality.

Using exit points and parameters to exit programs, you can control access to the various servers on the AS/400. Theoretically, you could interpret each SQL statement sent by client programs to determine whether or not the actions are permissible. However, there are several problems with this method.

One problem is that taking apart each SQL statement as it is executed requires considerable overhead and will slow performance noticeably. Also, the program required to interpret the SQL statements correctly would be quite complex and difficult to program. Furthermore, there are no guarantees that third-party ODBC drivers call programs registered in the IBM exit points.

Actually, there have been comments from IBM indicating there are no third-party ODBC drivers that honor the IBM exit-program methodology. This means that your data is only secure when people are using the Client Access ODBC drivers, and that isn't an acceptable solution. Therefore, you shouldn't use exit programs as a means of securing client server access to the AS/400.

Password "Sniffing" Using Trace

ODBC provides a means for tracing the "conversation" taking place between the driver and the host database. Used by developers for testing purposes, the tracing feature is designed to help programmers find out exactly what is going on and to help fix problems. But tracing also can be used by nefarious ne'er-do-wells to retrieve user passwords.

When tracing is enabled, communications with the host are written to a file. This includes the user ID and password, which are captured in plain-text format. Turning on tracing can be as simple as checking an option under the ODBC administrator (Figure 2-10).

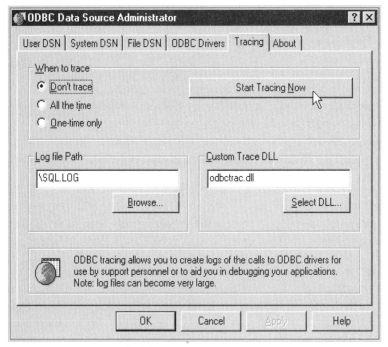

Figure 2-10: Turning on ODBC tracing.

How big of a problem is the misuse of tracing? According to Microsoft, it is not too big of a deal. After all, turning on tracing drastically slows down the application. Therefore, users would notice and call someone from MIS to diagnose their troubles. Balderdash! That's hardly a secure solution.

Another option is to delete the DLL (ODBCTRAC.DLL) that provides the tracing functionality. This DLL resides in the Windows directory. This is a limited solution, however, because any installs of new applications that use ODBC are likely to install that file again.

An automated deletion of that file, such as in the AUTOEXEC.BAT file or a network login batch file, would help further ensure that tracing could not be done. But this is still less than an ideal solution.

Windows NT also has some security measures that can be put in place. But these will not be of any help to Windows 95 users.

The only viable solution that works in all environments is for the application programmer to explicitly turn off ODBC tracing when logging on. This is done using ODBC programming calls. Once the logon is complete, tracing can be turned back on using those programming calls. In the real world, the problem with this method is that you cannot guarantee that third-party applications will do this.

Until turning off ODBC tracing becomes a standard practice, or Microsoft somehow addresses it in a different manner, ODBC will continue to have holes in this area. Keep in mind, however, that a relatively specific set of circumstances have to be in place for a security violation to occur. The misuse of tracing is not something that is likely to be exploited by just anybody. The user would have to know exactly what they are doing and have physical access to the machine on which they want to run the trace.

The bottom line is that all aspects of Client Access, including ODBC, by definition honor the AS/400 security model. This means that if your users have access to objects through their sign-ons, they most likely will be able to access them through Client Access. Conversely, it also means that if they don't have access to those objects through their AS/400 sign-on, they won't be able to access them within Client Access. Therefore, the recommended method of securing your system is to use the AS/400 object-level authority.

For more information on this subject, see the *Client Access for Windows 95/NT ODBC User's Guide* (Document Number SC41-3535-00).

ODBC TIPS AND TECHNIQUES

If IBM already had a function for transferring data to clients, why include ODBC? ODBC by itself does not transfer data to clients. It is merely a tool to enable the transfer of that data. Client programs are required to take the data from the AS/400 and put it into a format useful for the PC. In contrast, the data transfer function will by itself transfer data from the AS/400 to your PC hard drive. Both methods are useful in different circumstances. Use the data transfer function if:

❖ Offline data access is required or desired.

❖ No ODBC client utilities are available to perform the transfer.

❖ ODBC security is a concern.

Use ODBC if:

❖ Up-to-date information is required.

❖ The data is too big to exist on the PC.

❖ The data-transfer program does not provide the necessary functionality.

In addition, if you are doing application development, ODBC is really the best method when compared to the file-transfer function. While the file-transfer function performs static file transfers, ODBC can dynamically update records on the AS/400 in real time.

As explained in the Microsoft Office chapters of this book, many client applications work directly with ODBC databases. This seamlessly enables you to take advantage of the functionality of those applications without having to go to an external program to retrieve the data. This can be the real time saver in terms of ease of use and the capability to take advantage of the client functionality. For example, there are a large number of third-party tools that are ODBC-enabled to allow them to work directly with AS/400 data in ways that you might not have imagined.

Automating DSN Setup

Setting up a DSN involves a number of steps the users might or might not know how to do. Wouldn't it be nice if you could automate the process so you and your users could be spared the burden of doing the work manually? Well, luckily you can.

There are a few different methods that can be used to automate DSN setup. One method involves the Operations Navigator. Using the Operations Navigator and V3R7 or higher, it is possible to deploy "user" DSNs to other computers. To deploy DSNs to other PCs from your AS/400, perform the following steps.

1. Start the Operations Navigator.

2. Expand the tree on the right to find the DATABASE entry on the AS/400 system where you want to store the DSN. Expand the database entry.

    ⇨   Under the database entry, there is an entry for ODBC data sources. Clicking on this entry lists the DSNs, stored on your AS/400, in the window on the right-hand side of the screen.

3. Right-click the ODBC DATA SOURCES entry and select NEW DATA SOURCE from the menu (Figure 2-11).

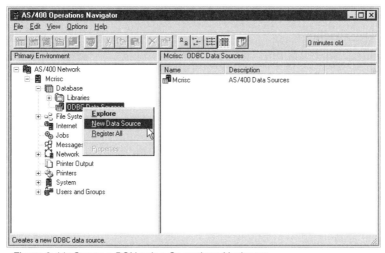

Figure 2-11: Create a DSN using Operations Navigator.

    ⇨   Clicking this entry brings up the standard ODBC DSN configuration screen. This screen is the same as the screens you've seen previously, but there is an additional option you can check to store the data source on the AS/400.

4. Configure the ODBC DSN as normal.

   ⇨ Use the methods discussed in this chapter to define your DSN.

5. Under the SERVER tab, there is a new option to manage the data source from the AS/400. Click the SERVER tab and select the MANAGE DATA SOURCE from the AS/400 option (Figure 2-12).

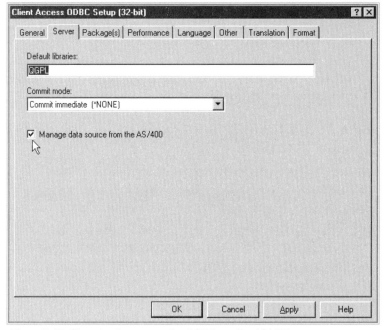

Figure 2-12: Choosing to manage the DSN from the AS/400.

The data source will be stored on the AS/400. You can then go to other computers and use the Operations Navigator to register the DSN as a user DSN by performing the following steps. To register the DSN on other computers:

1. On the target computer, start the Operations Navigator.

2. You are looking for the database entry.

3. Expand the tree to display the ODBC DATA SOURCES entry as you did before.

4. Click on the ODBC DATA SOURCES entry to display a list (Figure 2-13) of the DSNs defined on your AS/400 in the window on the right-hand side of the screen.

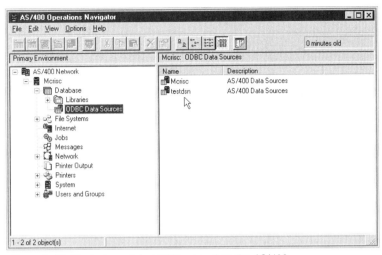

Figure 2-13: Displaying a list of DSNs stored on the AS/400.

5.   Select the DSN you want to register and right-click on it.

   ➪   This displays a menu of valid operations for managing the DSN (Figure 2-14).

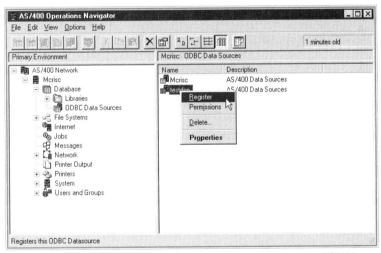

Figure 2-14: Displaying a menu for managing a DSN stored on the AS/400.

6.   Select REGISTER.

⇨ A user DSN will be created on the target PC.

That's how you manage the Operations Navigator to copy your user DSNs to other PCs. There are other methods of registering DSNs on target PCs. For example, you could edit the registry of the remote computers to create "user" and "system" DSNs. However, that is beyond the scope of this book. Also, you could copy the files that store the file DSNs around the network just like any other file. File DSNs have parameters that are stored in a file with the extension ".DSN."

Accessing Multimember Database Files

The AS/400 has the capability to store data in database files. These database files can be further divided into units called members. Many shops have their data stored in a one-member-per-database file. This works well with SQL and ODBC. However, there are AS/400 installations using software with many members per database file. Because neither SQL nor ODBC supports database members directly, determining how to access data in different members can be a little mysterious.

There are a few methods you can use to retrieve data from different members with ODBC. One method involves calling QCMDEXC as a stored procedure. This method is useful for programming. The other method involves creating logical files, which are pointers to the data that exists in the individual database members.

Accessing Database Members with QCMDEXC

Using ODBC, you can call programs, and one of the programs you can call is QCMDEXC. QCMDEXC can be used to run AS/400 commands. Using a call to OVRDBF, you can tell the AS/400 to use a specific member whenever a file (table) is retrieved through ODBC. Because the override can be active for the entire ODBC session, once the override is performed it will be valid until you disconnect from the ODBC database.

A call to QCMDEXC takes two parameters. One of the parameters is an AS/400 command to be run, and the other is the exact length of that command in a very specific 15,5 format. The syntax of the SQL statement that you send to the AS/400 is:

```
CALL QSYS.QCMDEXC( OVRDBF FILE(FILE1) MBR(MBR9) +
OVRSCOPE(*JOB) ,0000000044.00000)
```

Again, the second parameter is a count of the length of the string passed in the first parameter. The leading and trailing zeros are required or an error will occur. Does that seem a little odd to you? We know that computers are good at counting things. Why can't the AS/400 count the length of the first parameter? Also, why all the zeros? And why have a high-precision decimal number when all you are counting is characters? Has anyone ever seen a .00001th of a character? It must be very small. Anyway, that's the way you have to do it.

This SQL statement must be sent uninterpreted to the AS/400. Some ODBC tools, such as Microsoft Access, by default try to put their own spin on the SQL statements being sent to the backend databases. Make sure that this doesn't happen. If you are using Microsoft Access, you can use a passthrough query. See chapter 10 for details.

Once this command is executed, any references to FILE1 (through SQL or whatever) will actually refer to the member inside FILE1 called MBR9. This is valid until another override is made or the ODBC session ends.

Accessing Database Members with Logical Files

Another way to access different members through ODBC is to create a separate object for each member you want to access on the AS/400. This can be done by the creation of a logical file without actually duplicating the data itself.

Logical files are separate database objects that serve as pointers to data in database files. The many purposes for which logical files are used include having data presorted in a manner different than it is stored in the physical file (logical files and indexes), and "pre-joining" multiple files (logical files and views). You want them to point to the data in a particular member in a database file. To accomplish your goals of being able to access data in members, you must create a logical over each member you want to access.

You must use DDS to create a logical file. SQL has similar objects called *indexes* and *views* but, because SQL can't work with multiple members, you can't use it to create indexes or views that point to different members.

Making Data Updateable through ODBC and JET

ODBC can be used to update data on the AS/400 as well as read data. With ODBC, you use SQL to update the data. There are no special considerations other than those imposed by SQL.

However, one of the primary means of accessing AS/400 data with Microsoft Office applications is the JET database engine. Microsoft Access and Visual Basic both use the JET engine by default to manipulate data on the AS/400. For more information on the JET engine, see chapter 10. Note that Microsoft Query does not use the JET engine.

If you are going to use the JET engine to update AS/400 data, you must create a unique key or index on the table you want to update. The JET engine uses the unique key—sort of like a crude record lock—as a means of ensuring that changes in a multi-user environment happen predictably.

If the file you are accessing already has a unique key, the JET engine will pick it up and allow updates (as long as you have sufficient authority) without any special requirements. The same goes if you have a unique logical file or index over the data; the JET engine will automatically use that as well.

However, if you don't have a unique key or a unique logical/index, you won't be able to update data using the JET engine. To make the data updateable through JET, you need to create a unique key over the file. This can be done using DDS or SQL. Using SQL, the syntax is:

```
CREATE UNIQUE INDEX <LIBRARY/NEWINDEXNAME> +
ON <LIBRARY/FILE> (FIELD1, FIELD2,  )
```

where <LIBRARY/NEWINDEXNAME> is the name of the new index and the library where it is to be created, and <LIBRARY/FILE> is the name of the file that you are creating the index over. The fields used to create the index are placed in parenthesis and commas separate multiple fields if you have more than one.

You can run this statement from the AS/400 or the PC. You just have to make sure that, if you run it on the PC, the SQL you typed is actually the SQL that gets sent to the AS/400. This is done in Access with a "passthrough" query and in Microsoft Query with the EXECUTE SQL option on the FILE menu (Figure 2-15).

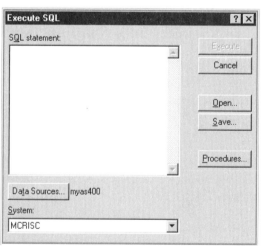

Figure 2-15: You can execute an SQL statement by selecting Execute SQL from the File menu of Microsoft Query.

Summary

ODBC is a powerful means of accessing your AS/400 data. It is very widely supported in Windows applications that use external data. It allows front-end applications such as Access and MS Query to access data regardless of where it is stored. The Client Access ODBC driver is a capable driver that allows you to retrieve data from the AS/400 for use in Office and other applications.

3

Retrieving AS/400
Data with MS Query

Microsoft Query, the helper application included with Microsoft Office, helps Office applications such as Word and Excel read data from ODBC data sources. While Query retrieves and formats data for inclusion in the other Office applications, it isn't a widely known helper application because it is not installed by default by the Office setup program. Even if you opt to install it, Office does not give Query an icon in the Office folder.

The primary way for you to access Microsoft Query is through the Word and Excel menus. For example, in Word, when you access the MAIL MERGE HELPER from the TOOLS menu—and opt to get data from an external source by the selecting the OPEN DATA SOURCE option from the GET DATA drop-down list—Microsoft Query is started and used to retrieve that data from the database through ODBC.

In Microsoft Excel, when you choose GET EXTERNAL DATA from the data menu, and select CREATE NEW QUERY, Microsoft Query is started and used to bring data into the worksheet.

Because Microsoft Query is such a commonly used application, learning it can help you maximize productivity. Microsoft Query is the primary means used to bring external data into the Office applications. In turn, Microsoft Query uses ODBC to retrieve that data from the AS/400.

INTRODUCTION

This chapter helps you become familiar with ODBC and Microsoft Query terminology while explaining how to install Query. Practical examples show you how to create, save, and use queries and how to join tables and use filtering, grouping, totaling, and sorting. In addition, there are tips on how to speed up the design process and how to reduce performance issues with your AS/400. Along with the basics, there are advanced tips that specifically address Microsoft Query's interaction with the AS/400.

First, make sure that you have an ODBC data source (DSN) configured that points to the data you want to retrieve from your AS/400. See chapter 6 for information on how to configure an ODBC data source, and keep in mind that you have to configure a "file-type" DSN for Microsoft Query.

To help you learn Query, this chapter guides you through some examples using the sample data on the Web page created for this book. To complete these examples as shown, first load the sample data onto your AS/400. For instructions on loading the data on your AS/400, refer to appendix A.

These examples cover the basics as well as some of the more advanced applications of Microsoft Query. Because the examples in the sample data are as realistic as possible, you should be able to benefit immediately by using and applying this new knowledge to your own situation.

COMING TO TERMS

Before starting with MS Query, you should be aware of some terms used throughout this chapter. Some ODBC and SQL terms might not be familiar to programmers accustomed to AS/400 terminology.

When you are learning these new terms, it is helpful to imagine the data in an AS/400 file laid out in a spreadsheet-like format. When viewed in this format, the entire spreadsheet, or file, is referred to as a *table*. Each record in the table is referred to as a *row*. A particular field is referred to as a *column*. A collection of tables is referred to as a *database*. This is generally analogous to an AS/400 library.

INSTALLATION

Before you can work with MS Query, it has to be installed on your system. Unfortunately, there usually isn't a shortcut that enables you to start this program by itself. You can determine if MS Query is installed on your system by searching for a program called MSQRY32.EXE. If you're sure that MS Query is installed on your system, you can, of course, skip this step. But if you are not sure, it would be wise to take a look before you get started on the examples.

To search your computer for this program, click the START menu, select FIND, and then select FILES OR FOLDERS. See Figure 3-1.

In the NAMED textbox, enter MSQRY32.EXE. In the LOOK IN box, select MY COMPUTER. Click the FIND NOW button to begin the search. If the search finds the program, it will be listed in the box at the bottom of the find screen. See Figure 3-2.

If the program is found on your computer, skip the "Installation" section and continue with the "Creating A Shortcut" section. If the program isn't found, you must install it.

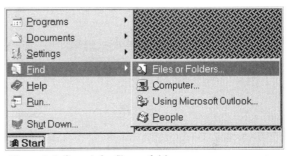

Figure 3-1: Search for files or folders.

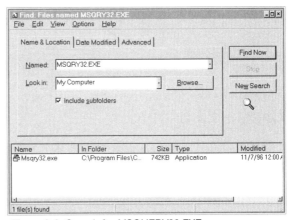

Figure 3-2: Search for MSQUERY32.EXE.

INSTALLING MICROSOFT QUERY

If you didn't find MS Query on your system, install it by running the Office 97 setup program. MS Query is found under the data access OPTIONS checkbox (Figure 3-3). Make sure that this option is checked and that the MICROSOFT QUERY option, found by clicking the CHANGE OPTION button, is also selected. Proceed through the setup program to install MS Query. Once Query is installed, the next optional step is to create a shortcut to the program.

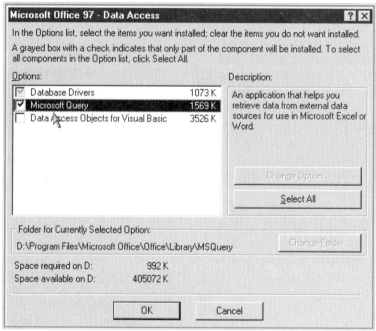

Figure 3-3: Office 97 setup.

CREATING A SHORTCUT

Usually, there is no shortcut to MS Query that allows you to start the program directly. Creating a shortcut on your desktop to MS Query allows users to quickly run the program without having to go into Word or Excel. One technique for creating a shortcut is to drag-and-drop using the right mouse button.

Click the MS Query entry in the search box results window with the right mouse button. Without releasing the right mouse button, drag the file to the desktop. When you let go of the right mouse button, a menu appears. From the menu, select CREATE SHORTCUT(S) HERE (Figure 3-4).

You will now have a shortcut on the desktop that you can use to fire up MS Query without having to open any of the other Office applications.

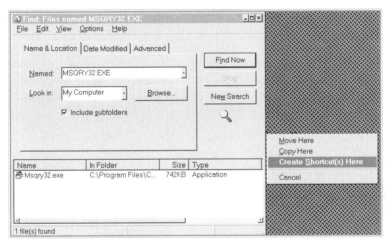

Figure 3-4: Creating a shortcut.

A QUICK LESSON

There are two basic methods to create a query within Microsoft Query. The easiest method is to use the Query Wizard to create a query by answering questions about the data you want to retrieve. However, this method doesn't provide you with all the available options. To access all the facilities available in Microsoft Query, you need to use the "manual" (for lack of a better term) method of creating a query.

Note that it is possible to use a combination of the two methods by creating a query with the wizard and then manually adding any additional features that aren't created by the wizard. So that you can choose the option that works best in your situation, both methods of creating queries are explored in the following sections.

Let's jump right to work with the MS Query program. Start with the basics by creating a simple query with the Wizards and save it. To start MS Query, double-click its icon on the desktop.

MS Query loads and presents a blank workspace. To create a new query, click on the NEW QUERY button (Figure 3-5), on the left side of the toolbar, or select NEW QUERY from the FILE menu.

 Figure 3-5: The New Query button.

The first step in creating a new query is selecting a database. The databases listed in the CHOOSE DATA SOURCE dialogue box are the file DSNs that you create as explained in chapter 6. The data source points to the library where the data that you want to access resides. See Figure 3-6.

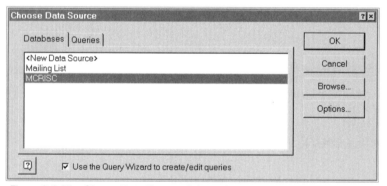

Figure 3-6: The Choose Data Source dialogue box.

If you don't see your ODBC data source on this screen, it's because you either have not created it or you created a DSN that was not a file DSN. In either case, review the steps in chapter 6 for creating a DSN.

The OPTIONS button on this screen allows you to set which directories will be searched for file DSNs. Click on the OPTIONS button to display the DATA SOURCE OPTIONS screen (Figure 3-7).

The directories on your system currently set are listed in the box at the bottom of this screen. The defaults should be sufficient for most installations. If you are an administrator and you want to store your file DSNs in a central location (like a network server), you could point to it

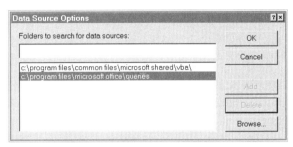

Figure 3-7: The Data Source Options screen.

here. For now, you can click the cancel button to return to the CHOOSE DATA SOURCE screen.

If you need to create a new DSN, select NEW DATA SOURCE from the database list (Figure 3-6) and click the ok button. You also can create queries and save them for later recall using MS Query. To load a previously saved query, click the QUERIES tab at the top of the CHOOSE DATA SOURCE window. If you have any saved queries, they will be listed n this box. You can now click on the DATABASES tab to return to the previous screen.

CREATING A SIMPLE QUERY USING THE WIZARD

Did you notice the option to use the Query Wizard to create and edit your queries (Figure 3-6)? Check this option; you're going to use the Query Wizard for your first query. With this option checked, select a DSN and click the ok button to create a new query. At this point, you may be presented with an ODBC logon screen. If so, enter your user ID and password to sign on.

Now that you have signed on, you will see the first screen: QUERY WIZARD - CHOOSE COLUMNS. On this screen, you can select the tables and

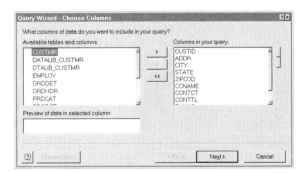

Figure 3-8: The Query Wizard - Choose Columns screen.

columns you want to use in your query by choosing them from the list on the left and clicking the top button. The button is located in the center of the query-wizard screen and has a single arrow pointing to the right (Figure 3-8).

You can expand the table entries to see a list of columns in the table by clicking on the plus sign to the left of the table name. On some systems, the plus (+) sign doesn't show up. In that case, click the area to the left of the table name to open the field list.

If you accidentally add a table you don't want, you can select it in the right-hand list and click the middle button, located in the center of the screen, with the arrow pointing left. To remove all tables from the right-hand list, click on the bottom button that has two left-pointing arrows.

For this example, accept all the columns from your customer table by clicking the NEXT button at the bottom of the screen. This brings up the filter data screen (Figure 3-9).

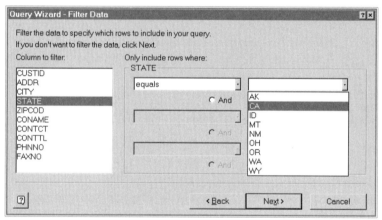

Figure 3-9: The Query Wizard - Filter Data screen.

On this screen, you can filter records based on values in the columns. For example, if you want to send letters to only the customers in a certain state, you can do it here. Let's say you want to select only customers from California. To do so, you would select STATE in the left-hand list.

Next, select an operator for the filter by using the pull-down menu named ONLY INCLUDE ROWS WHERE: STATE. Click on the right-hand arrow and select EQUALS from the list. You will notice that this action activates the box on the right-hand side of the screen.

Use this box to specify the value for which you want to filter. In this example, the goal is to select only customers that are in California. Therefore, you select CA from the drop-down list. At this point, you could enter up to two more filters on this screen. Because this example uses only one filter, you can now click on the NEXT button at the bottom of the screen. This brings you to the sort screen (Figure 3-10).

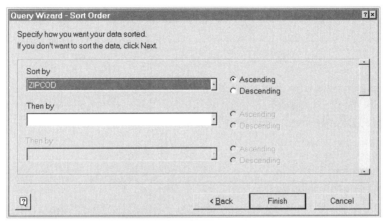

Figure 3-10: The Query Wizard - Sort Order screen.

On this screen, you can specify how you want the data sorted. For the example, you will sort by ZIP code. The option buttons to the right of the SORT BY box allow you to choose either ascending or descending sort order. For this example, use ASCENDING sort order. At this point, you can, if you want, sort by multiple fields. When you are done, click the FINISH button.

Once you define the query, the program builds the query and retrieves the data. The selected data is displayed in the lower window. The tables are displayed in the boxes at the top of the window, and the criteria are displayed in the center. See Figure 3-11.

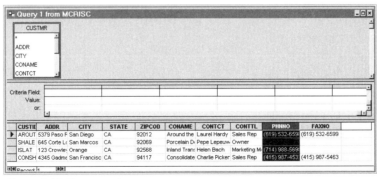

Figure 3-11: Query results.

CREATING A QUERY WITHOUT THE WIZARD

Now let's delve into creating a query without using the wizard. This method of query creation sacrifices speed and simplicity for flexibility and power. And the sacrifices of speed and simplicity aren't really that large, either. As you'll see, it's still very easy to create a query.

If it isn't already running, the first step is to start the MS Query program. When you start Query, you will be presented with a blank workspace. You can click the NEW QUERY button or click on the FILE menu and select NEW as you did for the last query.

The database selection screen appears again (Figure 3-6). This time, you will want to make sure the option to use the Query Wizard is not selected. Select your AS/400 DSN and click the OK button.

Once you do this, MS Query will work for a moment or two and then present you with a list of tables available to your data source. On the ADD TABLES screen (Figure 3-12), you will see the tables that you are authorized to use from the databases specified in the DSN setup.

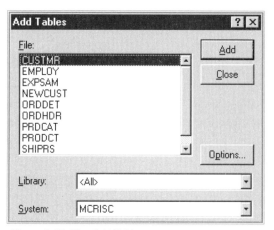

Figure 3-12: The Add Tables screen.

The OPTIONS button allows you to specify whether you want to see tables, views, system tables, or synonyms (Figure 3-13). You usually won't need to make changes to the options.

Click on CANCEL to return to the ADD TABLES screen (Figure 3-12). Here you simply select the tables you want to use for the query and press the ADD button. You add

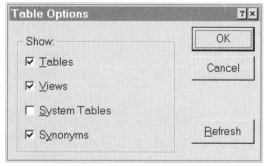

Figure 3-13: The Table Options screen.

tables to the query one at a time. When the tables are added, they appear in the table pane of the query workspace view. When you have the tables you need, click the CLOSE button. For this example, select just one table—the customer (CUSTMR) table. Click the ADD button followed by the CLOSE button.

The remaining screen is the query workspace. The top section of the screen is called the *table pane*, and it is here where you see representations of the data tables used in your query. The bottom section of the screen is called the *data pane*. This is where the data returned by the query is displayed.

To complete the creation of the query, add some fields to it. To add all of the fields in the table to your query, select the asterisk in the table and drag it to the data pane.

After a delay, MS Query returns all rows and columns from this table (Figure 3-14). If you don't see the data at this point, click the QUERY NOW button on the toolbar. See Figure 3-15.

Figure 3-14: Query results.

 Figure 3-15: The Query Now button.

SAVING THE QUERY

Now you can save your work. To save a query, click on the diskette icon on the toolbar or click on the FILE menu and select the SAVE option.

If this is the first time this query has been saved, you will be prompted to enter a filename (Figure 3-16). Type MYQUERY in the filename field and click the OK button. The query is now saved for later retrieval. If you want to save the query with a different name, you can select the SAVE AS option under the FILE menu.

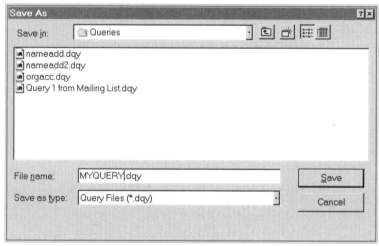

Figure 3-16: Save query.

SORTING RECORDS

Now that the basics have been covered, you're ready to learn about the additional capabilities of MS Query. You've already learned how to select records from a table, but what if you want to sort them? The quickest way to create a sort is to select a column and press the SORT

Figure 3-17: The sort ascending button and the sort descending button.

ASCENDING button or the SORT DESCENDING button on the toolbar. See Figure 3-17.

To select a column in the query you just created, click on the STATE column title in the data pane. The background of the column turns black when the column is selected. Then click the SORT ASCENDING button on the toolbar to sort by that column.

> Tip: To determine the name of a button on any toolbar, you can hold the mouse pointer over each button on the toolbar to display a tool tip that tells you the name of the button.

You can also specify more complex sorts using the SORT option under the RECORDS menu item. This allows you to specify exactly which fields should be included in the sort and which direction they should be sorted. Click on the RECORDS menu and select the SORT option. This displays the SORT dialogue box, where you can enter your sort criteria (Figure 3-18). You can see the sort you've already added in the SORTS IN QUERY list box. To remove that sort, you can select it and click the REMOVE button.

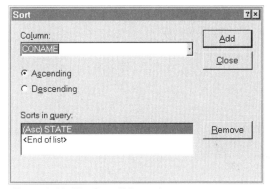

Figure 3-18: The Sort dialogue box.

To add a new column to the sort, select the column from the COLUMNS drop-down list box.

Select either ASCENDING or DESCENDING to determine the order of the sort. Click the ADD button to add the sort to your query. You can do this as many times as necessary to get the data sorted in the order you want. To finish, click the CLOSE button.

SPEEDING UP THE DESIGN PROCESS

As you may have noticed, every time you change something in the query, the data automatically gets refreshed (meaning it is read again from the AS/400). This can be a slow process. To speed up the creation of queries, you can turn off the AUTO-QUERY option. Do this by clicking on the Auto-query button on the toolbar.

This button is a toggle that changes each time you click on it. To turn off auto-query, leave the button in the "up" position.

After you have set up the query to your liking, press the QUERY NOW button on the toolbar. This refreshes the data from the AS/400.

> Note: Throughout this chapter, whenever you see a reference to *refreshing the query,* it means pressing the QUERY NOW button on the toolbar.

FILTERING RECORDS

You also can tell MS Query to retrieve only the records that you want to see. For example, you can create a list of all customers in California by entering a search criterion for the STATE column requesting only records that have CA in the state column be returned.

To do this, you must add a criterion to your query. The quickest way to do this is to highlight the row you want by clicking on it and then pressing the CRITERIA EQUALS button (Figure 3-19) on the toolbar.

 Figure 3-19: The criteria equals button.

To find all the customers in California, locate a row in the data pane that has the value CA in the state column. Click on that cell and then click the CRITERIA EQUALS button on the toolbar.

This opens up a new pane, called the *criteria pane*, on the display where the selection criteria of your query are displayed. When you refresh the query by clicking on the QUERY NOW button on the toolbar, you see only the customers from California listed (Figure 3-20).

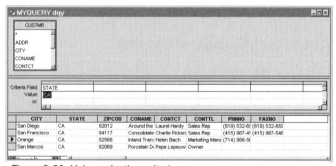

Figure 3-20: Using selection criteria.

You can add multiple criteria just as you can add multiple sorts. One way to add another criteria to a query is to select ADD CRITERIA from the CRITERIA menu. This displays the ADD CRITERIA dialogue box (Figure 3-21).

To add more criteria, enter the information for the criteria and press the ADD button. This example adds a criterion to restrict the records to customers in the city of Orange, California. In the field list box, choose CITY. Leave the OPERATOR set at EQUALS.

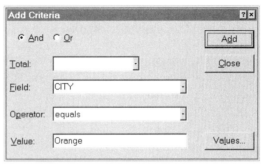

Figure 3-21: The Add Criteria dialogue box.

Then click on the VALUES button. Clicking this button lists all the current values in the database for the field selected (Figure 3-22). Use this button carefully. Sometimes the list can be large and can take a while to be retrieved from the AS/400. (I don't often use this button, but it's good to know it's there).

Select ORANGE and press the OK button to put ORANGE in the VALUE field. Click the ADD button in the ADD CRITERIA box and then the CLOSE button. Click on the QUERY NOW button to display only the records from the customer table with addresses located in Orange, California.

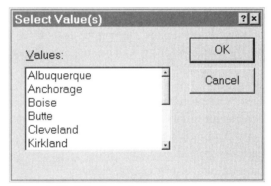

Figure 3-22: Selecting values.

That's how easy it is to create criteria to limit your queries to only the records you want to see. One use of this feature is to select records for a particular time frame. This allows you to restrict reports with a lot of detail to just the period on which you want to focus. Another use would be to filter out orders for a particular product. There are endless possibilities.

The next two steps explain how to join tables and how to create totals. In creating queries to report on data in a relational database system, these are the most important steps.

JOINING TABLES

The *relational model* is a method of dividing data into logical, non-repeating units. This is usually one of the most efficient ways to store data.

For example, in a typical relational business system, information about customers is stored in the customer table. Information about products is stored in a product table. Information about orders is stored in two tables. One table, called the *order header table*, holds information common to the order, such as the ordering customer, the order date, the order taker, etc. The other order table, a *detail table*, holds the contents of the order (in other words, the items the customer wants). There may be several items per order and, because it would be inefficient to store the order-header information for each item on the order, separate tables are used. The tables are linked using a special field called a *key field*. If this seems confusing, just follow along with the examples and it will become clearer.

Let's create a query that shows all the items ordered from customers in Portland, Oregon. To do that, you need information from three of the tables in your sample database. The tables are the customer (CUSTMR) table, the order header (ORDHDR) table, and the order detail (ORDDET) table.

First, start a new query by clicking on the NEW QUERY icon on the Microsoft Query toolbar. Select your AS/400 DSN and click OK. Then you will need to add these three tables to the query. You do this by selecting each one from the list (CUSTMR, ORDHDR, and ORDDET) and pressing the ADD button after each one. After the last table is added to the query, press the CLOSE button. See Figures 3-5 and 3-12.

Now you can see all three tables in the table pane of the query window (Figure 3-23). To retrieve information from these tables correctly, the relationship between them has

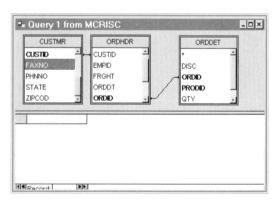

Figure 3-23: Joining tables.

to be described to Microsoft Query. The relationship between the tables is called the *join specification* or the *join criteria*.

With some databases, Microsoft Query does its best guess and it tries to supply the join criteria for you. On others, you have to tell Query how the tables are related. You learn how to tell Query about your tables by manually adding the join specification.

As you might know, tables in a relational database are joined by common fields. Using Microsoft Query, the simplest way to specify a join is to drag a common field from one table to its complement in the other table. The following sections explain this technique using the customer and order-header tables.

First, find the CUSTID field in the customer table. Then drag it and drop it over the CUSTID field in the order-header table.

A line appears joining the field in the customer table to the field in the order-header table. This tells Microsoft Query that the records in the order-header table in effect belong to the records in the customer table.

With this so-called *one-to-many relationship*, one record in the customer table can have many records in the order-header table. This makes logical sense because a customer can have more than one order, but it would not normally make sense for an order to have more than one customer.

There is a similar relationship between orders in the order-header table and the items on the order in the order-detail table. One order can have many items, but one particular order item cannot be on more than one order.

The order-header table and the order-detail table are joined by the ORDID field. Find the ORDID field within the order-header table and drag it to the ORDID field in the order-detail table.

Now, as shown in Figure 3-23, there are relationships between all the tables shown by lines connecting the related fields.

Let's add some fields to this query to see some data. Rather than looking at all the fields in all three tables, take a look at just a select few. The fields from the customer table are: CONAME, CITY, and STATE. Drag these fields to the data pane to add them to the query.

By holding down the Control key, you can select multiple fields from the table and drag them to the data pane in one go. You also want to see the order date from the order-header table. Therefore, drag the ORDDT field to the data pane. From the order-detail table, take the QTY, UPRICE, and DISC fields.

Refreshing the query by clicking on the QUERY-NOW button returns a lot of records, and many of the values seem to repeat themselves on the screen. Notice that there is one row for every item ordered on every order (Figure 3-24). That's a lot of information. Let's add some criteria that helps limit the records to just what you want to see.

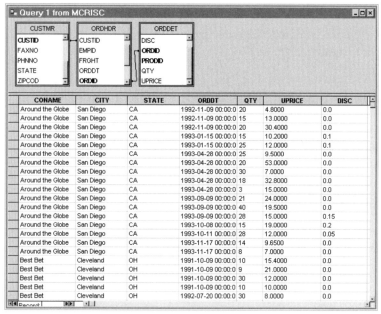

Figure 3-24: Query results.

First, select ADD CRITERIA from the CRITERIA menu. Next, you can limit the STATE field to OR for Oregon and limit the CITY field to "Portland." Notice that the fields listed in the field drop-down list box are now prefixed by the name of the table from which they come. This is to allow distinction of fields with the same name that are in different tables.

Select the CUSTMR.STATE field and set the operator text box to EQUALS, set the VALUE text box to "OR," and press the ADD button. This limits the query to customers located in Oregon.

To further limit the query to the city of Portland, select the CUSTMR.CITY field. Again, leave the operator text box set at EQUALS. Then type "Portland" in the value text box. Make sure you use the correct case when entering the city. For this example, use an uppercase "P" and leave the rest lowercase (Figure 3-25).

Now press the ADD button followed by the CLOSE button.

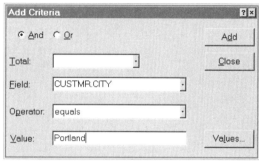

Figure 3-25: The Add Criteria screen.

When the query is refreshed, you see a list of all items ordered by any customers located in Portland, Oregon. Did you notice that there is no extended price field in the order-detail table? This is because the extended price needs to be calculated. Fortunately, Microsoft Query can do that as well.

To add a calculated field, select the ADD COLUMN or INSERT COLUMN option from the RECORDS menu (it will say "add" or "insert" depending upon what is selected at the time). The example used here displays the ADD COLUMN dialogue box (Figure 3-26).

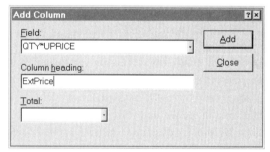

Figure 3-26: The Add Column dialogue box.

In the FIELD box, type: QTY*UPRICE. This is called an *expression*, and expressions are used to create calculated fields. For the column heading, enter EXTPRICE , press the ADD button, and then press the CLOSE button.

> Tip: Once you become familiar with Microsoft Query, be sure to read the help section in Query on the subject of expressions. Expressions provide powerful tools for obtaining information you want.

When you refresh the query by clicking on the QUERY NOW button, you see the extended price for each item ordered. See Figure 3-27. Expression fields can be used in almost any way that you can use a regular field.

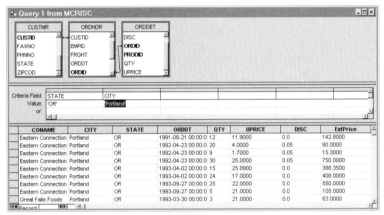

Figure 3-27: Extended price added to the query.

TOTALING AND GROUPING

So far, you have used MS Query to produce information in the form of detailed lists. This is useful in manipulating mailing lists and labels, but it is not very useful in analyzing data. To analyze data in a more useful manner, records must be totaled and grouped based on how you want to see the data. For example, it might be useful to know the total sales by state or the total sales by customer. Performing these kind of queries using Microsoft Query is easy.

To start, create a new query by selecting NEW from the FILE menu or by clicking on the NEW QUERY button on the toolbar. Choose your AS/400 data source and press the OK button. Then, from the list of tables, add the customer (CUSTMR), order-header (ORDHDR), and order-detail (ORDDET) tables and press the CLOSE button.

Join the tables as shown in Figure 3-23. The customer table should be joined with the order-header table by the CUSTID field. The order-header table should be joined to the order-detail table with the ORDID field. To create a grouping query, you have to choose the fields by which you want to group. For this example, choose the STATE field from the CUSTOMER table. Drag the field to the data window to add it to your query. Click on the QUERY NOW button to run the query.

To sort this field in ascending order, highlight the column by clicking on the header, and then press the SORT ASCENDING button on the toolbar.

Now you can create a summary field for the dollar amount of each order. Under the RECORDS menu, select INSERT COLUMN to bring up the INSERT COLUMN dialogue box (Figure 3-28).

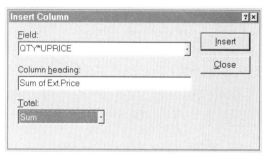

Figure 3-28: The Insert Column dialogue box.

In the FIELD box, type QTY*UPRICE and in the column heading box enter SUM OF EXT.PRICE. Then, in the TOTAL field, select SUM from the drop-down list. Next, click on the INSERT and then the CLOSE button to close the INSERT COLUMN dialog box.

When you refresh the query, you see the list of states with the total sales for each state listed next to it (Figure 3-29). The detailed information is summarized to give a total value.

You also can get averages, counts, and minimum and maximum value statistics on summary data. These statistics are useful for creating reports that will help you spot trends in your data.

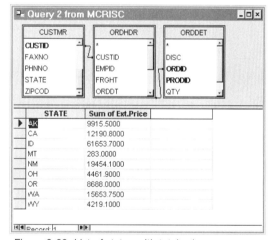

Figure 3-29: List of states with total sales.

In general, summaries should be to the right-hand side of the grouped data. In fact, that is how Microsoft Query works. When you create a summary field, the data is grouped by all the fields to the left-hand side of the summary field.

PERFORMANCE CAUTIONS

As described in this chapter, Microsoft Query can be an excellent tool for exploring data. However, please bear in mind a few words of caution. Because it is possible to retrieve a very large set of data using Query, you must be careful how you design your requests so that you do not affect the performance of the AS/400 for other users. Here are a couple of tips to help ensure that you don't get more than you asked for:

❖ Try to minimize the amount of data that will be retrieved before you refresh the query. That will lower the workload on the AS/400.

❖ Also, if you do not need to sort data, then do not specify a sort. This will allow the AS/400 to process the data in the order that is most efficient. Requiring the AS/400 to sort a large amount of data can adversely affect the performance, and you should avoid large shorts whenever possible.

❖ If you do need to sort a large amount of data, add a logical file to the AS/400 table that requires sorting. This allows the AS/400 to have the data sorted before you request it (meaning the AS/400 does not have to perform the sort on the fly). If you do not know how to add a logical file, ask your system administrator if a logical file can be added.

❖ Think before you query. You will generally avoid the wrath of your fellow AS/400 users if you query responsibly.

SUMMARY

This chapter explains many ways for using Microsoft Query to retrieve AS/400 data. It is a visual query-building tool that offers many powerful options for data retrieval. Because it is used as a "glue" application that shuttles data from the AS/400 to the Office Applications such as Word and Excel, taking the time to understand Query is very important.

4

Using AS/400 Data with Word

Microsoft Word is the word processor included with Microsoft Office. While Word stands on its own as an application—it doesn't need data from the external world—when combined with data from your AS/400, Word can become a truly powerful tool for today's business world.

With Word, you can easily use external data to create mailing labels, form letters, and reports. In the past, when bringing external data into a word processor, the standard procedure was to use complex document-formatting commands. Wizards make using external data with Word much easier. With wizards, the program guides you step-by-step through the process of retrieving the data, freeing you from having to memorize complex commands. This chapter explores three ways to use AS/400 data with Word. You'll find out how to:

❖ Create mailing labels from the customer data on the AS/400.

❖ Create properly formatted form letters using the customer data from the AS/400.

❖ Import data from an AS/400 table into a table in your Word documents. These imported tables can then be used in such things as monthly reports.

All AS/400 data used in the following examples is retrieved using ODBC and Microsoft Query. This section presumes you are familiar with MS Query. If you aren't familiar with using Microsoft Query with AS/400 data, please review chapter 7 before proceeding.

CREATING MAILING LABELS

To begin creating mailing labels using AS/400 customer data, first close any currently open documents by repeatedly selecting CLOSE from the FILE menu until there are no open documents. Next, open your Microsoft Word application and create a new blank document. To create a new blank document, select NEW from the FILE menu. Then select BLANK DOCUMENT from the GENERAL tab and click on the OK button (Figure 4-1).

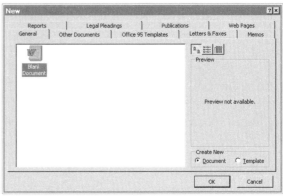

Figure 4-1: Creating a new document.

A blank document now appears in the Word window. To begin the process of creating mailing labels, click on the TOOLS menu and select MAIL MERGE. This will start the MAIL MERGE HELPER (Figure 4-2).

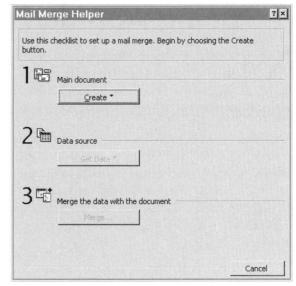

Figure 4-2: the MAIL MERGE HELPER screen.

The MAIL MERGE HELPER screen shows that there are three main steps to creating mailing labels. Step 1 is to set up the main document (CREATE). Step 2 is to select your data source (GET DATA). Step 3 is to perform the actual merge of the document and the data (MERGE). The following sections go through each of these steps in detail.

STEP 1: CREATE

Begin step 1 by clicking on the CREATE button. When the drop-down menu appears, select MAILING LABELS from this menu (Figure 4-3).

Word next prompts you to choose between using the active document window or creating a new document window (Figure 4-4). Because you don't have anything in your existing document, use it. Click on the ACTIVE WINDOW button. Word will use your new blank document to create your mailing labels.

You will notice that a new button with the title SETUP now appears in step 1 next to the CREATE button. This button is grayed for the moment; therefore, you cannot click on it. That completes step 1 of the process.

STEP 2: GET DATA

Begin step 2 by clicking on the GET DATA button. Another drop-down menu appears below the button asking whether you want to create a data source, use an existing one, or set the header options.

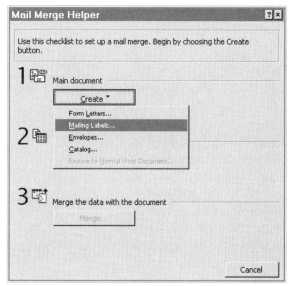

Figure 4-3: Creating mailing labels.

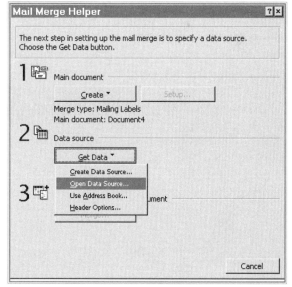

Figure 4-4: Selecting the ACTIVE WINDOW.

Because you've already defined a data source to your AS/400 data, select OPEN DATA SOURCE. See Figure 4-5.

A file-open dialog box appears (Figure 4-6). By default, Word wants to obtain its external data from another Word document. Therefore, Word is asking you to locate the Word document that will provide the data from the current directory. Because this example won't use a Word document as the data source, click on the MS QUERY button on the right-hand side of the dialogue box. Bringing up MS Query allows you to grab some data from your AS/400.

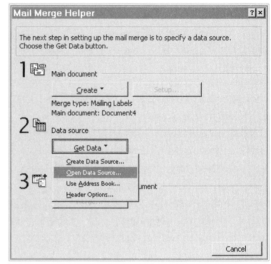

Figure 4-5: Getting data.

You must be familiar with the features of MS Query to continue with step 2. If you aren't familiar with MS Query, be sure to read chapter 3 before continuing.

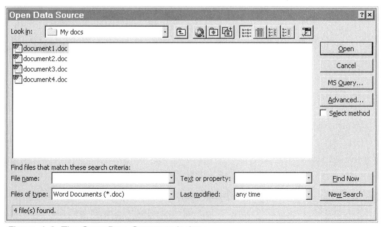

Figure 4-6: The OPEN DATA SOURCE window.

After MS Query loads, select your AS/400 ODBC data source from the list of available data sources and click on the OK button (Figure 4-7).

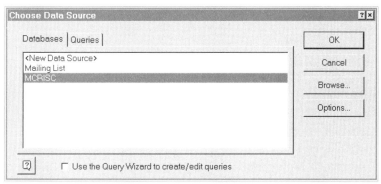

Figure 4-7: The CHOOSE DATA SOURCE screen.

MS Query presents you with a list of tables from your data source. Select the customer (CUSTMR) table, press the ADD button, and then click the CLOSE button (Figure 4-8).

The customer table is now displayed in the table pane of the query window. To add all fields to the data pane, drag the asterisk from the customer table and drop it in the data pane. Note that you can add criteria as necessary to limit the data to the records you want. This example walks you through the process to create mailing labels for all customers.

Let's sort the query by ZIP code. To do] this, click on the ZIP code field column header and click the SORT ASCENDING button on the toolbar.

Refresh the query by clicking on the QUERY NOW button on the toolbar. The data is retrieved from the AS/400. Be sure to review the data to make sure it is exactly what you want.

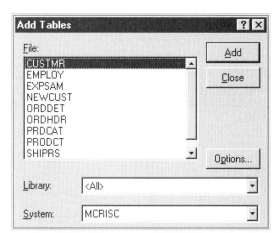

Figure 4-8: The ADD TABLES screen.

When you are satisfied with the query, you can return to Word by selecting RETURN DATA TO MICROSOFT WORD from the FILE menu (Figure 4-9).

Now that you have returned to your Word document, a dialog box appears telling you that you have to set up your main document (Figure 4-10). Because there's only one choice, click the SET UP MAIN DOCUMENT button now.

You are now presented with a dialog box where you are prompted to specify the type of label to be used (Figure 4-11). Here you can customize the label specification to exactly match the labels you want to use. You can also specify printer options. Select your label type from the list by clicking on it and then click on the OK button.

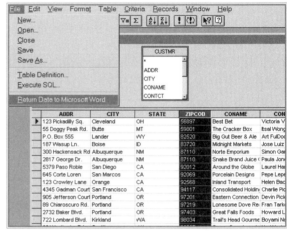

Figure 4-9: The RETURN DATA TO MICROSOFT WORD screen.

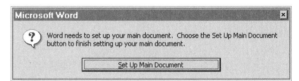

Figure 4-10: The SET UP MAIN DOCUMENT button.

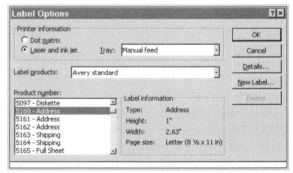

Figure 4-11: LABEL OPTIONS.

If you don't see your mailing labels here, you can create a custom label specification by clicking on the NEW LABEL button or DETAILS button (Figure 4-12). You will be prompted to add the specifications—including margins, label size, and layout on the page—for your label. You then type in a name for your new label and click the OK button. Click the OK button again to close the LABEL OPTIONS dialogue box.

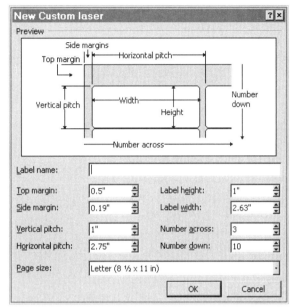

Figure 4-12: A new custom label.

The CREATE LABELS dialogue box appears (Figure 4-13) and this is where you create the actual layout of the data on the label. To add a field to the label, click on the INSERT MERGE FIELD button to display a menu showing the available fields from your data source.

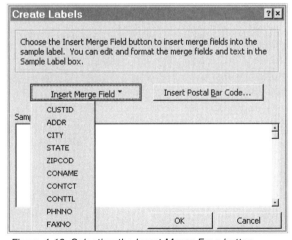

Figure 4-13: Selecting the Insert MERGE FIELD button.

First, add the company name. Do this by selecting the CONAME field from the menu. See Figure 4-14.

The field drops down to the first line in the label workspace, surrounded by the Word field delimiters. The data from this AS/400 field is substituted in this location for each record in your query. You can position the field using spaces and hard returns.

You also can change the formatting of one or more fields by selecting them and clicking your mouse's right button. To change fonts, spacing, shading, and many other formatting options, select the FONT option and the PARAGRAPH option from the menu (Figure 4-15).

Now you're ready to add the rest of the fields to your label. Put the name CONTCT and the title CONTTL on the second line separated by a dash. The address (ADDR) goes on the third line. The next line holds the city (CITY) followed by a comma and a space, the state (STATE), another space, and the ZIP code (ZIPCOD) all together on the same line. Press the Enter key to add a new line. When you're finished, your screen should look like the one shown in Figure 4-14.

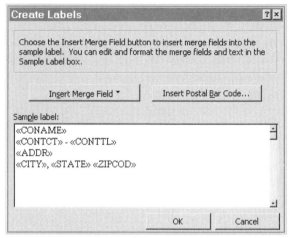

Figure 4-14: Selecting CONAME from the CREATE LABELS menu.

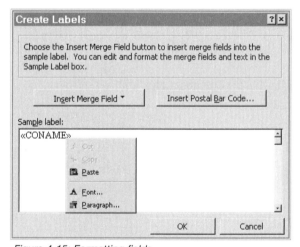

Figure 4-15: Formatting fields

You also can insert a postal barcode for the ZIP code field. To do this, click on the INSERT POSTAL BAR CODE button. Select the ZIP code (ZIPCOD) from the first drop-down menu, select the address (ADDR) from the second drop-down menu, and click on OK (Figure 4-16). You will notice a line added to your mailing list fields that reads DELIVERY POINT BAR CODE WILL PRINT HERE!

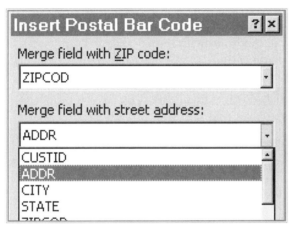

Figure 4-16: The INSERT POSTAL BAR CODE window.

When you have finished laying out the label, click on the OK button. You have now completed the first two steps of the mailing-label process. You will notice that you have a label layout on your screen that looks like Figure 4-17. The next step merges your customer data to create the labels.

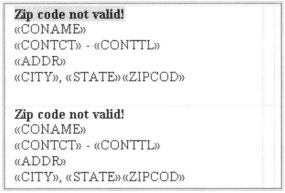

Figure 4-17: Label layout screen.

STEP 3: MERGE

The third step is to merge the data to create the labels. Do this by clicking on the MERGE button on the MAIL MERGE HELPER screen. When the MERGE dialog box appears, you can specify more options for how the labels will look and print.

Click on the MERGE TO drop-down box to display the options that allow you to specify the destination for the merged labels. The most common option is to merge them to a new document. You also can choose to merge them directly to the printer or to electronic mail. For this example, select the MERGE TO "New document" option. See Figure 4-18.

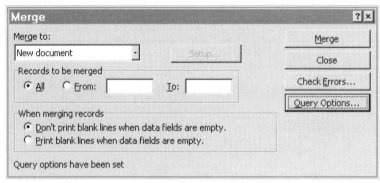

Figure 4-18: The MERGE TO dialogue box.

Another option on this screen allows you to specify which labels you want merged. This allows you to specify a numerical range of labels to print. This option is useful if your label printing has been interrupted for some reason and you need to start printing again from a specific label number.

You can also specify whether or not blank lines are printed when the field data is blank. This is useful in cases where you have a second address field that is sometimes blank. If this option is on, Word automatically omits the blank lines from the labels so they appear correct when printed.

For this example, leave all the options set at their defaults and press the MERGE button. Word goes to work and creates the labels from your AS/400 data source. When finished, your labels are in the form of a Word document that you can edit and print as needed. Using MS Query and Word makes it a breeze to create labels using your AS/400 data. See Figure 4-19.

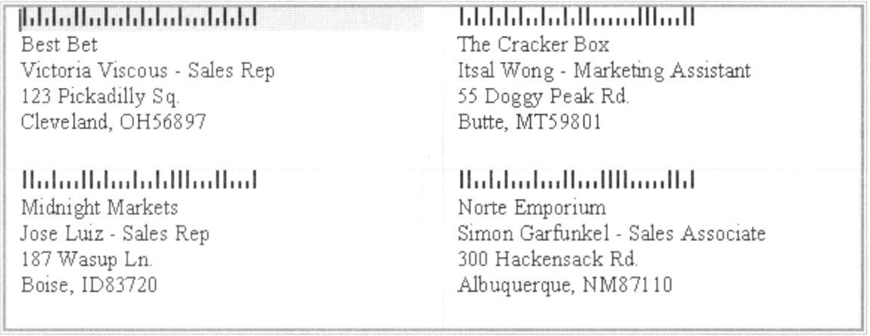

```
|l.l.l..ll.l..l.l.l.l.l..l.l.l.l.l|          l.l.l.l.l..l.l.l.ll.....lll...ll
```
Best Bet   The Cracker Box
Victoria Viscous - Sales Rep   Itsal Wong - Marketing Assistant
123 Pickadilly Sq.   55 Doggy Peak Rd.
Cleveland, OH56897   Butte, MT59801

```
ll..l..ll.l..l.l.lll..ll..l                 ll..l.l..l..ll..lll....l.l.l
```
Midnight Markets   Norte Emporium
Jose Luiz - Sales Rep   Simon Garfunkel - Sales Associate
187 Wasup Ln.   300 Hackensack Rd.
Boise, ID83720   Albuquerque, NM87110

Figure 4-19: Completed labels.

CREATING FORM LETTERS

Now you are ready to move on to form letters. Creating a form letter in Word is almost as easy as creating mailing labels. The process to tell Word which data to use is the same. The main difference is in the document layout. As with the mailing labels, there are three steps to creating a form letter. Step 1 is to set up the main document (CREATE). Step 2 is to select your data source (GET DATA). Step 3 is to perform the actual merge of the document and the data (MERGE). The following sections explain how to create a mail-merge letter to inform all your existing customers of a special sale you are holding just for them.

STEP 1: CREATE

Begin by creating a new blank document (Figure 4-1) in Word and selecting the MAIL MERGE option from the TOOLS menu.

On the MAIL MERGE HELPER screen, click on the CREATE button and select FORM LETTERS from the menu. See Figure 4-2.

When prompted to select ACTIVE WINDOW or NEW MAIN DOCUMENT choose ACTIVE WINDOW (Figure 4-4) to create a form letter in the current document.

STEP 2: GET DATA

Begin step 2 by clicking the GET DATA button on the MAIL MERGE HELPER screen. Then choose OPEN DATA SOURCE from the drop-down menu (Figure 4-5).

Once again, Word will prompt you to select a data source from your list of Word documents. Because you will use your AS/400 data, click on the MS QUERY button to start the Microsoft Query application. See Figure 4-6.

When MS Query starts, select your AS/400 data source that you used previously to create mailing labels (Figure 4-7). Because you are going to build the query manually, make sure the Query Wizard option is not checked, and press the OK button.

When the list of tables is presented, choose the customer table (CUSTMR), press the ADD button, and then press the CLOSE button. See Figure 4-8.

In the QUERY WINDOW, drag the asterisk from the table pane to the data pane to select all columns from all rows in the file. Refresh the query by clicking the QUERY NOW button on the toolbar. Under the FILE menu, choose the RETURN DATA TO MICROSOFT WORD option (Figure 4-9). To this point, everything you do to create a form letter is exactly the same as for creating mailing labels.

As shown in Figure 4-20, you are returned to Word and are presented with a dialog box that informs you that Word found no merge fields. Because you haven't created any merge fields yet, seeing this message is normal. The only option is to edit the main document. Click the EDIT MAIN DOCUMENT button to continue.

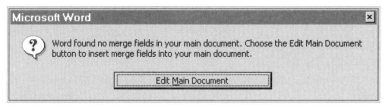

Figure 4-20: The EDIT MAIN DOCUMENT option.

Word displays a blank document with a new MERGE toolbar (Figure 4-21). You now can create the address portion of your letter.

Figure 4-21: The MERGE toolbar.

Click on the INSERT MERGE FIELD button, on the left-hand side of the MERGE toolbar, and select contact (CONTCT) from the drop-down menu (Figure 4-22). The contct field will appear in your document with the field delimiters around it. Press the Enter key to start a new line and use the INSERT MERGE FIELD button again to add the company name (CONAME) field.

Continue adding the fields for the address (ADDR, CITY, STATE, and ZIPCOD). Remember to add a comma and a space after the city and to add the appropriate state and ZIP code to the same

Insert Merge Field
Insert Word Field
CUSTID
ADDR
CITY
STATE
ZIPCOD
CONAME
CONTCT
CONTTL
PHNNO
FAXNO

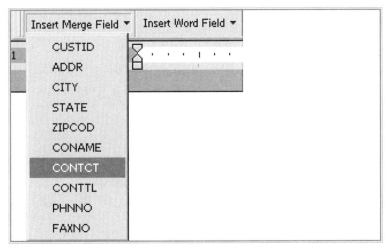

Figure 4-22: Select the INSERT MERGE FIELD button.

line. Press the Enter key to move to a new line. You will now have an address block that looks similar to the mailing labels you created earlier.

To add the date and the salutation, press the Enter key a couple of times to leave some space for your margin and then type in the current date. Press the Enter key a few more times to move down a couple of lines and type "Dear". Then leave a space and insert the CONTCT field in the document using the INSERT MERGE FIELD button. When the merge is performed, the name from the AS/400 will be substituted in the text right after the salutation ("Dear"). End the line with a comma.

Now you can insert a few line spaces and start typing the body of your letter. For this example, type the sentence "How is life in" and add a space. Then insert the city field by once again using the Insert Merge Field. Add a question mark to finish the sentence. Your page should look like the example shown in Figure 4-23.

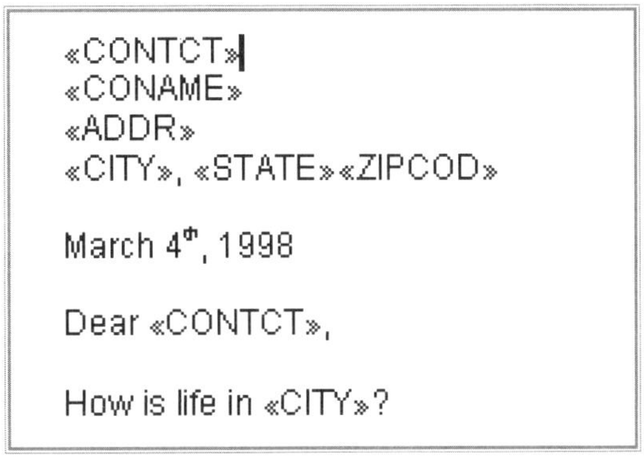

«CONTCT»
«CONAME»
«ADDR»
«CITY», «STATE»«ZIPCOD»
March 4th, 1998
Dear «CONTCT»,
How is life in «CITY»?

Figure 4-23: A form letter page setup.

You can write an entire multi-page letter, using fields from the database, wherever appropriate. At any time you can review your work by clicking on the VIEW MERGED DATA toggle button (Figure 4-24) on the toolbar.

This shows you how your data looks when it is substituted into the letter (Figure 4-25). Click the button again to go back to field-view mode, or click on the FIRST, PREVIOUS, NEXT, or LAST record buttons on the merge toolbar to move to different records in the database.

Figure 4-24: The VIEW MERGED DATA button.

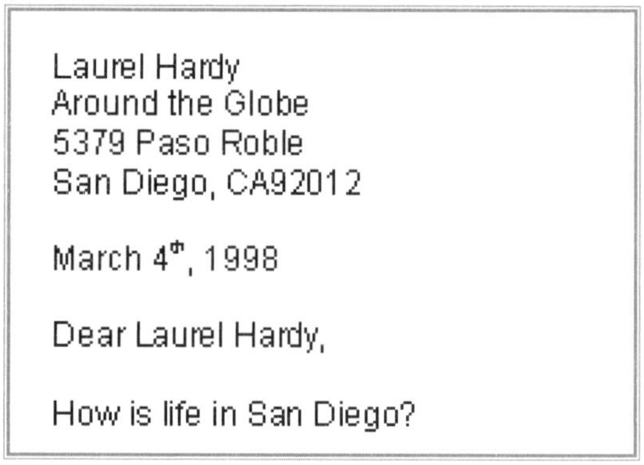

STEP 3: MERGE

When you are finished creating your letter, you can merge it to a new document, merge it to the printer, edit your data source, or view the mail merge helper screen by clicking on the appropriate button on the merge toolbar.

Laurel Hardy
Around the Globe
5379 Paso Roble
San Diego, CA92012

March 4th, 1998

Dear Laurel Hardy,

How is life in San Diego?

Figure 4-25: Form letter with merged data.

For this example, merge the data and the form to a new document. Click on the MERGE TO NEW DOCUMENT button (Figure 4-26) on the merge toolbar and wait for Word to create a new document with separate sections for each record.

Figure 4-26: The MERGE TO NEW DOCUMENT button.

When Word finishes the task, you will see the completed document with all the data merged. Each record retrieved is located in a separate section.

Creating form letters with Word and AS/400 data isn't too difficult. There are endless possibilities for creating advanced mail merge letters with Word and MS Query. With Word, you can add conditional fields to substitute "Mr." or "Ms." where appropriate. With MS Query, you can create total records and then create a letter in Word, confirming the customer's order, with the exact dollar amount of the order substituted in the appropriate place. The possibilities are tremendous.

CREATING ADDRESSED ENVELOPES

To create addressed envelopes using AS/400 customer data, first open your Microsoft Word application and create a new blank document. See Figure 4-1. To begin the process of addressing envelopes, click on the TOOLS menu and select MAIL MERGE to start the MAIL MERGE HELPER. See Figure 4-2.

From the MAIL MERGE HELPER screen, you can see that there are three main steps to addressing envelopes. Step 1 is to set up the main document (CREATE). Step 2 is to select your data source (GET DATA). Step 3 is to perform the actual merge of the document and the data (MERGE). The following sections detail each of these steps.

STEP 1: CREATE

Begin step 1 by clicking on the CREATE button. When the drop-down menu appears, select ENVELOPES from this menu. Word then prompts you to choose between using the active document window or creating a new document window (Figure 4-4). Because you don't have any data in your existing document, you can simply click on the ACTIVE WINDOW button. Word will now use your new blank document to create your addressed envelopes.

STEP 2: GET DATA

Begin step 2 by clicking on the GET DATA button. Another drop-down menu appears below the button asking whether you want to create a data source or use an existing one (Figure 4-5). Select OPEN DATA SOURCE because this example uses an existing AS/400 data source.

A file-open dialog box appears (Figure 4-6). Once again, Word defaults to obtaining its external data from another Word document. Because you don't want to use a Word document as your data source, click on the MS Query button on the right-hand side of the dialogue box. This will open MS Query and allow you to grab data from your AS/400.

After MS Query loads, select your AS/400 ODBC data source from the list of available data sources and click on the OK button (see Figure 4-7). MS Query presents you with a list of tables from your data source. Select the customer table (CUSTMR), press the ADD button, and then the CLOSE button (Figure 4-8).

The customer table is now displayed in the table pane of the query window. To add all fields to the data pane, drag the asterisk from the customer table and drop it in the data pane. Note that you can add criteria as necessary to limit the data to the records you want. For this example, you will create addressed envelopes for all customers.

Let's sort the query by company name. To do this, click on the company name field column header (CONAME) and click the SORT ASCENDING button on the toolbar.

Refresh the query by clicking on the QUERY NOW button on the toolbar. The data is retrieved from the AS/400. Review your data to ensure that it is correct. When you are satisfied with the query, return to Word by selecting RETURN DATA TO MICROSOFT WORD from the FILE menu (see Figure 4-9).

Now you have returned to your Word document. A dialog box appears telling you that you have to set up your main document. Because there is only one choice, click the SETUP MAIN DOCUMENT button (Figure 4-10).

You are now presented with the ENVELOPE OPTION box (Figure 4-27A) where, on the Envelope Options tab (Figure 4-27B), you are prompted to specify the size of envelope to be used. Here you can customize the envelope specification to exactly match the envelopes you want to address. You can specify the font and font size for both the delivery and, if required, the return address.

Click on the PRINTING OPTIONS tab to select a feed method for your envelopes that is correct for your printer. Once you have set all your options, click on the OK button.

The ENVELOPE ADDRESS dialogue box is where you create the actual layout of the data that will appear on the envelope. This dialogue box is the same as the CREATE LABELS dialogue box used to create mailing labels (Figure 4-13). To add a field to the envelope, click on the INSERT MERGE FIELD button.

A menu displays the available fields from your data source. First, add the customer's company name by selecting the CONAME field from the menu.

The field drops down to the first line in the envelope workspace, surrounded by the Word field delimiters. The data from this AS/400 field is substituted in this location for each record in your query. You can position the field using spaces and hard returns.

You also can change the formatting of one or more fields by selecting them and clicking the right-mouse button (Figure 4-15). This will allow you to change fonts, spacing, shading, and many other formatting options.

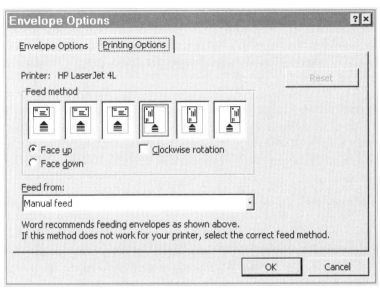

Figure 4-27A: The ENVELOPE OPTION box.

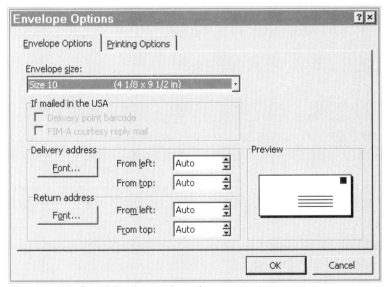

Figure 4-27B: Specifying the envelope size.

Now you are ready to add the rest of the fields to your envelope. Put the name CONTCT and the title CONTTL on the second line separated by a dash. The address (ADDR) goes on the third line. The next line holds the city (CITY) followed by a comma and a space, the state (STATE), and the ZIP code (ZIPCOD) all together on the same line. When you are finished, your screen should look like the example shown in Figure 4-14.

You also can insert a postal bar code for the ZIP code field. To do this, click on the INSERT POSTAL BAR CODE button (Figure 4-16). Select ZIP code (ZIPCOD) from the first drop-down menu, select the address (ADDR) from the second drop-down menu. When you have finished laying out the envelope, click on the ok button.

Now you are ready to verify the return address that will appear in the top left-hand corner of the envelope. Click on the EDIT button next to CREATE on the MAIL MERGE HELPER window (Figure 4-28).

Then click on the envelope's MAIN DOCUMENT. Verify that the return address is correct; you can correct it here if necessary. If you do not require a return address on your envelope because you have "pre-printed" envelopes, you can delete the return address here (or leave it blank if there is no return address set up). The return address you enter here will be printed on all your envelopes. When you have completed your return address, your envelope should look like the example shown in Figure 4-29. Click on the TOOLS menu and select MAIL MERGE to return to the MAIL MERGE HELPER dialogue box. You have now completed the first two steps of the envelope process.

STEP 3: MERGE

The third step is to create the addressed envelopes by clicking on the MERGE button on the MAIL MERGE HELPER screen. The MERGE dialog box appears as shown in Figure 4-18. Here you can specify more options for how the printed envelopes will look.

Click on the MERGE TO drop-down box to display the options that allow you to specify the destination for the merged envelopes. The most common option is to merge them to a new document. You can also choose to merge them directly to the printer or to an electronic mail system. For this example, choose the new DOCUMENT option.

Other options on this screen allow you to specify which envelopes you want merged and to specify a numerical range of envelopes to print. The latter option is useful if your envelope printing has been interrupted for some reason and you need to start printing again from a specific envelope number.

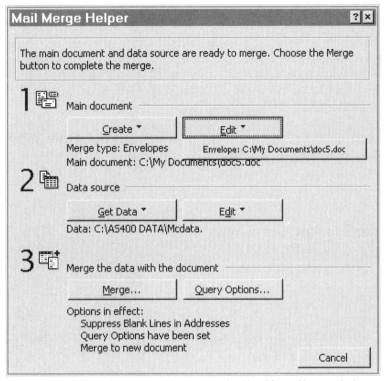

Figure 4-28: Editing the return address using the MAIL MERGE HELPER window.

Figure 4-29: Envelope layout.

You also can specify whether or not blank lines are printed when field data is blank. This would be useful in cases where you have a second address field that is sometimes blank. If this option is on, Word automatically omits the blank lines from the envelopes so they appear correct when printed. For this example, leave all the options set at their defaults and press the MERGE button.

Word goes to work and creates the envelopes using the customer data from your AS/400 data source. When finished, your envelopes are in the form of a Word document that you can edit and print as necessary.

You have now completed all three steps used in creating addressed envelopes. Processing addressed envelopes using your AS/400 data is fast and easy when using MS Query and Word.

INSERTING DATA INTO A TABLE

Word can also use MS Query to produce a document table from an external database. This function is useful for creating lists that can be used as reports. The following section explains how to create a report that shows the name, city, and state of each of your vendors.

Begin by opening a new blank document (Figure 4-1) in Word. To insert data into a table, use the database toolbar by right-clicking anywhere on the existing toolbars and selecting DATABASE from the displayed list (Figure 4-30).

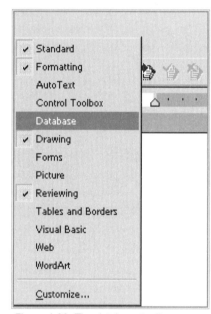

Figure 4-30: The database toolbar.

An alternate method for displaying the database toolbar is to click on the VIEW menu; select the TOOLBARS option (Figure 4-31), and then select DATABASE from the list.

Figure 4-31: The database toolbar.

Once you have the database toolbar displayed at the top of your screen, click the INSERT DATABASE button (Figure 4-32) on the database toolbar.

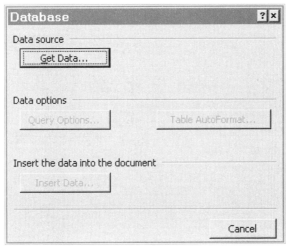

Figure 4-32: The INSERT DATABASE button.

This brings up the DATABASE dialog box (Figure 4-33). Click on the GET DATA button. Word assumes that you want to use another Word document as the data source, and it displays the file-open dialog box (see Figure 4-6). Press the MS Query button to start the MS Query program.

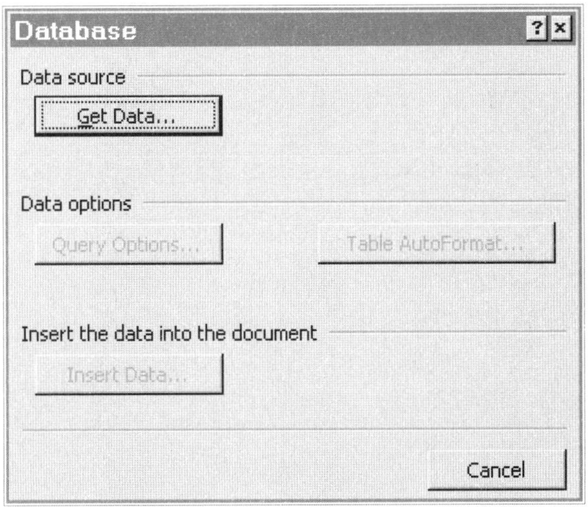

Figure 4-33: The DATABASE dialogue box.

After MS Query starts, select your previously defined AS/400 data source (Figure 4-7). Make sure the option to use the query wizard is not selected. Click OK and wait for the list of tables to be displayed. From the list that appears, select the Vendor Master (VNDMST) table. Click the add button and then the CLOSE button.

Next, select the fields that you want MS Query to use to build your table. Select and drag the CONAME, CITY, and STATE fields from the vendor table to the data pane. Using the Control key you can select and drag all three items at once. When you refresh the query by clicking on the QUERY NOW button on the toolbar, your screen should look like the example shown in Figure 4-34.

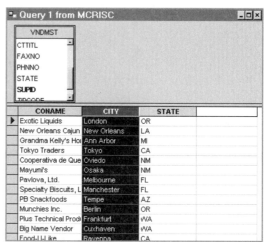

Figure 4-34: Vendor master table query results.

When you are satisfied that you have all the correct information displayed in the data pane, return the data to Word by selecting RETURN DATA TO MICROSOFT WORD from the FILE menu.

This will bring you back to the DATABASE dialog box in Word. It's easy to create a professional look for your table by clicking on the TABLE AUTOFORMAT button. With the TABLE AUTOFORMAT dialogue box (Figure 4-35), you can choose the look you want for your table.

The TABLE AUTOFORMAT options allow you to customize the look of your table. You can experiment by

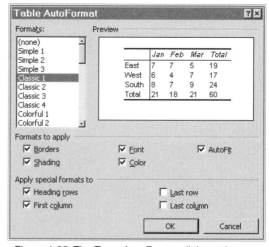

Figure 4-35: The TABLE AUTOFORMAT dialogue box.

selecting different standard formats from the displayed list and customizing them to your liking by using the checkboxes in the FORMATS TO APPLY and APPLY SPECIAL FORMATS TO sections of the screen. For this example, choose the CLASSIC 1 format from the list and accept the default settings by pressing the OK button. This will return you to the DATABASE screen. Click the INSERT DATA button.

Word prompts you to select which records to insert (Figure 4-36). If you want to limit the report to, for example, the first 10 vendors, you can click on the From button, then enter a 1 in the FROM box and a 10 in the TO box. For this example, choose ALL and press the OK button.

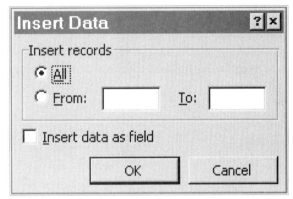

Figure 4-36: Select records to insert.

Word inserts the data into your document in tabular form (Figure 4-37). Note that with the options you chose, the data is no longer linked to the AS/400.

CONAME	CITY	STATE
Exotic Liquids	London	OR
New Orleans Cajun Delights	New Orleans	LA
Grandma Kelly's Homestead	Ann Arbor	MI
Tokyo Traders	Tokyo	CA
Cooperativa de Quesos 'Las Cabras'	Oviedo	NM
Mayumi's	Osaka	NM
Pavlova, Ltd.	Melbourne	FL
Specialty Biscuits, Ltd.	Manchester	FL
PB Snackfoods	Tempe	AZ
Munchies Inc.	Berlin	OR
Plus Technical Products	Frankfurt	WA
Big Name Vendor	Cuxhaven	WA
Food-U-Like	Ravenna	CA

Figure 4-37: Results Table.

SUMMARY

This chapter explains how to create mailing labels, format form letters, address envelopes, and how to insert data into tables. Combined with MS Query, Word offers extremely powerful solutions to assist you in formatting your data into almost any presentation format appropriate for the task at hand.

There are many ways you can use your AS/400 data with Microsoft Word. The flexibility provided by ODBC, MS Query, and Word allows you to easily accomplish many things that previously were difficult or complex tasks. In the context of using AS/400 data with a word processor, the possibilities with Word seem almost endless.

5

Analyzing
AS/400 Data with Excel

Microsoft Excel is probably the most powerful data-access and analysis tool in the standard edition of Microsoft Office. (Note that Access is offered as part of the professional edition of Microsoft Office.) Excel allows for easy creation of lists, graphs, and reports, and it provides many exceptional features to help make advanced data analysis simple.

This chapter explores using Microsoft Excel to analyze AS/400 sales data. First, you'll find out how to bring data, in the form of a list, from the AS/400 into Excel. Then you can use that data to create a chart. Also examined is how to create and use an Excel PivotTable. A PivotTable is a very powerful tool for analyzing large amounts of data. And there is information on the Client Access Excel add-in feature as well.

Excel spreadsheets are organized into so-called *books*. Books are collections of individual sheets (or pages). A separate spreadsheet can be on each sheet of the book.

When you first start Excel, a new book is created and the first sheet of the book is displayed for you. To change to another page in the book, you simply click on the sheet tabs at the bottom left of the screen (Figure 5-1).

RETRIEVING DATA IN A LIST

Begin by starting Excel. When the program has finished loading, a new book is displayed with the first sheet showing. Let's move right into bringing in the AS/400 data. To retrieve data from the AS/400, use Microsoft Query. First, click on DATA, and then select the GET EXTERNAL DATA menu option. Next, select CREATE NEW QUERY from the submenu (Figure 5-2).

After MS Query loads, it asks you to specify a data source. Select the data source for your AS/400 data and press the OK button (Figure 5-3).

After a moment, the list of tables is displayed (Figure 5-4). To retrieve the total dollar sales by product, select the product (PRODCT) and the order detail (ORDDET) tables by clicking on each table, one at a time, and selecting the ADD button. When both tables have been added to the query, click the CLOSE button to close the dialog box.

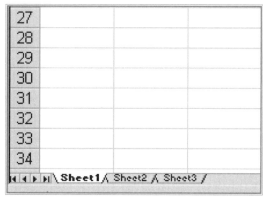

Figure 5-1: Sheet tabs.

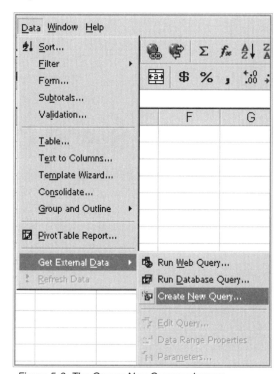

Figure 5-2: The CREATE NEW QUERY submenu.

The product and order detail tables are now displayed in the table pane of your Query 1 (Figure 5-5).

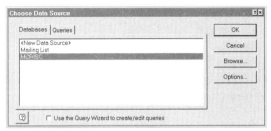

Figure 5-3: Selecting the data source screen.

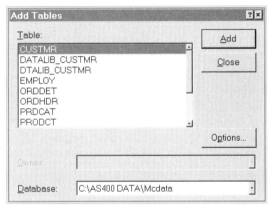

Figure 5-4: Adding tables.

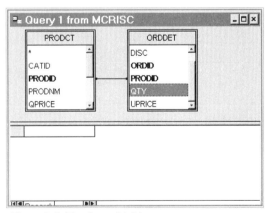

Figure 5-5: The Query1 table pane.

Now you have to tell MS Query how to join these tables. Join the product table to the order detail table by selecting the PRODID field from the product table and dragging it to the PRODID field in the order detail table. When this is done, a line, indicating the join, appears between the tables.

Now, you can add the fields to the query. Select the Product Name (PRODNM) field from the Product table and drag it down into the data pane.

To add the summary field that calculates the gross extended sales for the product, try a new shortcut for MS Query. First, click on the empty column header to the right of the product name column. Type "sum(qty*uprice)" and press the Enter key (Figure 5-6). This adds a calculated field that is the sum of the quantity sold times the unit price.

Double click on the column header you have just created. The EDIT COLUMN window appears. Change the column heading to "Sales" and click the OK button (Figure 5-7).

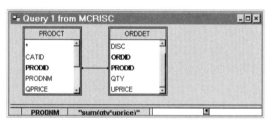

Figure 5-6: Adding the summary field.

Press the QUERY NOW button (Figure 5-8A) on the toolbar.

The query is displayed (Figure 5-8B). As you can see, it is sorted alphabetically, by product, with the total dollar amount of product sold next to the product name.

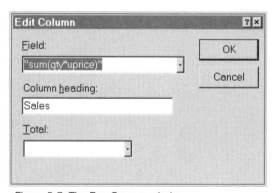

Figure 5-7: The EDIT COLUMN window.

Click on the file menu and select RETURN DATA TO MICROSOFT EXCEL. When Excel reappears, the RETURNING EXTERNAL DATA TO MICROSOFT EXCEL dialog box is displayed (Figure 5-9).

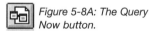

Figure 5-8A: The Query Now button.

There are a few options that can be set on this screen. Click the

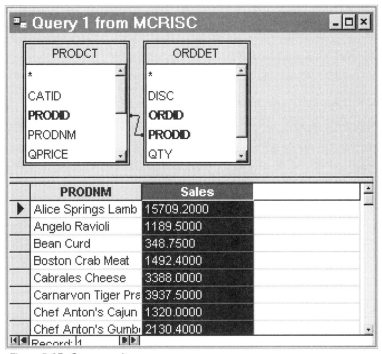

Figure 5-8B: Query results.

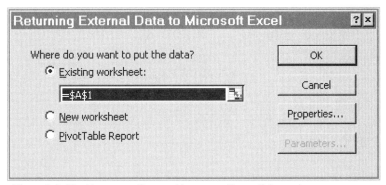

Figure 5-9: The RETURNING DATA TO MICROSOFT EXCEL dialogue box.

PROPERTIES button. Make certain the SAVE QUERY DEFINITION box is checked on the External Data Range Properties dialog box (Figure 5-10). After you have reviewed the options on this screen, and confirmed that they are correct, click the OK button to finish.

You are now back at the RETURNING EXTERNAL DATA TO MICROSOFT EXCEL dialog box. You can select a destination for the data either by typing the range into the destination field textbox or by clicking on the appropriate sheet and location in your Excel book.

One of the nice features of Excel is that you can choose destinations with the mouse, by pointing and clicking, even when a dialog box is displayed on top of the spreadsheet.

Choose "A1" of SHEET1 as the location to put your data. Do this by clicking on the top left cell of SHEET1 of your book. Notice that the text in the destination field in the dialog box changes to "=Sheet1!A1".

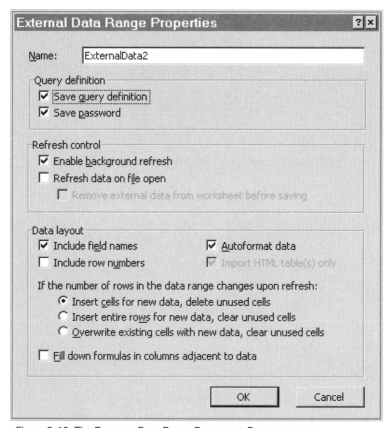

Figure 5-10: The EXTERNAL DATA RANGE PROPERTIES DIALOGUE screen.

Don't worry. Excel won't place all your data in that one cell. Rather, the destination cell refers to the location where Excel should start when placing data into the workbook spreadsheet.

Click the OK button to accept your options. With the exception of the column headings, the data appears in the spreadsheet (Figure 5-11) much as it appears in the MS Query data pane.

A	B	C
PRODNM	**Expr1001**	
Alice Springs Lamb	15709.2	
Angelo Ravioli	1189.5	
Bean Curd	348.75	
Boston Crab Meat	1492.4	
Cabrales Cheese	3388	
Carnarvon Tiger Prawns	3937.5	
Chef Anton's Cajun Seasoning	1320	
Chef Anton's Gumbo Mix	2130.4	
Cloudberry Liqueur	4256.4	
Courdavault Raclette Cheese	6736.5	
Dharamsala Tea	3006	
Dutch Chocolate	153	
Escargots from Burgundy	1100.25	

Figure 5-11: An Excel spreadsheet.

A new toolbar appears. You can use the EXTERNAL DATA toolbar (Figure 5-12) to edit the query, set properties for the range, and refresh the query to retrieve new data.

Figure 5-12: The EXTERNAL DATA toolbar.

At this point, you cannot update your data from within Excel. You can use the retrieved data, just as you would any other data in Excel, with some additional capabilities. One of those capabilities is to refresh the data to update any changes that might have occurred on the AS/400. To do this, simply:

❖ Click anywhere in the list.

❖ Click on the DATA menu.

❖ Select REFRESH DATA from the submenu (Figure 5-13).

As an alternative method for updating data, you also can click the REFRESH button on the EXTERNAL DATA toolbar. Either way, Excel uses MS Query in the background to refresh

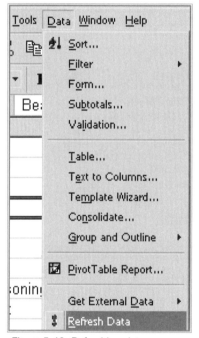

Figure 5-13: Refreshing data.

the data from your AS/400 data source. This feature can be very useful in producing monthly reports or year-to-date reports.

You also can edit the query used to produce your product list. There are two ways to do this. The quickest way is to click the EDIT QUERY button on the left-side of the EXTERNAL DATA toolbar. MS Query then loads and you can change the query as appropriate.

The other way is to single click inside the data and then click on the DATA menu. Select the GET EXTERNAL DATA option and then the EDIT QUERY option on the submenu (Figure

5-14). This allows you to edit the query and also allows you to change some of the options associated with the query.

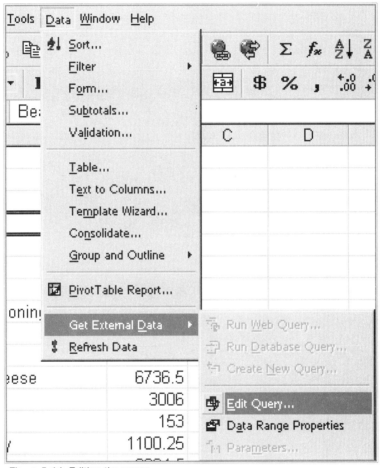

Figure 5-14: Editing the query.

CREATING A CHART FROM AS/400 DATA

A list of products with their total sales is hardly exciting. Let's create a bar chart that shows the sales of the top 10 items in your list. To do this, you need to sort the data by the dollar amount in descending order.

PREPARING THE DATA

First, while holding the shift key, highlight both columns of the query by clicking on the column headers. Then, from the DATA menu, select the SORT option.

The SORT dialog box is displayed. If the SORT WARNING dialog box (Figure 5-15) appears, you did not select both columns of data correctly. Check the EXPAND THE SELECTION box to continue.

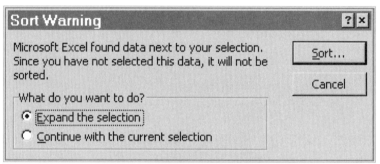

Figure 5-15: The SORT WARNING dialogue box.

In the SORT dialog box (Figure 5-16), you can specify up to three columns to SORT BY (either in ascending or descending order). In the first Sort by box, select the summary sales field from the drop-down list box. Note that because you did not name the field in MS Query, a unique name is assigned for this field. Click on DESCENDING to change the sort order to highest to lowest. Click the OK button and the list is sorted with the biggest-selling items at the top.

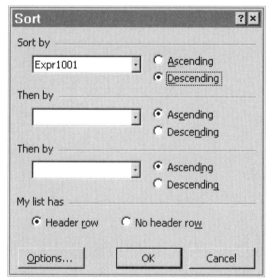

Figure 5-16: The SORT dialogue box.

Creating Charts

Because charts allow you to present data in a visual format, the significance of your data becomes easier to grasp. Before creating a chart from the preceding example data, you should change the headers to more meaningful names. Change the header for the total sales to read SALES. And change the PRODNM header to read PRODUCT. Do this by clicking on each header and replacing the text in the text box located on the toolbar above your workbook (Figure 5-17).

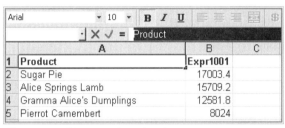

Figure 5-17: Change column headers.

As the first step in creating a chart, select the first 10 rows of data on your worksheet. You must carefully select both the product name and the total sales dollar amount columns, as well as the headers for both columns. Including the header, you actually will be selecting 11 rows. Click on the PRODUCT header. Then, holding down the shift key, click on row 11 of the SALES column (Figure 5-18). This selects the first 10 rows of your data.

	A	B
1	Product	Sales
2	Sugar Pie	17003.4
3	Alice Springs Lamb	15709.2
4	Gramma Alice's Dumplings	12581.8
5	Pierrot Camembert	8024
6	Uncle Bob's Organic Dried Pears	7926
7	Malaysian Coffee	7624
8	Sir Rodney's Marmalade	7354.8
9	Perth Meat Pies	6778.3
10	Courdavault Raclette Cheese	6736.5
11	Manchego La Pastora Cheese	6688
12	Shepard's Pie	5421.6
13	Giovanni's Mozzarella	4963.9

Figure 5-18: Selecting the first 10 rows of data.

Now click on the CHART WIZARD button (Figure 5-19A) on the toolbar.

Figure 5-19A: The CHART WIZARD button.

The CHART WIZARD - STEP 1 OF 4 - CHART TYPE screen is displayed (Figure 5-19B). If Office Assistant also opens, you can close it by clicking on the NO DON'T PROVIDE HELP NOW option.

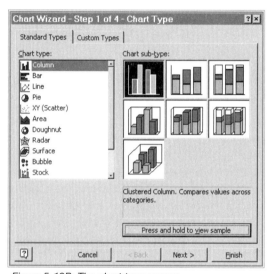

Figure 5-19B: The chart type screen.

Select a type of chart for your data. The STANDARD tab lists the major types of charts on the left side of the screen. Each major type of chart also has corresponding subtypes. These are shown on the right side of the screen. To select a type of chart, you must select both a major type and a subtype.

Selecting the PRESS AND HOLD TO VIEW SAMPLE button displays your data in the selected format (Figure 5-20). This is great for quickly previewing your chart to make sure it is exactly as you want it. To find what you are looking for, you can click through the various types of charts.

You can also check out the types of charts available under the CUSTOM TYPES tab located at the top of the view sample screen. As indicated in Figure 5-21, there are some interesting chart formats available.

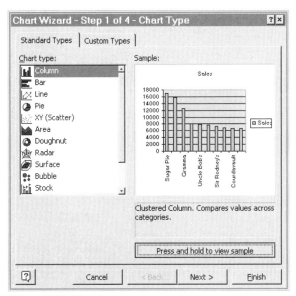

Figure 5-20: The view sample screen.

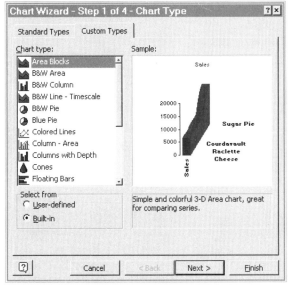

Figure 5-21: The custom types screen.

For this example, select the COLUMN option for the major type and the CLUSTERED COLUMN option (top left) for a subtype. These options are both located under the STANDARD tab. After you have selected your chart type, click the NEXT button to proceed to the next screen.

The CHART WIZARD - STEP 2 OF 4 - CHART SOURCE DATA screen (Figure 5-22) asks you which data you want to graph. There are various options located under the DATA RANGE and SERIES tabs. The data you previously selected is already chosen. You can accept these options by clicking the NEXT button to continue.

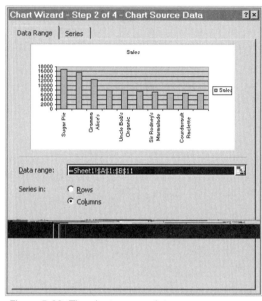

Figure 5-22: The chart source data screen.

The CHART WIZARD - STEP 3 OF 4 - CHART OPTIONS screen is displayed as shown in Figure 5-23. On this screen, you can set many of the chart's options. Among other things, you can specify such things as the title, the legend, axes, gridlines, and labels for the data. Clicking on the tabs along the top of the screen display allows you to control the settings. For this example, accept the defaults and proceed to the next step by clicking the NEXT button.

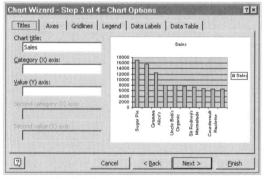

Figure 5-23: The chart options screen.

On the CHART WIZARD - STEP 4 OF 4 - CHART LOCATION screen (Figure 5-24), you tell Excel where you want the chart placed. You can place it in a new sheet or place it as an object in an existing sheet.

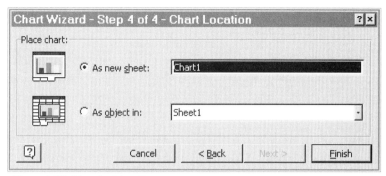

Figure 5-24: The chart location screen.

Because you aren't really concerned with the details of the data and just want to see the chart, let's place it in a new sheet. Do this by selecting the AS NEW SHEET option. Clicking the FINISH button places the chart in a new sheet.

Your chart is returned on a new sheet (Figure 5-25). You still can customize the chart using all of Excel's tools.

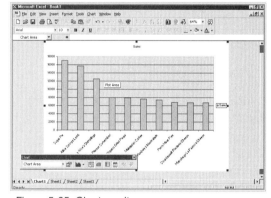

Figure 5-25: Chart results.

You also will notice that a new CHART toolbar (Figure 5-26) appears on the screen.

When you want to refresh the data in the chart, you do so by refreshing the underlying query from which that the chart was created.

Figure 5-26: The CHART toolbar.

To refresh the data, go to SHEET1—by clicking the SHEET1 tab at the bottom left of the screen—where your data is listed. On SHEET1, refresh the data by clicking the REFRESH DATA button on the EXTERNAL DATA toolbar. The query is refreshed in the background.

You can tell the refresh is happening because there will be a spinning green globe in the status bar at the bottom of the screen.

Unfortunately, you will now have to resort the list using Excel. Your list is now sorted alphabetically again and not by volume of sales. In this instance, the data could not be sorted easily in MS Query because the combination of MS Query and the Client Access ODBC driver does not allow for sorting by a calculated field.

It is possible to sort the query by directly entering the SQL for the correct sort into MS Query. However, directly editing SQL is a topic that is beyond the scope of this book. There are some workarounds that can be used if you encounter this problem.

1. Enter the SQL directly into MS Query, as mentioned above.

2. Create an Excel macro that refreshes the query and then sorts the data once it is returned to Excel.

3. Create a logical file or view on the AS/400 that is sorted correctly.

CREATING A PIVOTTABLE

An interesting feature of Excel, PivotTables can be useful for analyzing trends in large amounts of data. PivotTables are so called because they take raw data in row and column format and pivot it around a core data area to provide you with different views of the data. The PIVOTTABLE WIZARD can be used to create a PivotTable that summarizes which products each sales-person sold in each state. There are four steps to this process.

STEP 1

Begin with a new workbook by clicking on the NEW icon on the toolbar or by selecting NEW from the FILE menu. Clicking on the DATA menu and selecting the PIVOTTABLE REPORT option starts the PIVOTTABLE WIZARD (Figure 5-27). Again, if the office assistant also opens, you can close it by clicking on the NO DON'T PROVIDE HELP NOW option.

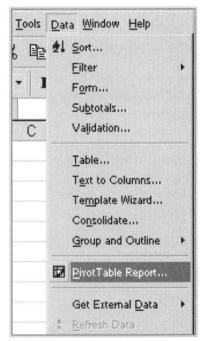

Figure 5-27: Selecting the PIVOTTABLE REPORT from DATA menu.

In Step 1 of the PivotTable wizard sequence, Excel asks "where is the data you want to analyze" (Figure 5-28). As in the other examples, use MS Query to bring the data in from the AS/400. To do this, select EXTERNAL DATA SOURCE and click on the button labeled NEXT.

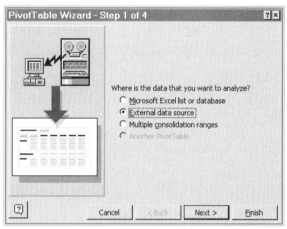

Figure 5-28: The PivotTable report from Step 1.

STEP 2

In Step 2, to retrieve your data, click on the GET DATA button (Figure 5-29).

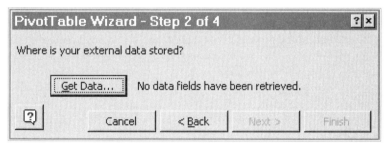

Figure 5-29: Step 1 of the PivotTable report.

After MS Query loads, choose your AS/400 data source and click the OK button (Figure 5-30).

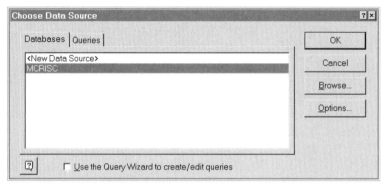

Figure 5-30: The CHOOSE DATA SOURCE screen.

When the list of tables appears, choose the customer (custmr), order header (ORDHDR), order detail (ORDDET), product (PRODCT), and the employee (EMPLOY) tables by selecting them and clicking the ADD button. When all five tables have been added, click the CLOSE button to finish.

With your five tables displayed in the table pane, you now need to join all the tables. Use the tables' primary keys by dragging:

❖ CUSTID field from the CUSTOMER table to the CUSTID field on the ORDER HEADER table.

❖ ORDID field from ORDER HEADER table to the ORDID field on ORDER DETAIL table.

❖ EMPID field from EMPLOYEE table to the EMPID field on ORDER HEADER table.

❖ PRODID field from the ORDER DETAIL table to the PRODID field on the PRODUCT table.

When completed, the tables will be joined together as shown in Figure 5-31. The EMPLOYEE table in this example is used to retrieve the name of the salesman for a particular order.

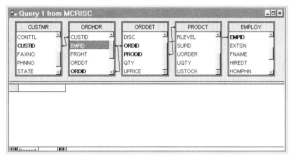

Figure 5-31: Linking tables in a table pane in Step 2.

The goal of this query is to produce a list that shows the employee name, the state where the sales were made, and a total dollar amount of each product sold. To add these fields to the query, drag from the table pane to the data pane:

❖ LNAME from the EMPLOYEE table.

❖ STATE from the CUSTOMER table.

❖ PRODNM FROM THE PRODUCT table.

Add a summary total field by clicking in the empty header field to the right of PRODNM in the data pane. Type "sum(qty*uprice)" and press the Enter key. Then refresh the query by clicking on the QUERY NOW button on the toolbar.

When the query refreshes, you will see a summary query that shows the total amount of each product sold by each salesperson in each state (Figure 5-32).

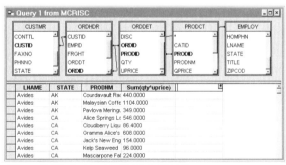

Figure 5-32: Query results from Step 2.

Select RETURN DATA TO MICROSOFT EXCEL from the FILE menu to return to Excel. When Excel reappears, click the NEXT button on the PIVOTTABLE WIZARD dialog box (Figure 5-29) to go to step 3.

STEP 3

Step 3 of the PIVOTTABLE
WIZARD (Figure 5-33) is
where the bulk of the
action takes place. Here
you define exactly how
you want the PivotTable
to look. You can create a
pivot table that allows the
selection of a specific
salesperson and shows the
sales by state and product
for that salesperson.

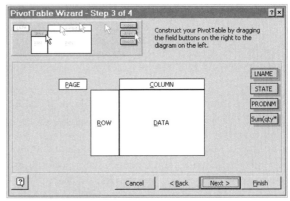

Figure 5-33: The PIVOTTABLE WIZARD from Step 3.

From the right-hand side
of the screen, drag the last-name field (LNAME) to the box with the word PAGE in it. This
designates the last name as the PAGE field, which means that a new page is created for
each different salesperson.

Next, drag the product-name field (PRODNM) to the box with the word ROW in it. This
creates a row for each product sold by the salesperson.

Then drag the STATE field to the box marked COLUMN. This creates a column for each
state in which a sale was made.

To finish the layout, drag
the expression field
"sum(qty*uprice)" to the
DATA section of the
PivotTable. The
expression field is the
summary field that you
create by summing the
quantity-sold field. Your
screen should look like
the example shown in
Figure 5-34. To continue
to Step 4, click on the
button marked NEXT.

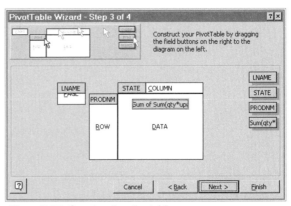

Figure 5-34: Constructing the table.

STEP 4

Step 4 allows the setting of several options (Figure 5-35). One of those options is the location of the PivotTable in the workbook. When specifying the location, you can use your mouse to navigate to the spot where you want to position the table and click in the cell where the upper left corner of the table should be. For this example, click in the "A1" cell (top left of your screen).

Figure 5-35: The PIVOTTABLE WIZARD from Step 4.

By clicking the OPTIONS button (Figure 5-36), you can specify the options for the PivotTable. Set the title of your PivotTable to "Sales by State" by entering the text in the PIVOTTABLE OPTIONS NAME textbox. Other options you can set include:

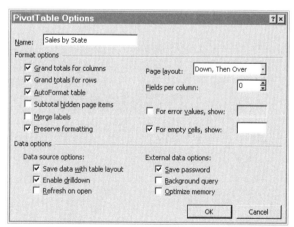

Figure 5-36: Step 4 options.

❖   Whether or not you want totals on the rows and columns.

❖   If you want to save the data with the PivotTable.

❖   If you want the automatic layout option on when the table is created.

For this example, leave all these options checked and press the OK button.

By clicking the FINISH button, the PivotTable is created and placed on your screen (Figure 5-37).

A	B	C	D
LNAME	(All) ▾		
Sum of Sum(qty*uprice)	STATE		
PRODNM	AK	CA	ID
Alice Springs Lamb	624	546	4953
Angelo Ravioli		780	
Bean Curd			
Boston Crab Meat			977.6
Cabrales Cheese			980
Carnarvon Tiger Prawns			
Chef Anton's Cajun Seasoning			
Chef Anton's Gumbo Mix		640.5	
Cloudberry Liqueur	900	266.4	2370

Figure 5-37: PIVOTTABLE results.

As shown in Figure 5-38, a new PivotTable toolbox comes on the screen.

Figure 5-38: The PIVOTTABLE toolbox.

Notice the drop-down list box in the cell next to the LNAME box on your worksheet. If you drop the list box down and choose a different salesperson, the PivotTable changes to reflect the data for the salesperson you indicate. You also can choose ALL from this list box to display all data from all salespeople. See Figure 5-39.

A	B	C
LNAME	(All)	
	(All)	
Sum of Sum(qty*uprice)	Avides	
PRODNM	Clay	CA
	Drew	
Alice Springs Lamb	Jackson	548
Angelo Ravioli	Joplin	780
Bean Curd	Mito	
Boston Crab Meat	Redfurd	

Figure 5-39: The EMPLOYEE list box.

You can make this table more presentable by changing some of the titles from the raw field name to something more meaningful. Double-click on the LNAME gray box.

The PIVOTTABLE FIELD dialog box appears (Figure 5-40). Here you can change the name, orientation, and other information for that field. Change the field to LAST NAME and click the OK button. You can change the other field names in the same manner.

You now have completed all four steps used in creating a PivotTable with the PivotTable wizard. As you can see, PivotTables are a quick, easy, and powerful way to view your data in ways that aren't as easily accomplished using traditional reporting techniques.

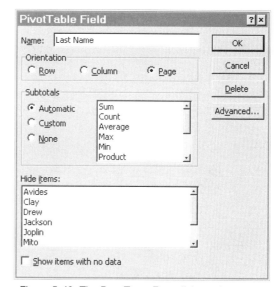

Figure 5-40: The PIVOTTABLE FIELD dialogue box.

THE CLIENT ACCESS EXCEL ADD-IN

Client Access for Windows 95/NT includes an Excel add-in specifically designed to retrieve data from the AS/400. *Add-ins* are helper programs used by Excel to perform specialized tasks. There are some add-in included with Excel and others are provided by third parties such as IBM (Client Access).

One advantage that the Client Access Excel add-in has is that it can very easily be used to retrieve data from members. With MS Query and ODBC, this process is a little more difficult because ODBC is SQL based, and SQL on the AS/400 doesn't support members.

A disadvantage of the add-in is that, once the data is transferred, it is treated in Excel as if you had entered it using the keyboard. In other words, Excel's external data options do apply. This means that there will be some additional steps (more than just clicking on the REFRESH button) to re-retrieve the data. Armed with that knowledge, let's explore how you can install and use the Excel add-in.

INSTALLING THE CLIENT ACCESS EXCEL ADD-IN

Two different scenarios apply to installing the Client Access Excel add-in. If Excel was installed on your computer before Client Access was installed, the add-in will be installed automatically. No further installation work is required.

If you installed Excel after Client Access was installed, you must identify the Client Access add-in to Excel so that it can be used. Perform the following steps to append the add-in to Excel. Once the add-in is loaded, you're ready to begin using it.

1. Begin with Excel loaded, and select ADD-INS from the TOOLS menu.

   ⇨ This displays the Add-Ins dialog box (Figure 5-41) used to manage your Excel add-ins.

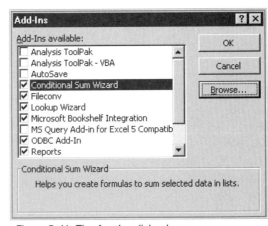

Figure 5-41: The ADD-INS dialog box.

2. On the ADD-INS dialog box, click the BROWSE button.

    ⇨ This brings up a standard File Open screen.

3. Find and select the CWBTFXLA file (Figure 5-42).

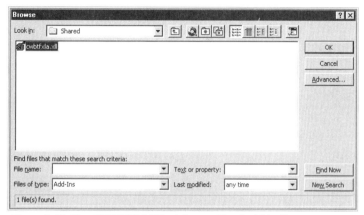

Figure 5-42: The CWBTFXLA Client Access Excel add-in file.

⇨ This is the add-in provided with Client Access, and it will be located in the shared directory underneath the directory where you installed Client Access. For example, if you installed Client Access on your C drive, the default path will be "C:\Program File\IBM\ClientAccess\Shared."

4. Highlight the file and click the OK button.

    ⇨ This will load the add-in into Excel, as shown in Figure 5-43.

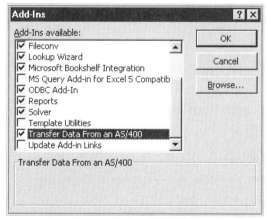

Figure 5-43: The Add-In is now loaded into Excel.

USING THE CLIENT ACCESS EXCEL ADD-IN

The Client Access Excel Add-In shows itself in the form of a new Excel toolbar (Figure 5-44). As you can see from the figure, there is only one button on this toolbar. Excel toolbars are very flexible. They can be viewed in many ways. In Figure 5-44, I've detached the toolbar into a floating window so it can be seen easily. Your setup might look a little different.

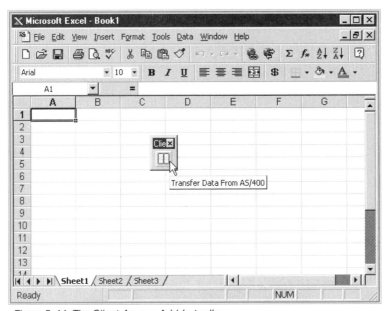

Figure 5-44: The Client Access Add-In toolbar.

To display toolbars, move your mouse over a toolbar that is already showing and then right-click. A menu will appear listing the toolbars that can be displayed. An alternative is to select VIEW and then TOOLBARS from the taskbar menu and then select the name of the toolbar you want to see.

To begin using the Add-In feature, click the TRANSFER DATA FROM THE AS/400 button (it's the only button on the toolbar). This brings up the TRANSFER REQUEST dialog box as shown in Figure 5-45.

On the screen shown in Figure 5-45, you must supply the name of the transfer request and where you want the data to be placed. You also can select whether or not to include column headings.

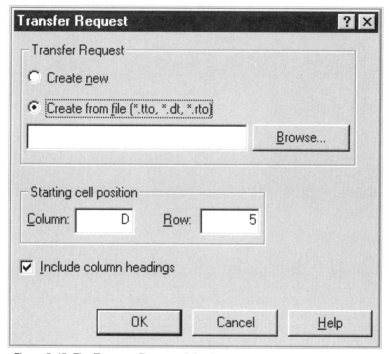

Figure 5-45: The TRANSFER REQUEST dialog box.

If you have a transfer request already built, select it by clicking the CREATE FROM FILE (*.TTO, *.DT, *.RTO) option. The next step is to locate the existing transfer request. Click the BROWSE button to find your request. If you are building a new transfer request, select the CREATE NEW option.

Enter the column and row where you want the data to be placed, whether or not you want to include column headings, and click the OK button. If you are using an existing request, it will be loaded and you can perform the transfer without having to specify the transfer options again.

If you are creating a new request, the DATA TRANSFER FROM AS/400 dialog box will appear (Figure 5-46). On this screen, select the AS/400 from which you want to retrieve the data and click the NEXT button.

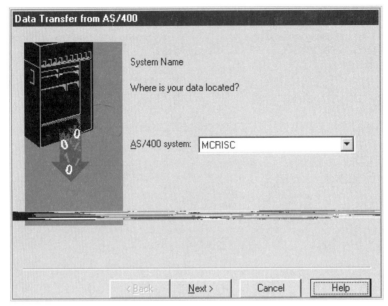

Figure 5-46: Creating a new transfer request.

On the next screen (Figure 5-47), select the library, file, and (optionally), the member from which you want data to be transferred.

Note: If you want to specify more than one file, separate each entry with a comma. The format of the entry is "LIBRARY/FILE(MEMBER)."

If you click the BROWSE button, the screen shown in Figure 5-48 is displayed. On this screen, you can visually find the files from which you want to obtain your data. You also can select more than one file from your AS/400 (if you need to retrieve data from multiple files).

Note: If you want to select from a particular library, and that library doesn't show up when you click the BROWSE button, type the name of the library in the screen shown in Figure 5-47 and then click the BROWSE button.

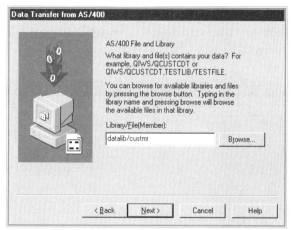

Figure 5-47: Specifying the library, file, and member from which to transfer.

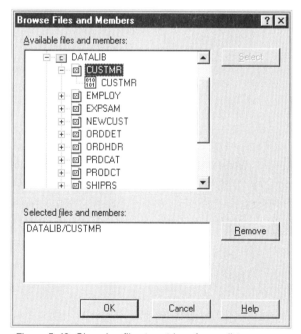

Figure 5-48: Choosing files to retrieve from a list.

To complete this exercise, choose the Customer (CUSTMR) table from the sample data and click the NEXT button. The next screen (Figure 5-49) allows you to set options for your data-transfer request.

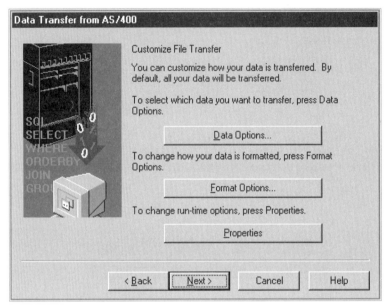

Figure 5-49: Setting transfer options.

The DATA OPTIONS screen brings up the data transfer function's filter screen, where you can refine your query further by filtering data and specifying how multiple files are joined. The FORMAT OPTIONS button brings up a screen where you can set the appearance options for your data. The PROPERTIES button brings up the data-transfer screen where you specify the options for the transfer. All of these screens are covered in detail in chapter 9.

Once you have the options set according to your preferences, click the NEXT button. The next screen (Figure 5-50) is where you can save your transfer request if you want to use it again. If you want to save the request, enter the filename and path to save the request.

The last step is to click the FINISH button. The Client Access "waiting" animation will play for a moment, and the data will appear in your spreadsheet (Figure 5-51). At this point, the data is completely separated from the AS/400. There is no way to refresh it except to run the request again by going through the previous steps (which are shortened considerably if you save the transfer request).

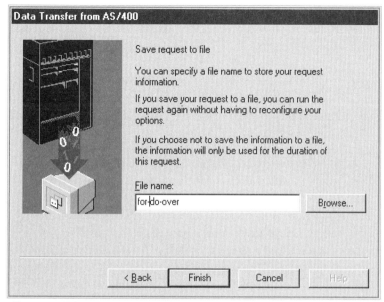

Figure 5-50: Saving the transfer request.

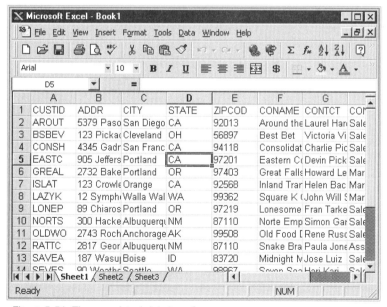

Figure 5-51: The completed data transfer.

That's how you use the Client Access Excel Add-In. Its wizard functionality makes it easy to use and the existing transfer requests can be a real time saver for you and your users.

SUMMARY

The methods outlined in this chapter are the main methods for importing AS/400 data into Excel. The two primary methods are using ODBC and MS Query, and using the Client Access Excel add-in and the data-transfer function.

There are many ways of using your data once you have brought it into Excel. For example, you can use the data in other calculations just as with any other Excel data. Try experimenting with the SUBTOTALS option under the DATA menu. This option allows you to create summary reports that can be expanded and collapsed to give the exact view of the data you want. You also can use advanced features such as Excel macros and Visual Basic for Applications to create reports that automatically refresh the data from the AS/400 and use it in complex calculations. The possibilities are really limited only by time and your imagination. Have fun experimenting!

6

Expanding Your Options with Access

Microsoft Access has many features that make it one of the most powerful database products available for the PC. When integrated with AS/400 data, Access offers unique functionality that is not possible using the AS/400 or Access independent of each other.

This chapter explores how to link your tables to an Access database so you can view live AS/400 data. You also will discover how to import your AS/400 tables for local processing, create and edit Access queries, and create forms for custom data display, including graphs of your AS/400 data. You will find out how to create reports in Access, to transform your raw AS/400 data into information, and find tips for speeding up database Access, securing your data on the AS/400, and more. Let's get started!

TERMINOLOGY

This chapter contains numerous terms that might not be familiar to traditional AS/400 users. In order to understand and follow the examples, you'll need to become familiar with these terms.

In Access (and many other database systems), a *data file* is called a *table*. This is in contrast with the standard AS/400 term (which is *file*). When a reference is made to a "table" on the AS/400, this refers to an AS/400 database file.

Also, the terms *library* and *collection* are used interchangeably. The AS/400 ODBC driver refers to "collections" as "libraries." Be aware of this to avoid confusion.

In addition, the terms *index* and *view* are used to refer to objects that are highly similar to AS/400 logical files

USING AS/400 DATA

There are two ways to get to AS/400 data using Microsoft Access. The first method is called *linking* tables. The other method is called *importing* tables. Each method has advantages and disadvantages. This chapter explains how each method works and provides guidelines to help you decide which method you should select for each specific situation.

What Is Linking?

When you "link" AS/400 tables to an Access database, Access stores a link to the AS/400 data in the database. The data itself is still on the AS/400, but an image of the table structure is kept within the Access database. Therefore, a linked table in a Microsoft Access database is basically a pointer to a table on your AS/400.

Because it is read directly from the table on the AS/400, data in linked tables is the most current data available from the AS/400. When records change on the AS/400, the changes are reflected immediately in the Access database. Similarly, when a linked table is updated through Access, the update takes place directly to the AS/400 table.

Keep in mind that you can use linked tables just like any other tables within Access. For example, you could use them in queries, reports, forms, and Access programs.

Be aware that, if you make any changes to the structure of your AS/400 database, such as adding a field, or even adding a new index to the file, you must relink the table in your Access database in order for the changes to be picked up.

Note: In earlier versions of Access, "linking" is referred to as "attaching."

Linking Step by Step

Let's link an AS/400 table to an Access database using an example. The first step is to open an existing Access database or to create a new one. For this example, create a new database for your practice work. When Microsoft Access is loaded, select BLANK DATABASE from the Microsoft Access dialogue box (Figure 6-1) and click OK.

Figure 6-1: Opening a blank database.

You also can open a new database by clicking on the NEW DATABASE button (Figure 6-2A) on the toolbar or by selecting the NEW DATABASE option from the FILE menu.

Figure 6-2A: The new database button.

Then on the "new" screen, choose BLANK DATABASE, on the GENERAL tab, and press the OK button (Figure 6-2B).

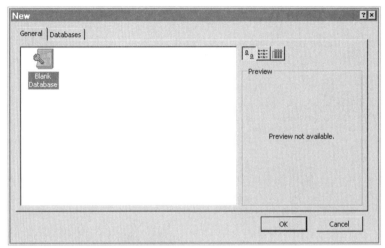

Figure 6-2B: An open blank database.

Access prompts you to name your new database. Call the new database PRACTICE by typing "practice" in the filename textbox. Notice that, on this screen (Figure 6-3), you can specify in which directory you want to place the new database. Once you have selected which directory you want to use for your practice database, click the CREATE button.

Figure 6-3: Creating a new database.

Your new database is now created as the PRACTICE :DATABASE window appears (Figure 6-4).

Figure 6-4: The practice database window.

To add some data to your blank database, click on the FILE menu, select GET EXTERNAL DATA, and select the LINK TABLES option (Figure 6-5).

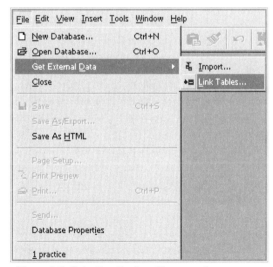

Figure 6-5: Selecting the LINK TABLES option.

Access displays the LINK dialogue box (Figure 6-6), indicating where the database must be pointed in order to be linked. In the FILES OF TYPE parameter, choose ODBC DATABASES at the bottom of the list.

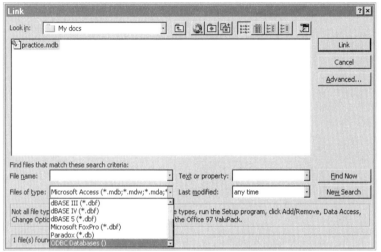

Figure 6-6: The LINK dialogue box.

On the SELECT DATA SOURCE screen (Figure 6-7), choose your AS/400 data source and click the OK button. If your ODBC driver requires a user ID and password, the system will request that information now.

When your list of tables is displayed, choose the Customer (CUSTMR) table (Figure 6-8). There is an extra parameter on this screen. The SAVE PASSWORD option saves your ODBC password so that you will not have to enter it each time you open the linked table. If you're concerned about security for the linked tables, do not check this option

When you press the OK button, Access gathers information about the table. It then displays a screen asking you to select a unique record identifier (Figure 6-9). Access displays the list of fields in the file you have chosen. From the list of fields, you should choose a combination of fields that will allow Access to identify individual records within the table. This is sometimes referred to as the *primary key* of the table.

In your Customer table, choose the CUSTID field because it is unique for every record. You don't have to choose a unique record identifier if you don't want to. If you don't, however, you most likely won't be able to update the AS/400 table. If you don't want to choose a unique identifier, click the CANCEL button and the AS/400 table will still be linked to the Access database. For this example, you do want to choose a unique identifier. Therefore, choose CUSTID and click the OK button.

Figure 6-7: The SELECT DATA SOURCE screen.

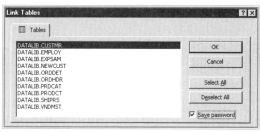

Figure 6-8: The LINK TABLES screen.

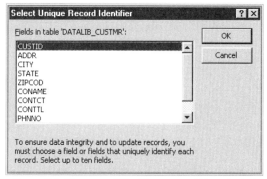

Figure 6-9: The record identifier screen lists selected fields.

When Access has finished gathering the table structure from the AS/400, you will see the table appear, with a small icon next to it, in the list of tables in the database window (Figure 6-10). The icon indicates that the table is a linked table.

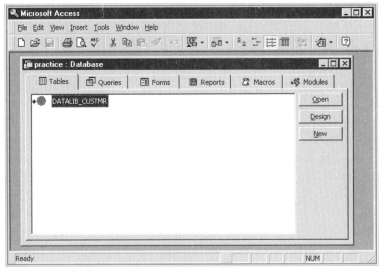

Figure 6-10: A linked table in a database window.

Note: One of the features of linking tables to Microsoft Access is the capability to rename the linked table within the Access database without affecting the table on the AS/400. The result is you can link your AS/400 tables and rename them to something more meaningful without breaking the link.

To rename a linked table, select the table from the tables list in the database window. Then right-click the mouse button. This brings up a menu of actions that can be performed on this table (Figure 6-11). Select RENAME from the menu. Enter "Customers" as the new name for your table. When you click off of the table name or hit the Enter key, the table will have a new name in your practice Access database.

Now you know how simple it is to link tables into an Access database.

What Is Importing?

When you *import* an AS/400 table into an Access database, the table structure and its data are copied into the Access database. This means that the Access table is roughly the same size as the AS/400 table.

When tables are imported, all the data is stored locally. Therefore, any updates made to the table are not reflected on the AS/400. Similarly, any changes made to the AS/400 table will not show up in the table in the Access database unless you explicitly reimport it. However, because the data is stored locally on the PC, it can usually be accessed more quickly.

When the data in an imported table is accessed, no AS/400 resources are required. Therefore, AS/400 performance is not impacted by long-running operations.

Importing Step by Step

To import an AS/400 table into a Microsoft Access database, first start your practice database (see Figure 6-4). Click on the FILE menu, select GET EXTERNAL DATA, and select the IMPORT option (Figure 6-12).

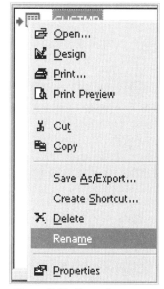

Figure 6-11: Renaming a linked table.

This brings up the IMPORT dialogue box that asks you which table you want to import. Again, under the FILES OF TYPE parameter, choose ODBC DATABASES from the bottom of the list.

The SELECT DATA SOURCE screen shows the available ODBC data sources. The tab at the top of the screen controls which types of DSNs are displayed in the list. Select

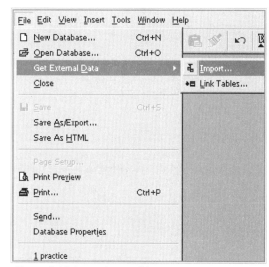

Figure 6-12: Importing a table.

your AS/400 DSN and press the OK button (see Figure 6-7). If your ODBC driver requires any logon information, enter it now and then press the OK button.

After a moment, a list of tables appears. The list of tables is built from the libraries you specified in the DEFAULT LIBRARIES parameter of the ODBC driver configuration screen. Here is where you choose the table, or tables, you want to import. You can select multiple tables on this screen just by clicking on them. To deselect a table, just click on it again.

For this example, select the Vendor Master (VNDMST) table and click the OK button. You will see that the tables are copied from your AS/400 to the Access database. You can rename this table in your Access database—in the same way you rename linked tables—by right-clicking the mouse on the table and selecting the RENAME option (see Figure 6-11).

Linking Versus Importing

Because there are two methods of accessing AS/400 data from within Access, you need to know when each method is appropriate. The following lists offer some general guidelines to help you decide whether it's better to link your data or import it.

Importing an AS/400 table is the best choice in several circumstances. For instance if:

❖ The table is small.

❖ The table does not change frequently on the AS/400.

❖ You don't need to change the data in the table on the AS/400.

❖ You want to perform operations without affecting or relying upon the AS/400.

However, you will want to link the AS/400 table, instead of importing it, under the following circumstances if:

❖ The table is very large.

❖ You need access to the most up-to-date information on the AS/400.

❖ You need to change data in the AS/400 table.

Deleting Tables

To delete tables from your Access database, simply click on the table in the database window and press the Delete key. You also can delete tables from the database window by right-clicking on the table and selecting DELETE from the list (Figure 6-13).

Don't worry. When you delete this way, you're not deleting anything from the AS/400. The table is removed only from the Access database. This is acceptable for linked tables

Figure 6-13: Deleting a Table.

because they can just be re-linked and no data is lost. For imported and other Access tables, the data (in the local database) also will be lost. Be careful.

For this example, delete the Vendor Master Table (VNDMAST) that you imported to your database in the preceding section. First, click on the VNDMST table in the database window and press your keyboard's Delete key. When Access asks you to confirm this deletion (Figure 6-14), press the YES button. The table is deleted from your database.

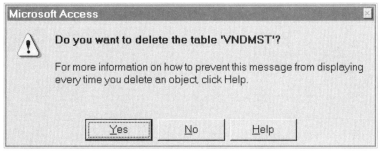

Figure 6-14: Confirming the deletion of a table.

THE DATASHEET VIEW

When you open a table in the TABLES tab, it provides a view that looks like a spread-sheet. This is called the *Datasheet View*; you will be seeing it frequently. To view a table this way, either double click on the table you want to open or select it and click the OPEN button on the right side of the database screen (Figure 6-15).

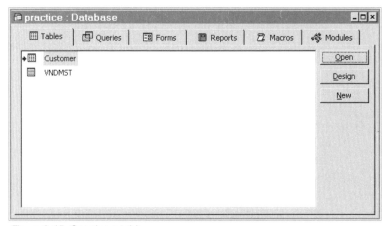

Figure 6-15: Opening a table.

In the Datasheet View, there is one column for each field in the table (Figure 6-16A). Each row represents a record in the table. You can move around within the datasheet using the scroll bars and arrow keys.

CUSTID	ADDR	CITY	STATE	ZIPCOD	CONAME	CONTCT	CONTTL	PHNNO	FAXNO
AROUT	5379 Pa:	San Diego	CA	92012	Around the	Laurel Hardy	Sales Re	(619) 532-6	(619) 532
BSBEV	123 Pick	Cleveland	OH	56897	Best Bet	Victoria Visc	Sales Re	(598) 898-6	(598) 987
CONSH	4345 Ga:	San Franc	CA	94117	Consolidate	Charlie Pick:	Sales Re	(415) 987-4	(415) 987
EASTC	905 Jeffe	Portland	OR	97201	Eastern Co:	Devin Pickle	Sales Ac	(503) 654-9	(503) 356
GREAL	2732 Bal	Portland	OR	97403	Great Falls	Howard Lera	Marketin	(503) 555-7	
ISLAT	123 Crow	Orange	CA	92568	Inland Trans	Helen Bach	Marketin	(714) 988-5	
LAZYK	12 Symp	Walla Wal	WA	99362	Square K C	John Will St:	Marketin	(509) 555-7	(509) 555
LONEP	89 Chiar:	Portland	OR	97219	Lonesome [	Fran Tarkent	Sales M:	(503) 555-9	(503) 555
NORTS	300 Hacl	Albuquerq	NM	87110	Norte Empc	Simon Garfu	Sales As	(505)564-8:	(505)568-
OLDWO	2743 Ro:	Anchorage	AK	99508	Old Food D	Rene Ruso	Sales Re	(907) 555-7	(907) 555
RATTC	2817 Ge:	Albuquerq	NM	87110	Snake Bran	Paula Jones	Assistan	(505) 555-5	(505) 555
SAVEA	187 Was	Boise	ID	83720	Midnight M:	Jose Luiz	Sales Re	(208) 555-8	
SEVES	90 Weatl	Seattle	WA	98967	Seven Seas	Hari Kari	Sales M:	(989)988-9:	(989)695-
SHALE	645 Cort:	San Marc:	CA	92069	Porcelain D	Pepe Lepeu:	Owner		
SPLIR	P.O. Bo:	Lander	WY	82520	Big Gut Be:	Art FulDodg:	Sales M:	(307) 555-4	(307) 555
THECR	55 Dogg:	Butte	MT	59801	The Cracke	Itsal Wong	Marketin	(406) 555-5	(406) 555
TRAIH	722 Lom	Kirkland	WA	98034	Trail's Head	Boyami Nag:	Sales As	(206) 555-8	(206) 555

Figure 6-16A: The Datasheet View.

Even though many records are displayed on the screen at once, there is only one "current" record. A small arrow on the left side of the screen indicates the current record. You can change the current record by clicking on the record you want to select inside the sheet. Then type the record number in the navigation bar at the bottom of the screen and press the Enter key or use the arrow buttons in the navigation bar.

If you have the proper permissions, the current record is the one you can update. To change data on the AS/400 from a linked table, all you have to do is click in the field you want to change and enter your changes. As soon as you move off of the record, the changes are written to the AS/400. This is powerful but it can also be very dangerous. There are ways to protect your data by preventing your users from updating tables this way. For more information, see the security section at the end of this chapter.

To add a record in the Datasheet View, click the NEW RECORD button (Figure 6-16B) on the toolbar.

 Figure 6-16B: The NEW RECORD button.

This moves you to a blank record, at the end of the datasheet, where you can enter field values for the new record. Again, as soon as you move off the record, it will be added to the AS/400. Of course, this happens only if you have the proper AS/400 authority to add records.

Deleting records is just as easy as adding them. If you have the authority to delete records, simply click the row header (left-most) column of the record you want to delete and press the Delete key. A dialogue box asks you to confirm the deletion (Figure 6-17).

Figure 6-17: At this point, the records are already removed from the AS/400. Answering "NO" has no effect!

Unfortunately, on my system, the record was already removed from the AS/400 at this point! If you click on "NO" at this point, the record is still gone (as long as you have the proper authority). Using the shift key and clicking rows allows you to select multiple records from the table for deletion. Again, this deletion of records is only possible if you have the proper authority to the database on the AS/400. This authority is based upon the user profile you used to sign on to Client Access and ODBC.

ACCESS QUERIES

One of the main tools for retrieving data with Microsoft Access is the *query*. Queries can be used for many functions within Access, including the retrieval of data for forms and reports. Among the several types of queries are.

❖ **Select Queries**. Select queries are used to return records based upon the query criteria.

❖ **Action Queries**. Action queries can be used to add, change, or delete records in database tables.

❖ **Crosstab Queries**. A crosstab query is a special type of selection query that can help you sift through mountains of data.

❖ **Pass-Through Queries**. Pass-through queries can be used to execute SQL statements directly on the AS/400, without going through the Access database engine.

In the following sections, you'll find out how to create and use queries. Because queries are used in the creation of reports and forms, a good understanding of them goes a long way toward helping you get the most from Access.

Select Queries

As the main type of query used when you want to view data, select queries can be used to retrieve data in a specific order, summarize data, group data, and perform calculations on data. You can use select queries to combine information from several files to obtain the results you need. Select queries also are the basis for more advanced data-retrieval functions such as reports and graphs.

The simplest type of select query returns data from a single table in a list format. To create a simple select query from your AS/400 tables, open your practice database (see Figure 6-4) and click on the QUERIES tab in the database window. Then click on the NEW button on the right side of the window (Figure 6-18).

The NEW QUERY dialogue box appears asking you which type of query you want to create (Figure 6-19). The first option (DESIGN VIEW) creates a query from scratch without using a wizard. In order to create this query from scratch, click on the DESIGN VIEW button and then click OK.

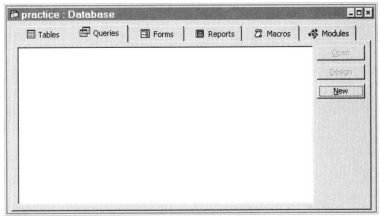

Figure 6-18: Creating a simple query.

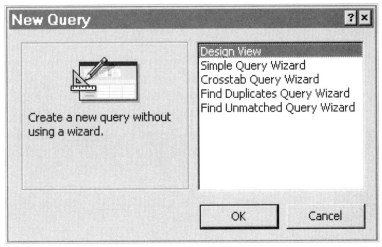

Figure 6-19: The NEW QUERY dialogue box.

Access displays a SHOW TABLE screen (Figure 6-20) containing a list of the tables in the database. Select the CUSTOMER table and press the ADD button and then the CLOSE button.

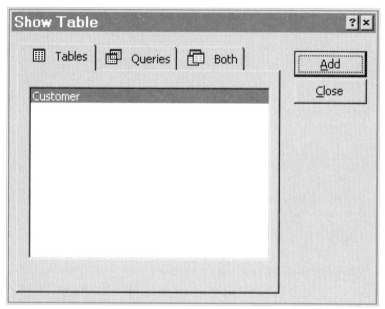

Figure 6-20: The SHOW TABLE screen.

When Access displays the SELECT QUERY window (Figure 6-21) in the top half of the query window, your selected tables(s) will appear with a list of the fields in each table.

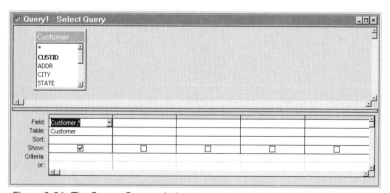

Figure 6-21: The SELECT QUERY window.

The bottom section of the query window is where the fields that are selected for the query will appear. Called the *Query By Example* (QBE) *grid*, this is where any selection criteria are added to the query.

Drag the asterisk from the CUSTOMER table in the top portion of the window down to the FIELD box in the lower portion of the window. This adds all the fields from the CUSTOMER table to the query (see Figure 6-21).

To display the data, run the query by clicking on the Run button (Figure 6-22A) on the toolbar.

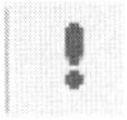

Figure 6-22A: The *Run button.*

Access returns a list of all the records in the CUSTOMER table on your AS/400. Your screen should look like the example shown in Figure 6-22B.

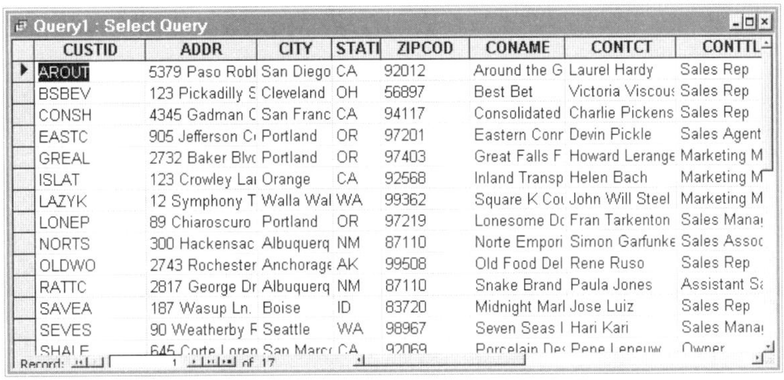

Query1 : Select Query

CUSTID	ADDR	CITY	STATI	ZIPCOD	CONAME	CONTCT	CONTTL
AROUT	5379 Paso Robl	San Diego	CA	92012	Around the G	Laurel Hardy	Sales Rep
BSBEV	123 Pickadilly S	Cleveland	OH	56897	Best Bet	Victoria Viscous	Sales Rep
CONSH	4345 Gadman C	San Franc	CA	94117	Consolidated	Charlie Pickens	Sales Rep
EASTC	905 Jefferson C	Portland	OR	97201	Eastern Conr	Devin Pickle	Sales Agent
GREAL	2732 Baker Blvc	Portland	OR	97403	Great Falls F	Howard Lerange	Marketing M
ISLAT	123 Crowley La	Orange	CA	92568	Inland Transp	Helen Bach	Marketing M
LAZYK	12 Symphony T	Walla Wal	WA	99362	Square K Cou	John Will Steel	Marketing M
LONEP	89 Chiaroscuro	Portland	OR	97219	Lonesome Dc	Fran Tarkenton	Sales Mana
NORTS	300 Hackensac	Albuquerq	NM	87110	Norte Empori	Simon Garfunke	Sales Assoc
OLDWO	2743 Rochester	Anchorage	AK	99508	Old Food Del	Rene Ruso	Sales Rep
RATTC	2817 George Dr	Albuquerq	NM	87110	Snake Brand	Paula Jones	Assistant Sa
SAVEA	187 Wasup Ln.	Boise	ID	83720	Midnight Marl	Jose Luiz	Sales Rep
SEVES	90 Weatherby F	Seattle	WA	98967	Seven Seas I	Hari Kari	Sales Mana
SHALE	645 Corte Loren	San Marc	CA	92069	Porcelain De	Pepe Lepeuw	Owner

Record: 1 of 17

Figure 6-22B: Query results.

Viewing Queries within Access

The three ways to view queries within Access are the:

- Design View.
- SQL View.
- Datasheet View.

The view you probably will use most often when creating a query is called the *Design View*. To look at a query in Design View, click on the arrow (Figure 6-22C) to the right of the VIEW button (on the left side of QUERY toolbar) when the query is open and select DESIGN VIEW (Figure 6-22D) from the drop-down list.

Figure 6-22C: The arrow
icon to the right of the VIEW button.

Figure 6-22D: Selecting
DESIGN VIEW.

As a result, you can see the now-familiar SELECT QUERY screen (see Figure 6-23). The Design View is used to visually build the SQL statements that execute the query. You can view and modify those SQL statements by selecting SQL VIEW from the VIEW drop-down list on the Query toolbar (Figure 6-22D). This view changes the query window into a screen where you can view and edit the SQL statement of your query.

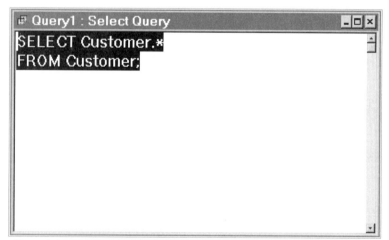

Figure 6-23: The SELECT QUERY screen.

The third way to view your query is in the Datasheet View (Figure 6-22D) mode. To display this view, press the RUN button on the toolbar. The Datasheet View shows you how your query looks when it is populated with data.

You can save the query as an object in the database for later recall. To do this, you can either click on the save icon (Figure 6-24A) on the toolbar, select the Save option from the File menu, or press the keyboard's Control and S keys at the same time when the query window is open.

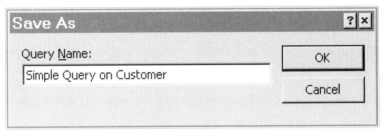

Figure 6-24A: The SAVE icon.

The first time the query is saved, Access brings up the SAVE AS dialogue box (Figure 6-24B) and asks you to name the query. For this example, type "Simple Query on Customer" in the QUERY NAME textbox and press the OK button.

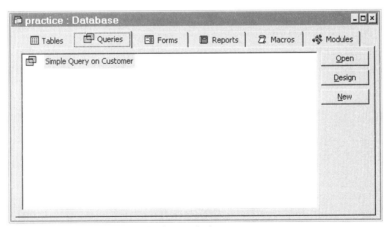

Figure 6-24B: The SAVE AS dialogue box.

Now close the query window. The query you just created shows up under the QUERIES tab in the database window (Figure 6-25).

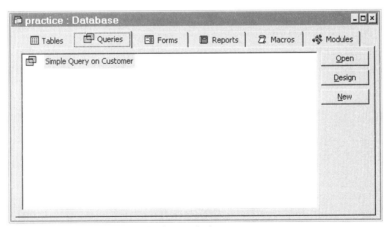

Figure 6-25: A query in the database window.

Sorting and Filtering Data

Queries are useful for sorting and filtering data. With queries, you can sort information from many fields in either ascending or descending order, and you can select only the records you want displayed. For an example, create a query that selects and sorts records from your CUSTOMER table.

First, make sure that your practice database (see Figure 6-4) is open. Next, create a new query by clicking on the QUERIES tab in the database window. Then click the NEW button (see Figure 6-18). Click on DESIGN VIEW on the NEW QUERY screen (see Figure 6-19), and again you will see a list of linked tables from the AS/400 that you can add to the query. Select the CUSTOMER table and press the ADD button and then the CLOSE button (see Figure 6-20).

Next, select the Contact (CONTCT) field from the table and drag it to the FIELD box in the first column of the QBE grid. This adds that field to the query. Continue by adding the contact title (CONTTL) field, the city (CITY) field, the state (STATE) field, and the ZIP code (ZIPCOD) field by dragging each field to the next available FIELD column available on the grid. When you have finished, the display should look like the example shown in Figure 6-26.

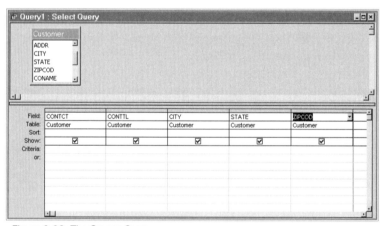

Figure 6-26: The SELECT QUERY screen.

So that you can see which customers are in which states, now sort the data by state. On the SORT row of the column containing the STATE field, click in the cell. Then click on the arrow on the right side of the cell, and select ASCENDING from the drop-down list (Figure 6-27).

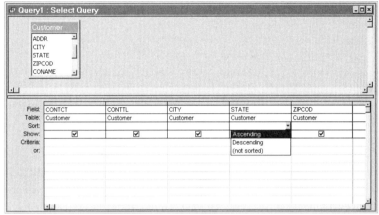

Figure 6-27: Sorting by state.

This tells Access to sort the contents of the state field in ascending order. Now take a look at the data in your query by pressing the RUN button on the toolbar (Figure 6-22A) or by selecting the DATASHEET VIEW from the VIEW button options on the toolbar (Figure 6-22D). As you can see in Figure 6-28, the data is now sorted by the STATE field.

CONTCT	CONTTL	CITY	STATE	ZIPCOD
Rene Ruso	Sales Rep	Anchorage	AK	99508
Charlie Pickens	Sales Rep	San Francisco	CA	94117
Pepe Lepeuw	Owner	San Marcos	CA	92069
Helen Bach	Marketing Mana	Orange	CA	92568
Laurel Hardy	Sales Rep	San Diego	CA	92012
Jose Luiz	Sales Rep	Boise	ID	83720
Itsal Wong	Marketing Assis	Butte	MT	59801
Simon Garfunke	Sales Associat	Albuquerque	NM	87110
Paula Jones	Assistant Sales	Albuquerque	NM	87110
Victoria Viscou	Sales Rep	Cleveland	OH	56897
Howard Lerange	Marketing Mana	Portland	OR	97403
Devin Pickle	Sales Agent	Portland	OR	97201
Fran Tarkenton	Sales Manager	Portland	OR	97219
Boyami Naggy	Sales Associat	Kirkland	WA	98034
John Will Steel	Marketing Mana	Walla Walla	WA	99362
Hari Kari	Sales Manager	Seattle	WA	98967
Art FulDodger	Sales Manager	Lander	WY	82520

Record: 1 of 17

Figure 6-28: The Datasheet View.

Return to the design mode by selecting the DESIGN VIEW option from the View button drop-down list on the toolbar.

When you specify sorts within the Access select query design window, be aware that, when a field sort is specified, Access sorts the fields in left-to-right order. In other words, if the CITY field is to the left of the STATE field, the CITY field is sorted before the STATE field. Therefore, if you want to sort by state first and city second, the STATE field needs to be positioned to the left of the CITY field in the QBE grid. There are two ways you can do this.

The first method is to click on the small column header of the STATE field. You will know when your cursor is in the right place because it will turn into a down arrow. After you click once on the header, the column background turns black. Then you will know it has been selected. You can now click again on the header and, by holding down the mouse button, drag the STATE column to the left of the CITY column. Let go of the mouse button when you see a black line along the left edge of the CITY column and the STATE column will be inserted here (Figure 6-29).

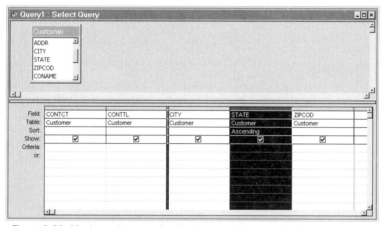

Figure 6-29: Moving columns using the drag-and-drop method.

The other way to move and change a column is to click in the STATE field and then click on the arrow that appears on the right side of the cell. This will display the full list of fields from your CUSTOMER table.

Select CITY from the list (Figure 6-30). You now need to do the same with your original CITY field to change it to a STATE field. When you use this method to move columns, you have to manually change all fields in the columns you change. For instance, the CITY field now contains the ASCENDING sort order you set up for the STATE field and the STATE field contains no sort order. You must change the CITY field to NOT SORTED and the STATE field to ASCENDING the sort order.

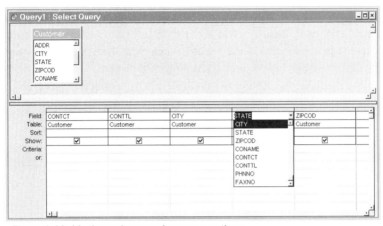

Figure 6-30: Moving columns using menu options.

When you are finished using either of these two methods, the STATE column will be located to the left of the CITY column.

Now you are ready to choose a sort order for the CITY field. Click in the SORT row of the CITY column. Click on the right-side arrow and choose DESCENDING from the list. Then click on the RUN button on the toolbar to view the results (Figure 6-31).

The records are sorted first by state then by city. But what if you want to have the CITY field to the left of the STATE

CONTCT	CONTTL	STATE	CITY	ZIPCOD
Rene Ruso	Sales Rep	AK	Anchorage	99508
Pepe Lepeuw	Owner	CA	San Marcos	92069
Charlie Pickens	Sales Rep	CA	San Francisco	94117
Laurel Hardy	Sales Rep	CA	San Diego	92012
Helen Bach	Marketing Mana	CA	Orange	92568
Jose Luiz	Sales Rep	ID	Boise	83720
Itsal Wong	Marketing Assis	MT	Butte	59801
Simon Garfunke	Sales Associat	NM	Albuquerque	87110
Paula Jones	Assistant Sales	NM	Albuquerque	87110
Victoria Viscou	Sales Rep	OH	Cleveland	56897
Howard Lerange	Marketing Mana	OR	Portland	97403
Devin Pickle	Sales Agent	OR	Portland	97201
Fran Tarkenton	Sales Manager	OR	Portland	97219
John Will Steel	Marketing Mana	WA	Walla Walla	99362
Hari Kari	Sales Manager	WA	Seattle	98967
Boyami Naggy	Sales Associat	WA	Kirkland	98034
Art FulDodger	Sales Manager	WY	Lander	82520

Figure 6-31: Sorting by state and city.

field in the results yet still sort by state and then city? The answer is to add the CITY field again, but make it not appear in the query results.

First, you need to return to the DESIGN VIEW by clicking on the VIEW button on the toolbar. For this example, move the STATE field back to its original position by dragging it to the right of the CITY field. Then clear the sort from the CITY field by selecting NOT SORTED in the SORT row of the QBE grid. Now the STATE field is the only field with a sort entry, and the CITY field is to the left of the STATE field (see Figure 6-27).

Now add another copy of the CITY field to the right side of the grid by dragging it again from the table in the table pane of the window. Then clear the SHOW entry under the new copy of the CITY field by clicking on the checkbox (Figure 6-32). This allows you to use this field in sorts and selections, but the field will not appear in the query data.

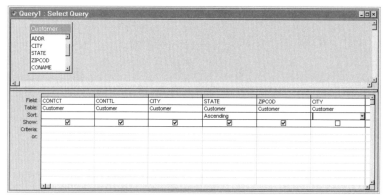

Figure 6-32: Clear the SHOW checkbox.

Next, choose DESCENDING for the sort order of the new CITY field (Figure 6-33). Note that Access is still sorting based upon the left-to-right order of the fields in the query design window, but the invisible CITY field is to the right of the STATE field.

Press the RUN button on the toolbar and check the results. As expected, the data is sorted by state and then by city within state (Figure 6-34). Now you know how to sort data using the SELECT QUERY DESIGN VIEW window.

You can continue to refine this query to retrieve exactly the data you need by adding some selection criteria to it so you can view, for example, only customers from the state of Washington. To do this, go back to query design mode by clicking on the VIEW icon on the toolbar. Click in the CRITERIA row in the STATE column on the QBE grid, and then type: ="WA". Note that Access will add the quotes to the state if you leave them out (Figure 6-35).

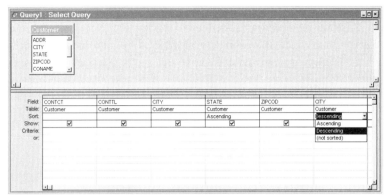

Figure 6-33: Sorting the new City column in descending order.

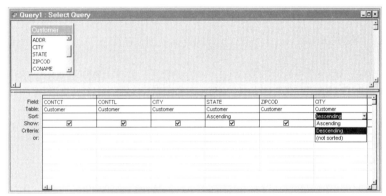

Figure 6-34: Datasheet View results.

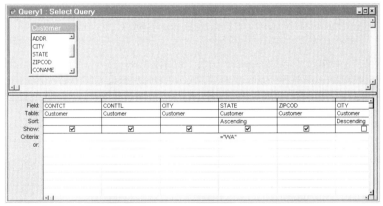

Figure 6-35: Adding criteria to a query.

This selection tells Access to return only the records that have the value "WA" in the STATE field. Click the RUN button on the toolbar to view the results. Access returns only the customers from the state of Washington, still sorted by state and city. Your screen should look like the example shown in Figure 6-36. You're now ready to create a more complex query.

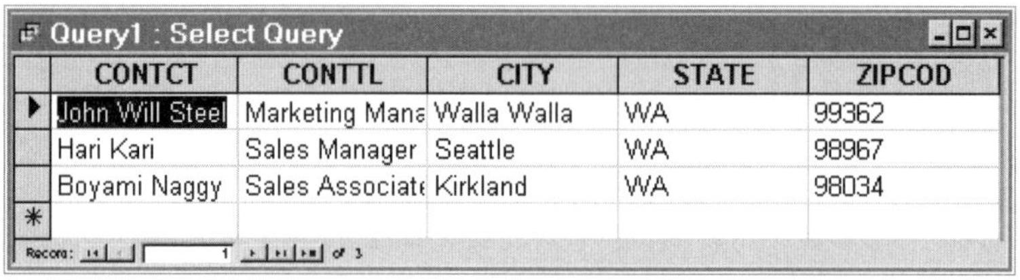

CONTCT	CONTTL	CITY	STATE	ZIPCOD
John Will Steel	Marketing Mana	Walla Walla	WA	99362
Hari Kari	Sales Manager	Seattle	WA	98967
Boyami Naggy	Sales Associate	Kirkland	WA	98034

Figure 6-36: Query results on customers located in Washington state.

Joining Tables

Joining tables and the next step, creating totals, are the most important steps in creating queries to report on data in a relational database system. Most business systems currently use the *relational model* to store data in their databases. The relational model is a method of dividing data into logical, non-repeating units. This is usually one of the most efficient ways to store data in computer systems.

In a typical relational business system, information about customers is stored in the Customer table and information about products is stored in a Product table. Information about orders is stored in two tables. The Order Header table holds information—such as the ordering customer, the order date, the order taker, etc.—common to the order. The other order table, a Detail table, holds the details about the order items the customer wants.

There could be several items per order and, because it would be inefficient to repeat the order header information for each item on the order, separate tables are used. The tables are linked using a special field called a *key field*. The following example makes this clearer.

First, load Access and open a new database by selecting this option from the dialogue box. You also can open a new database by clicking on the NEW DATABASE button on the toolbar or by selecting NEW DATABASE from the FILE menu, and selecting BLANK DATABASE (see Figures 6-1, 6-2A, and 6-2B).

Access prompts you to identify your new database. Name the new database by typing "practice2" in the filename textbox. Notice that, on this screen, you can specify in which directory you want to place the new database (see Figure 6-3). Once you have selected which directory you want to use for your practice2 database, click the CREATE button. Your new database is now created and the practice2 Database window appears (see Figure 6-4).

To add some data to your blank database, click on the FILE menu, select GET EXTERNAL DATA, and select the LINK TABLES option (see Figure 6-5). Access displays the LINK dialogue box (see Figure 6-6), indicating where the database must be pointed in order to be linked. In the FILES OF TYPE parameter, choose ODBC DATABASES at the bottom of the list.

On the SELECT DATA SOURCE screen (see Figure 6-7), choose your AS/400 data source and click the OK button. If your ODBC driver requires a user ID and password, the system will request that information now.

When your list of tables is displayed, choose the customer (CUSTMR) table, the order header (ORDHDR) table, and the order detail (ORDDET) tables (see Figure 6-8). Note that there is an extra parameter on this screen. The SAVE PASSWORD option saves your ODBC password so that you won't have to enter it each time you open the linked table. If you're concerned about security for the linked tables, don't check this option.

When you press the OK button, Access gathers information about the tables. It then displays a screen asking you to select a unique record identifier (see Figure 6-9). Access displays the list of fields in the file you have chosen.

From the list of fields, you should choose a combination of fields that will allow Access to identify individual records within the table. This is sometimes referred to as the primary key of the table. In your Customer table, choose the CUSTID field because it is unique for every record. In your Order Header and Order Detail tables, the ORDID field is unique for every record; so choose those. When you have chosen your primary keys, click the OK button.

Note: Astute database experts probably have already noticed that there is a problem with the structure of the test data. The Order Detail table should actually have another key to help uniquely identify the individual line items in an order. Because it's test data, we'll just leave it like it is.

You don't have to choose a unique record identifier if you don't want to. If you don't, however, you most likely will not be able to update the AS/400 table. If you don't want to choose a unique identifier, click the CANCEL button and the AS/400 table will still be linked to the Access database.

When Access has finished gathering the table structures from the AS/400, you will see the tables appear in the list of tables in the database window (Figure 6-37). The small icons next to each table indicate that they are linked tables.

Keep your practice2 database open. Begin a new query by clicking on the QUERIES tab in the database window and then clicking on the NEW button (Figure 6-18). Choose the DESIGN VIEW option and click OK (Figure 6-19). Add the Customer (CUSTMR), Order Header (ORDHDR), and Order Detail (ORDDET) tables to the query and press the CLOSE button (Figure 6-20). There are now three tables in the field-listing portion of the query design window (Figure 6-38).

Figure 6-37: The practice2 database window.

To retrieve the information from these tables correctly, you have to describe their relationship (or *join criteria*) to Access. With some

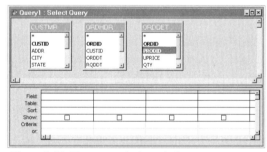

Figure 6-38: The query design window.

databases, Access guesses and supplies the join criteria for you. On others, you have to add them manually. The join criteria are simply a means of telling Access how common fields in different tables are related. The simplest way to create a join criterion is to drag a common field from one table to its complement in the other table.

In this example, use the manual method. Start with the Customer and Order Header tables. First find the CUSTID field in the Customer table. Then drag it and drop it over the

CUSTID field in the Order Header table. A line appears joining the field from one table to the field in the other table. This tells Access that the records in the Order Header table, in effect, belong to the records in the Customer table. This is called a *one-to-many relationship*.

One record in the Customer table can have many records in the Order Header table. This makes logical sense because a customer can have more than one order, but it usually would not make sense for an order to have more than one customer.

There is a similar relationship between orders in the Order Header table and the items on the order in the Order Detail table. The ORDERID field joins these tables. To join them, find the ORDERID field from the Order Header table and drag it to the ORDERID field in the Order Detail table. Now there are relationships between all three tables shown by lines connecting the related fields (Figure 6-39).

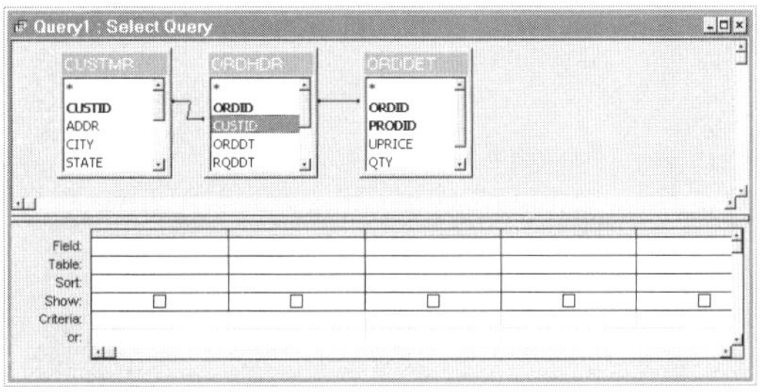

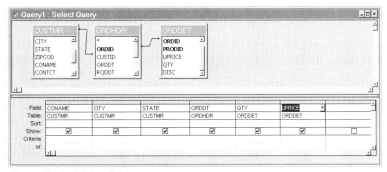

Figure 6-39: Joining tables.

Now you can add some fields to this query to see some data. Rather than looking at all the fields, in all three tables, take a look at just a select few. The fields you want to look at from the Customer table are company name (CONAME), city (CITY), and state (STATE).

Use your mouse to drag these fields to the QBE grid to add them to the query (Figure 6-40). You also want to see the order date from the Order Header table. Therefore, drag the order date ORDDT field to the QBE grid. Then, from the Order Detail table, add the QTY and UPRICE fields to your query.

Figure 6-40: Adding fields to a query.

To see your results, run the query by clicking on the RUN button on the toolbar. Your screen should look like the example shown in Figure 6-41.

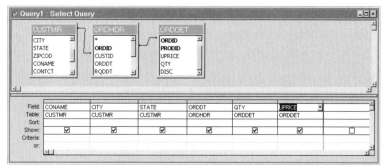

Figure 6-41: Query results.

When an SQL data query is run, the results of the query are returned in a tablelike format complete with rows and columns of data. This is sometimes called the *results table* or *result set*. It is also what you see in the Datasheet View when you run the query. However, it is not really a permanent table that exists on your AS/400. This is just the temporary results of your query.

> Note: Occasionally, when you are joining AS/400 tables with Access, you get an error message saying a particular field is not in the results table. This happens because sometimes Access generates SQL statements that the AS/400 does not support. For example, the AS/400 ODBC driver does not support sorting by a field that is not part of the results of a query. A side effect of this is that if you do not tell Access specifically which field to sort by, it might generate an invalid condition. This problem usually can be overcome either by putting the field in question into the results of the query or by specifying a sort on the query.

To specify a sort on the query to ensure that there are no problems, click on the VIEW button on the toolbar to return to the DESIGN VIEW. Then sort the company name field in ascending order (Figure 6-42).

Next, click on the RUN button again to return your results. The data is sorted alphabetically by company and should look like the example shown in Figure 6-43.

In this result set, there are a lot of records, and many of the values seem to repeat themselves on the screen. Notice that there is one row for every item ordered on every order. That's a lot of detailed information. You can perform some calculations and summary functions on the data to get a higher-level picture of customer orders.

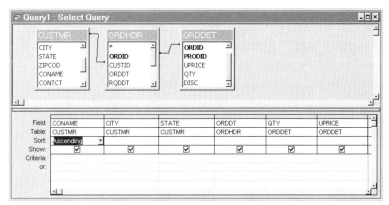

Figure 6-42: Sorting by company name.

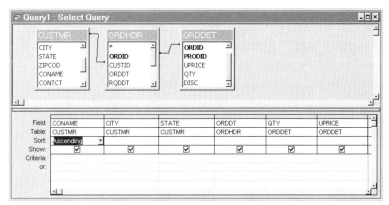

Figure 6-43: Results sorted by company name.

Did you notice that there is no extended price in your Order Detail table? Because the extended price can easily be calculated, there is no reason to store it. Let's add a calculated field for the gross extended price.

Return to the DESIGN VIEW by clicking on the VIEW button on the toolbar. Add your calculated field by clicking in the FIELD cell in the QBE grid in the column that is to the right of the last field in the query. Then type "QTY*UPRICE" and press the Enter key.

Access reformats the field to its liking so that what you just typed now looks something like the example shown in Figure 6-44. This is called an *expression field*. An expression field is a field that's calculated by Access using any of its built-in functions. Access has some very powerful facilities for creating complex expressions, and they can be very useful. When you are ready to learn more about expressions, consult Access HELP or the documentation. You will find it well worth the effort.

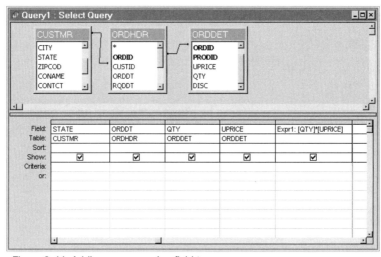

Figure 6-44: Adding an expression field to a query.

Now press the RUN button on the toolbar to take a look at the results of the query. As you can see, the expression field has been evaluated and the results are the quantity multiplied by the unit price (Figure 6-45). Because this is a rather unattractive, unformatted field, let's add some formatting to make the new field look more presentable.

First, click on DESIGN VIEW on the toolbar, and then right-click in the field cell containing the expression. Select PROPERTIES from the drop-down menu (Figure 6-46).

The PROPERTIES screen appears. Click in the FORMAT box; then click on the arrow that appears on the right. Access displays a list of predefined formats that can be applied to fields. Find the CURRENCY format and select it by clicking on it (Figure 6-47).

Figure 6-45: Query results with an expression field.

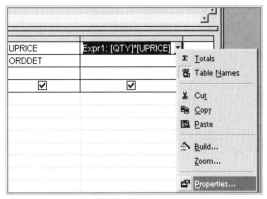

Figure 6-46: Selecting expression properties.

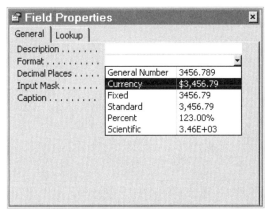

Figure 6-47: Selecting the CURRENCY format.

Then close the window to return to the query. Press the RUN button on the toolbar to see the new formatting. Now your results contain a properly formatted currency field (Figure 6-48).

CONAME	CITY	STATE	ORDDT	QTY	UPRICE	Expr1
Around the Glob	San Diego	CA	09-Sep-93	21	$24.00	$504.00
Around the Glob	San Diego	CA	09-Nov-92	20	$4.80	$96.00
Around the Glob	San Diego	CA	17-Nov-93	8	$7.00	$56.00
Around the Glob	San Diego	CA	17-Nov-93	14	$9.65	$135.10
Around the Glob	San Diego	CA	11-Oct-93	28	$12.00	$336.00
Around the Glob	San Diego	CA	08-Oct-93	15	$19.00	$285.00
Around the Glob	San Diego	CA	09-Sep-93	28	$15.00	$420.00
Around the Glob	San Diego	CA	09-Sep-93	40	$19.50	$780.00
Around the Glob	San Diego	CA	28-Apr-93	3	$15.00	$45.00
Around the Glob	San Diego	CA	28-Apr-93	25	$9.50	$237.50
Around the Glob	San Diego	CA	09-Nov-92	15	$13.00	$195.00
Around the Glob	San Diego	CA	09-Nov-92	20	$30.40	$608.00
Around the Glob	San Diego	CA	15-Jan-93	25	$12.00	$300.00

Figure 6-48: Results using the formatted Currency field.

Summary Queries

The step you have just completed shows the total for each line item, on each order, for each customer. But what if you want to see just the total for all the customers' orders? Getting this kind of information from Access is very easily achieved by creating a summary query.

To create a summary query, open (if it isn't already open) your practice2 database created in the preceding section (see Figure 6-37). Start with a new query by clicking on the QUERY tab in the database menu and then click on the NEW button (see Figure 6-18). Next, select the DESIGN VIEW option (see Figure 6-19). Then add the Customer, Order Header, and Order Detail tables to the query, and press the CLOSE button (see Figure 6-20).

Now you need to set the join specifications for the tables. The join specifications might already be set. If so, there will be a small line connecting each table indicating which fields are joined with which tables. If you don't see these lines when you create a query, it means you must create the join specifications manually (which is easy). This procedure is just like the one you used to join tables in the first query.

For this query, join the tables by dragging the CUSTID key field from the Customer table to the CUSTID field in the Order Header table. Then drag the ORDID field from the Order Header table to the ORDID field in the Order Detail table (see Figure 6-39).

To add some fields to the query, first add the CONAME field from the Customer table. Now you can add an expression. In the next column, in the FIELD row, enter the expression "QTY*UPRICE" followed by pressing the Enter key. Then format the total field by right-clicking in the field cell, selecting properties from the menu, clicking on FORMAT, then clicking on the right arrow to display menu, and then choose CURRENCY from the list (Figure 6-49).

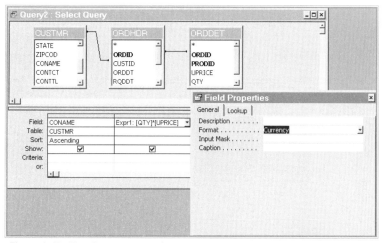

Figure 6-49: Entering an expression and sorting.

Now tell Access to sort the query by company name in ascending order. Click in the SORT row of the CONAME column, click on the arrow on the right, and select ASCENDING from the options (Figure 6-49). Everything you have done up to this point is the same as in the previous examples.

When you are creating a totals query, you must be able to see the TOTALS row in the QBE grid. To do this, click on the VIEW menu at the top of the screen and select TOTALS (Figure 6-50).

Figure 6-50: Displaying the TOTALS row in the QBE grid.

A new row now appears in the QBE grid (Figure 6-51). This row is where you tell Access how you want the information totaled. Notice that the field already has an entry of GROUP BY in this row. When a field has GROUP BY in this field, it is used as part of the grouping to get the total.

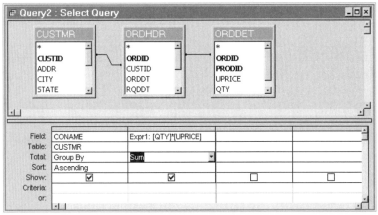

Figure 6-51: Adding SUM to the expression total.

To get the total sales for each company name, select SUM in the TOTAL row of your expression column (Figure 6-51). Doing this totals the expression field for each unique entry in the company-name field. Click the RUN button to display the total sales for each customer (Figure 6-52).

You also can get other statistics such as averages, counts, and minimum and maximum values on summary data. These statistics are useful for creating reports that help you spot trends in your data.

CONAME	Expr1
Around the Glob	$6,011.00
Best Bet	$4,461.90
Big Gut Beer &	$4,219.10
Consolidated Hd	$931.50
Eastern Connec	$2,439.45
Great Falls Foo	$4,116.55
Inland Transport	$5,248.30
Lonesome Dove	$2,132.00
Midnight Market	$61,653.70
Norte Emporiurr	$865.00
Old Food Delica	$9,915.50
Seven Seas Imp	$14,120.95
Snake Brand Ju	$18,589.10
Square K Count	$530.60
The Cracker Bo	$283.00
Trail's Head Gou	$1,002.20

Figure 6-52: Query results.

Parameter Queries

You can create Access queries, called *parameter queries*, that ask for values to be used to retrieve data when the query is run. Parameter queries are created almost exactly like any other query. The only difference is that, when you enter the criteria, you enter special values that Access uses to request values from the user when the query is run. The following example guides you through creating a parameter query.

First, create a new query by clicking on NEW under the QUERIES tab on your practice2 database dialogue box (see Figure 6-18). Select the DESIGN VIEW option (see Figure 6-19). Add the Customer, Order Header, and Order Detail tables and then press the CLOSE button (see Figure 6-20).

Join the tables as you did before (refer to the Joining Tables and Summary Queries sections of this chapter) by joining the Customer table and the Order Header table with the CUSTID field, and the Order Header and Order Detail tables with the ORDERID field (see Figure 6-39).

Now, from the Customer table, add the CONAME field and sort it in ascending order. From the Order Header table, add the ORDDT field. Then add the expression qty*uprice to the column to the right of the orddt field. Your screen should now look like the example shown in Figure 6-53.

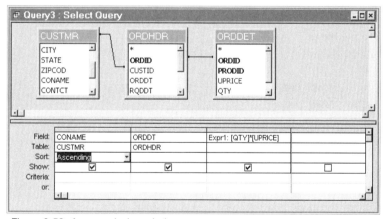

Figure 6-53: A query design window.

Make this a summary query by clicking on the VIEW menu and selecting TOTALS (see Figure 6-50). This will display the TOTALS row in the QBE grid. To summarize the extended price field, select SUM in the TOTAL row of the expression column (Figure 6-54).

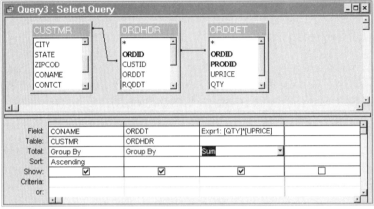

Figure 6-54: Adding SUM to the Expression column.

Now run the query by clicking RUN on the toolbar. Make sure everything so far is correct. In displaying the total sales to each customer for each day, your screen should look like the example shown in Figure 6-55.

Now go back to design mode and click in the CRITERIA row of the ORDDT column in the QBE grid. In this field, type a left square bracket, the words "Enter Date", and a right square bracket. Your screen should look like the example shown in Figure 6-56.

CONAME	ORDDT	Expr1
Around the Glob	09-Nov-92	$899.00
Around the Glob	15-Jan-93	$453.00
Around the Glob	28-Apr-93	$2,142.90
Around the Glob	09-Sep-93	$1,704.00
Around the Glob	08-Oct-93	$285.00
Around the Glob	11-Oct-93	$336.00
Around the Glob	17-Nov-93	$191.10
Best Bet	09-Oct-91	$803.00
Best Bet	20-Jul-92	$479.40
Best Bet	02-Feb-93	$1,328.00
Best Bet	15-Feb-93	$386.20
Best Bet	08-Apr-93	$139.80
Best Bet	09-Apr-93	$355.50
Best Bet	18-May-93	$477.00
Best Bet	08-Jun-93	$493.00
Big Gut Beer &	25-Jun-92	$48.00
Big Gut Beer &	02-Oct-92	$141.60
Big Gut Beer &	10-Nov-92	$864.00
Big Gut Beer &	21-Oct-93	$2,487.50

Figure 6-55: Query results.

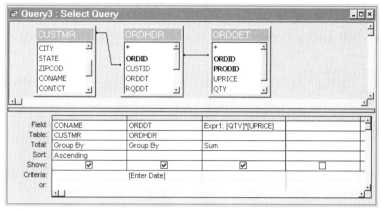

Figure 6-56: Entering date criteria.

The square brackets tell Access that you are using a field name. When Access encounters field names that it cannot find in the database, it treats them as parameters. Now, when you run the query again, Access displays a dialogue box asking you to provide the ENTER DATE information. Type the value "6/10/91" and press the OK button (Figure 6-57).

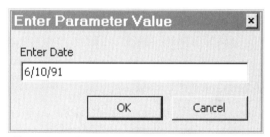

Figure 6-57: Entering the date dialogue.

Access then summarizes only the orders from June 10, 1991 (Figure 6-58).

As you can see, parameters are a useful feature of queries. You can use parameters in most of the same places you use literals within Access queries.

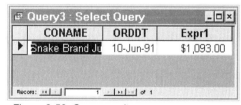

Figure 6-58: Query results.

Join Types

When you create queries that join tables, there are a couple of options for specifying how the tables are joined by Access. These options are important in helping you obtain the correct information from your database. Let's take a look at the different methods of joining customer data with order data.

When two tables are joined together in Access, the join is represented by a line that connects the fields that are used to join the tables. Double-clicking on the line, or right-clicking on the line and selecting JOIN PROPERTIES from the menu, brings up the JOIN PROPERTIES dialogue box. There the join method can be set to one of three different options (Figure 6-59). Return to DESIGN VIEW on your query and double-click on the join line between the Customer table and the Order Header table.

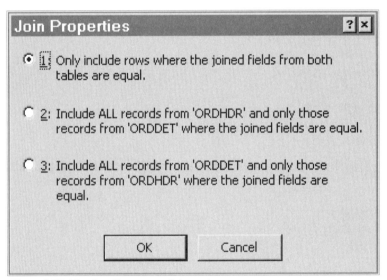

Figure 6-59: The JOIN PROPERTIES dialogue box.

The first option, called an *inner join*, is the default and it is the most commonly used type of join. It selects only records that have a matching field in both tables. The practical implication of an inner join, in the example of joining the CUSTMR and ORDHDR tables, is that only customers with orders will be returned in the query.

The second type of join is called a *left-outer join*. It selects all records from the left table (in this case, the Customer table) and any matching records in the right table (which is the Order Header table). The practical implication of this is that you will get all customers returned, whether or not they have any order records, in the query. The records in the result set that don't contain any order information will have null values in the fields included from the order table.

The third type of join is called a *right-outer join*. It selects all records from the right table (in this example, the Order Header table) and any matching records in the left table (the Customer table). The practical implication of this is that your results will include all orders (whether or not they have valid customers). This unusual method of joining tables is useful for finding invalid information in your database. All orders should have a matching customer. Otherwise, there is no way to know for whom the order is intended.

Action Queries

Action queries are a great way to manipulate data on the AS/400. Because they can be used to add, change, or delete large amounts of data, they are powerful tools, and they must be used with caution. Let's examine their use by working through an example that creates an update query that increases all prices in your product table by 10 percent.

Update Query

To create the update query, first open a new database. To do this, click on NEW DATABASE under the FILE menu. Select BLANK DATABASE from the Microsoft Access NEW dialogue box and click OK (see Figures 6-2A and 6-2B).

Access prompts you to identify your new database. Name the new database by typing "practice3" in the filename textbox (see Figure 6-3). On this screen, you also must specify in which directory you want to place the new database. Once you have selected where you want to locate your practice3 database, click the CREATE button.

To add some data to your newly created blank database, click on the FILE menu, select GET EXTERNAL DATA, and select the LINK TABLES option (see Figure 6-4).

Access displays the LINK dialogue box, indicating where the database must be pointed in order to be linked (see Figure 6-5). In the FILES OF TYPE parameter, choose ODBC DATABASES at the bottom of the list.

On the SELECT DATA SOURCE screen, choose your AS/400 data source and click the OK button (Figure 6-7). If your ODBC driver requires a user ID and password, the system will request that information now.

When your list of tables is displayed, choose the Product (PRODCT) table (see Figure 6-8). When you press the OK button, Access gathers information about the table. It then displays a screen asking you to select a unique record identifier (see Figure 6-9). Access displays the list of fields in the file you have chosen. For this example select PRODID and click the OK button.

When Access has finished gathering the table structure from the AS/400, you will see the table appear in the list of tables in the database window with the small "linked table" icon next to it.

Now you are ready to create your update query. First, click on the QUERIES tab and then click the NEW button (see Figure 6-18). In the NEW QUERY dialogue box, select DESIGN VIEW, and click the OK button (see Figure 6-19). In the SHOW TABLE dialogue box, select the Product (PRODCT) table, which is linked to your AS/400 product table (see Figure 6-20). Then click the ADD button and then the CLOSE button.

The query Design View is shown. Because Access defaults to creating a SELECT QUERY and you want to create an UPDATE QUERY, you must change this setting. Click on the QUERY menu and select the UPDATE QUERY option (Figure 6-60).

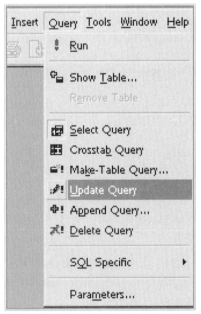

Figure 6-60: Changing to UPDATE QUERY.

You will notice that the screen changes slightly to reflect new parameters for an "update" type of query. In the FIELD drop-down list, select the QPRICE field (Figure 6-61).

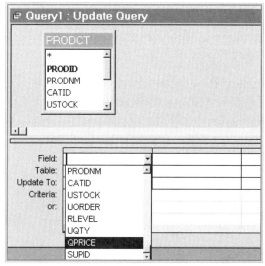

Figure 6-61: Selecting the QPRICE field.

Because the TABLE parameter has been automatically set for you, next you need to change the UPDATE TO parameter. Click in the UPDATE TO field and type "[QPRICE]*1.10". It should look like the example shown in Figure 6-62. The square brackets around the field name identify it as a field to Access. When the query is run,

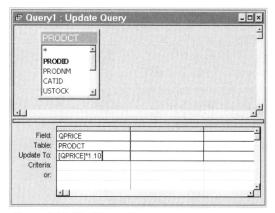

Figure 6-62: The UPDATE TO parameter.

this will change the QPRICE field in every record selected by the query to 10 percent higher than it was.

Please note that this changes all the records selected by the query. If necessary, you can add a filter to the query to select only certain records. Entering an expression in the CRITERIA parameter does this. In this case, because the price increase is across the board, you don't need to add a filter.

Now, to update the prices (if you have the authority), just run the query by clicking the RUN button on the toolbar. Access goes to work for a while. When it has completed the processing, it displays a warning telling you the number of rows that will be affected and that, once done, you cannot undo the change (Figure 6-63). As with the DELETE option mentioned previously, the records are already gone from the AS/400 at this point! Clicking "NO" has no effect and will not restore the data to its original form.

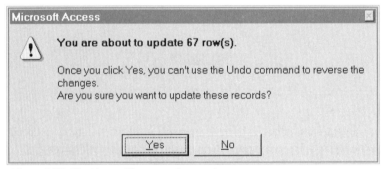

Figure 6-63: The UPDATE To parameter warning screen.

You also can use action queries to insert or delete large amounts of data. To create a query of this type, just select the appropriate choice (APPEND QUERY or DELETE QUERY) from the QUERY menu when you are in the DESIGN mode.

Wow! That's a lot of power to have at your fingertips. Of course, you can be trusted with such power, but not everyone is as benevolent and as wise as yourself. How do you protect your data from being updated by unauthorized users? The answer is to use OS/400 object-level authority to protect the data. If a user doesn't have the proper authority to the file on the AS/400, they won't be able to update the file with Access.

Performance Cautions

As you have seen, Microsoft Access is an excellent tool for exploring and manipulating your data. However, please pay close attention to these few words of caution. Because it is possible to retrieve a very large set of data using this tool, you must be careful in how you design your query so as not to affect the performance of the AS/400. Here are a couple of tips to help ensure that you don't get more than you asked for.

Try to minimize the amount of data that is retrieved before you refresh the query. This will reduce the workload on the AS/400. Do this by specifying only the fields you need in your queries. Retrieving extra fields causes more work for the AS/400, your PC, and your AS/400 link. Use the all-fields wildcard (*) sparingly if you are concerned about performance.

If you don't need to sort data, don't specify a sort. This allows the AS/400 to process the data in the order that is the most efficient for it. Whenever possible, avoid requiring the AS/400 to sort a large amount of data because excessive sorting can adversely affect performance.

The speed tips section of this chapter covers a technique called the pass-through query that can be used to speed up query processing and reduce some of the performance penalties.

ACCESS FORMS

Forms are used in Access to display data. In addition, forms can be used for inquiries, record maintenance, and to display graphs. You can customize forms to your own specification, including the use of graphics. This is especially useful for displaying company logos on your forms.

Forms can be created from tables and from queries. Access provides Wizards and AutoForms that help in the form-creation process and automates many of the tasks associated with form creation. This section examines how to use Wizards to manually create forms and then how to customize the forms to look exactly the way you prefer.

Form Types

Before you start to create a form, you must become familiar with the following different types of forms you can create in Access. The five types are the:

❖ **Columnar AutoForm**. The Columnar AutoForm creates a single-column form from a table or query. One record displays on the screen at a time.

❖ **Tabular AutoForm**. The Tabular AutoForm creates forms in a table-like format, so you can see multiple records on a single screen.

❖ **Datasheet Autoform**. The Datasheet AutoForm creates a form that looks like the Datasheet View shown in the table and query sections of this chapter.

❖ **Chart Wizard**. The Chart Wizard allows you to create a graph from a table or query.

❖ **PivotTable Wizard**. The PivotTable Wizard helps you create pivot table forms that are very useful for sifting through large amounts of data.

Creating a Form

Let's get started creating a form. First open your database. You can use your practice database for this example. See Figure 6-4. In the database window, click on the FORMS tab, and then click the NEW button (Figure 6-64).

Figure 6-64: Creating a new form.

This brings up the NEW FORM dialogue box where you select your table and choose whether you want to build the form from scratch or with the help of a wizard (Figure 6-65).

At the bottom of this window you will see a text box. Click on the arrow and select the Customer table from the drop-down list. Then select the FORM WIZARD option from the list at the top of the dialogue box and click the OK button.

The wizard displays the FORM WIZARD dialogue box that prompts you for the fields to include on the form (Figure 6-66).

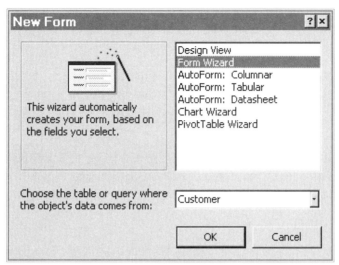

Figure 6-65: The NEW FORM dialogue box.

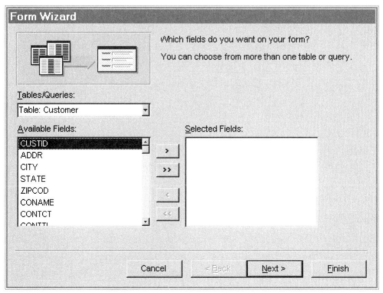

Figure 6-66: The FORM WIZARD setup.

The list on the left are the fields available from your table or query. The list on the right contains the fields you have selected for your form. This list is currently blank because you have not added any fields to your form, yet.

To add fields to your form, you can highlight individual fields in the left list and click on the single right-pointing arrow (>) button in the center of the window. Otherwise, you can move all the fields in one step by clicking the button with the double right-pointing arrows (>>).

Click on the double arrow to add all the fields to your form. When all the fields have moved from the left side to the right side of the window, press the Next button to advance to the next screen. The next screen asks you to choose the layout for your form (Figure 6-67).

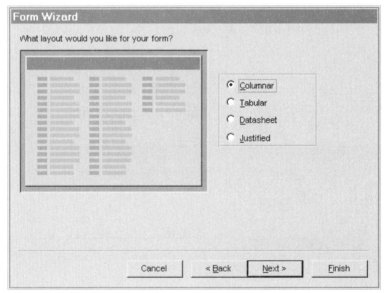

Figure 6-67: The FORM WIZARD layout.

Click on each one of the options to see a preview of the form layout on the left of the screen. For this example, choose COLUMNAR and press the NEXT button. The next dialogue box asks you to choose what style you want for your form (Figure 6-68).

Again, you can click on each option to see a preview of the style. For this example, choose the CLOUDS option, and press the NEXT button (Figure 6-68). The next screen is the last screen for this Wizard. Here you can give the form a title (Figure 6-69). For this example call your form CUSTOMER MAINTENANCE.

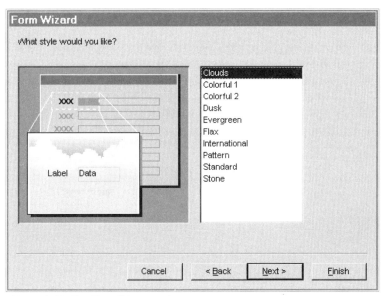

Figure 6-68: The FORM WIZARD style.

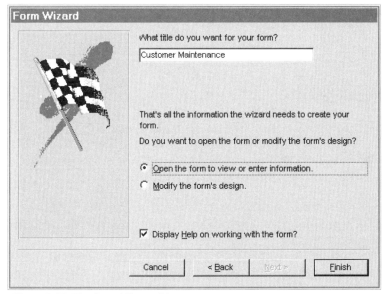

Figure 6-69: The FORM WIZARD title.

There also are options on this screen that allow you to decide what to do with the form once the wizard has created it. You can OPEN THE FORM TO VIEW OR ENTER INFORMATION or MODIFY THE FORMS DESIGN. Let's accept the default to view the form and press the FINISH button.

Access then creates the single-column CUSTOMER MAINTENANCE form for you, and opens it up populated with data from your AS/400 Customer table (Figure 6-70). Clicking on the navigation buttons at the bottom of the screen allows you to move around in the record set. Can you imagine how long it would take to code this in RPG?

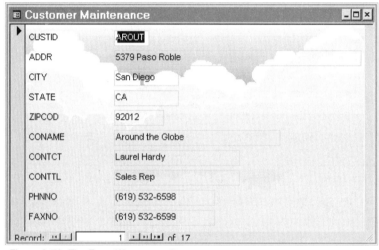

Figure 6-70: The FORM WIZARD results.

Customizing Forms

You can easily customize your form to give it the appearance you want. To do this, you will need to display the form in design mode. Click on the DESIGN VIEW button on the toolbar. You will notice that the CUSTOMER MAINTENANCE window has changed (Figure 6-71).

You also will notice that a TOOLBOX has appeared on the left of your screen. This toolbar can be moved and resized by clicking on it and dragging it to the desired location (Figure 6-72).

There are two columns in your table (Figure 6-71). The *label column* on the left and the *textbox column* on the right.

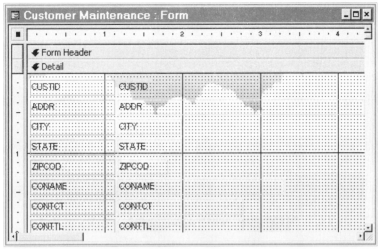

Figure 6-71: The FORM design view.

Figure 6-72: The form design TOOLBOX.

In design mode, almost every aspect of the form's design can be customized. For instance, you can change the field names to something more meaningful. Do this by clicking on the ADDR field label to the left of the address ADDR textbox (Figure 6-73).

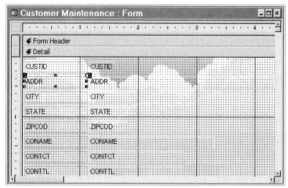

Figure 6-73: Selecting the address field label.

Click again in the center of the field label to position the cursor to this point. Then select the existing text ADDR and change the field title by typing "Address" in the label box (Figure 6-74). This can, of course, be done to all the fields.

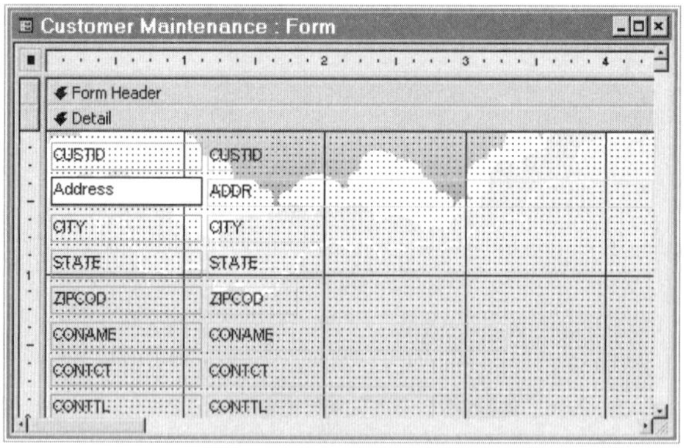

Figure 6-74: Replacing the label text.

You also can move the fields to the positions you like. For example, you can move the company name (CONAME) field to the top of the form and the customer ID (CUSTID) to the spot vacated by the company-name field. Do this by clicking on the CONAME textbox field to select it. You must be sure to click in the textbox portion of the field (not the label portion). Clicking in the textbox portion moves both the label and the textbox. Clicking on the label moves only the label itself.

Move the mouse slowly to the top edge of the field. When the mouse pointer becomes an open hand, hold down the left mouse button and drag the field to move it to its new location. For now, put it to the right of the Customer ID field (Figure 6-75).

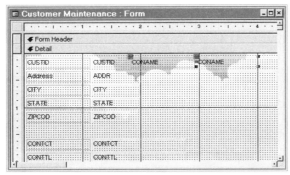

Figure 6-75: Moving form fields.

Then use the same method to move the Customer ID (CUSTID) field down to where the customer name field was. Next, move the customer name field to the left to line it up with the rest of the fields beneath it. Your form should now look like the example shown in Figure 6-76.

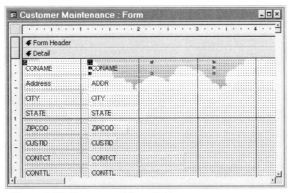

Figure 6-76: Rearranged form fields.

You also can use your mouse to change the size of the fields. For instance, you can make the address field a little smaller. To do this, click once in the address textbox. The field is highlighted and small black dots called *handles* appear around the field (Figure 6-73). To make the field smaller horizontally, click on the handle on the right side of the field and drag to the left.

You also can set the PROPERTIES of fields on your form. Properties you can change include the field's format (which controls how the data in the field is displayed). In addition, you can change the text in the status bar of a field. For this example, change the status bar text of the Address field to provide the user with help on which values to put in that field.

Start by selecting the ADDRESS textbox field and clicking with the right mouse button. This displays a popup menu (Figure 6-77). Make sure you select the textbox field and not the label field or Access will display the wrong dialogue box for you to make this change.

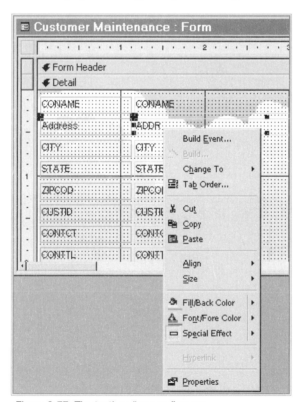

Figure 6-77: The textbox "pop-up" menu.

Select PROPERTIES from this menu to display the TEXT BOX properties dialogue box (Figure 6-78). Click on the OTHER tab or the ALL tab and in the STATUS BAR TEXT textbox. After typing "Enter the customer address", close the TEXT BOX dialogue box.

Now view your work by switching to FORM VIEW. Do this by clicking on the VIEW button on the toolbar and selecting FORM VIEW from the menu (Figure 6-79).

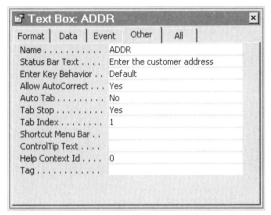

Figure 6-78: The TEXT BOX properties dialogue box.

Figure 6-79: Changing to FORM VIEW.

When you click in the address textbox, you will notice that the text you entered is displayed in the status bar text at the very bottom of your screen (Figure 6-80).

Tabular AutoForms

Tabular Autoforms display several records of data on the screen, at the same time,

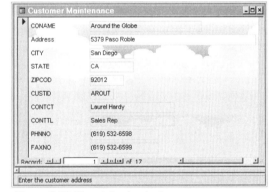

Figure 6-80: The status bar text.

similar to an AS/400 subfile and an Access datasheet. AutoForms are a combination of columnar forms and the Datasheet View.

The fastest way to create a tabular form is to use the Tabular AutoForms Wizard. First, select the FORMS tab in your practice database window and then press the NEW button.

Select the CUSTOMER table from the pull-down menu and select the AUTOFORM: TABULAR option (Figure 6-81). Then click the OK button.

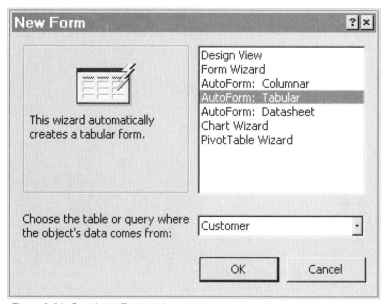

Figure 6-81: Creating a TABULAR AUTOFORM.

The form is created instantly (Figure 6-82). The form contains all the fields from the table you selected, and it uses the format you selected the last time you used the Forms Wizard.

CU!	ADDR	CITY	STA`	ZIP(	CONAME	CONTCT	CONTTL	PHNNO	FAXNO
AR	5379 Paso Roble	San [	CA	9201	Around the Gl(	Laurel Harc	Sales Rep	(619) 53	(619) 532
BSE	123 Pickadilly Sq.	Cleve	OH	568ς	Best Bet	Victoria Vis	Sales Rep	(598) 89	(598) 987
COl	4345 Gadman Court	San F	CA	9411	Consolidated ⊢	Charlie Pick	Sales Rep	(415) 98	(415) 987
EAS	905 Jefferson Court	Portle	OR	972(	Eastern Conne	Devin Pickle	Sales Ager	(503) 65	(503) 35E
GRE	2732 Baker Blvd.	Portle	OR	974(	Great Falls Foc	Howard Le	Marketing ℕ	(503) 55	
ISL,	123 Crowley Lane	Oran!	CA'	925E	Inland Transpc	Helen Bacr	Marketing ℕ	(714) 98	
LA;	12 Symphony Terrace	Walla	WA	993E	Square K Cour	John Will Sl	Marketing ℕ	(509) 55	(509) 55ς

Figure 6-82: Tabular Autoform results.

Great! You've got a one-click, subfile-style master file maintenance program, complete with scroll bars and update capability (provided the table or query is updateable). You can change the layout of this form to your liking in the same way you did with the single-column form by clicking the DESIGN VIEW button on the toolbar.

Creating Graphs with AS/400 Data

Graph forms display data from a table or query in a graphical format. This section describes how to create a graph showing the total sales of your company's products to each customer. This is a very useful feature of Access.

First, you must create a query that summarizes sales by customer. To do this, open your practice2 database (refer to the Joining Tables section of this chapter). Then click on the QUERY tab in the database window and press the NEW button (see Figure 6-18). SELECT DESIGN VIEW from the dialogue box (see Figure 6-19). Add the Customer, Order Header, and Order Detail tables to the query and press the CLOSE button (see Figure 6-20).

Again, the Customer table should be joined to the Order Header table by the CUSTID field, and the Order Header table should be joined to the Order Detail table by the ORDID field (see Figure 6-39).

You will need two fields—the customer name (CONAME) and the total sales—for this summary query. First, add the company name field from the Customer table to the query by dragging it from the table the to QBE grid. Then select ASCENDING order for the sort (Figure 6-83)

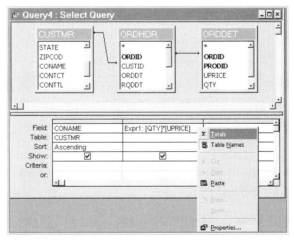

Figure 6-83: Displaying the summary row in a query.

In the column to the right of the CONAME column, add a calculated field of QTY*UPRICE for the field. As you know, this creates a field that calculates the gross price of each ordered item. Now display the summary row in the QBE grid by right-clicking in the extended price field and selecting TOTALS (Figure 6-83).

In the TOTAL row for the extended price field, select SUM from the pull-down menu. Let's also format this field so it looks good on the graph.

Format it as a currency field by right-clicking in the extended price column and selecting PROPERTIES from the menu (Figure 6-84).

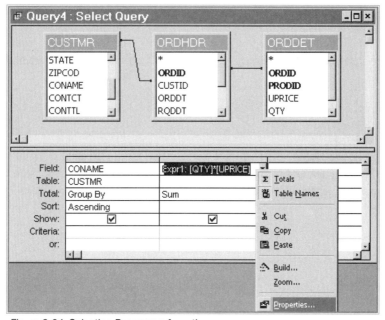

Figure 6-84: Selecting PROPERTIES from the menu.

In the FIELD PROPERTIES dialogue box, click in the FORMAT field, then click on the arrow that appears on the right side of the field, and select CURRENCY from the menu (Figure 6-85). Close the PROPERTIES window.

Now close the query and save it as CUSTOMER SALES (Figure 6-86).

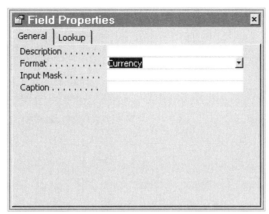

Figure 6-85: The FIELD PROPERTIES dialogue box.

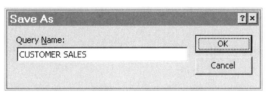

Figure 6-86: Saving a CUSTOMER SALES query.

Now you are ready to create a graph form. Start by clicking on the FORMS tab in the database window and clicking on the NEW button. Then select CHART WIZARD from the list, select the CUSTOMER SALES query, and click the OK button (Figure 6-87).

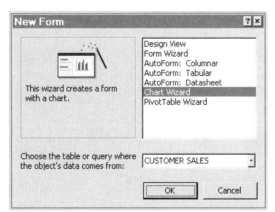

Figure 6-87: Creating a NEW FORM.

The CHART WIZARD dialogue box is displayed. Here, you need to select which fields you want to graph. Because you want to use both fields in this query, click on the

double-arrow (>>) button that points to the right (Figure 6-88). Then click on the
NEXT button.

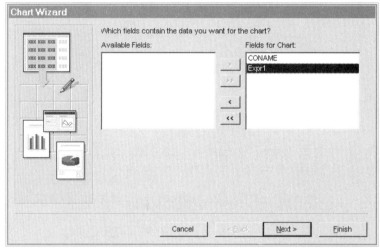

Figure 6-88: The CHART WIZARD setup.

On the next screen, Access displays the types of graphs available. Click on each chart type
to see a description. Take a look at each customer's sales as a percentage of the whole sales
by viewing your data as a 3D pie chart. Click on the 3D pie chart button that is located on
the bottom row, second from left (Figure 6-89). Then click on the NEXT button.

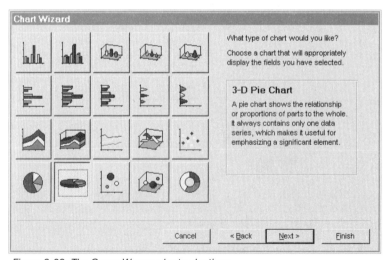

Figure 6-89: The CHART WIZARD chart selections.

On the next screen, you determine how the chart uses the data from the query (Figure 6-90). Access should have correctly guessed that you want to have the company name as the chart legend and the sum of the sales as the numeric data.

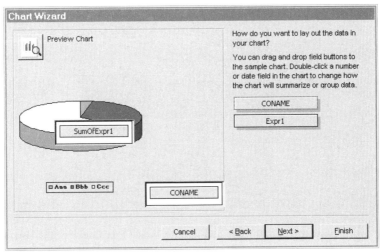

Figure 6-90: The CHART WIZARD layout.

You can click the PREVIEW CHART button to see what you have created so far (Figure 6-91). If your chart looks fine, click the CLOSE button and proceed to the next screen by clicking NEXT.

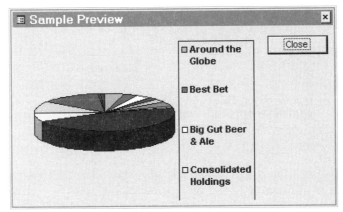

Figure 6-91: Chart Wizard - Preview.

On this screen, enter the title (SALES BY CUSTOMER) of your chart. in the textbox (Figure 6-92). To keep the chart's legend, leave the legend option selected. Accept the default to open the form with the chart displayed on it and click the FINISH button to view the chart.

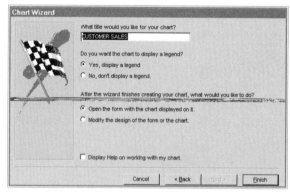

Figure 6-92: Selecting the CHART WIZARD title.

Your chart is displayed automatically and should look like the example shown in Figure 6-93.

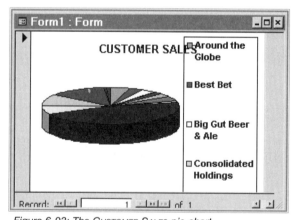

Figure 6-93: The CUSTOMER SALES pie chart.

Creating charts from your AS/400 data is a simple process using Microsoft Access. Forms provide many useful ways to display your data. For example, you can place command buttons on forms that execute code when pressed and you can attach code to user events such as modifying or deleting a record.

ACCESS REPORTS

Reports in Access are used to help provide information from raw data. While they are primarily geared toward printing information on paper, they can be used to display information on screen as well. There are many types of reports and many formatting options available. Because these options allow you to display your data in almost any format imaginable, Access is one of the most powerful reporting tools for AS/400 data.

As with the forms and queries, there are report wizards that make the creation of reports a matter of answering a few simple questions. The following sections describe how to use the wizards and what type of reports these wizards produce. You also will discover how to customize the results of the wizards to get the exact look you want for your reports.

Creating a Report

To create a master-file listing of the Customer table, first open your practice2 database and, in the database window, click the REPORTS tab and then click the NEW button (Figure 6-94).

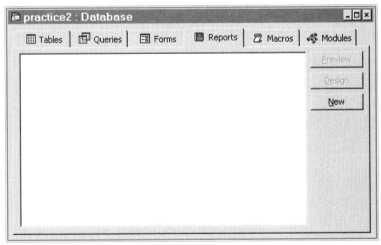

Figure 6-94: Creating a report.

On the NEW REPORT screen, select REPORT WIZARD from the list, choose the Customer (CUSTMR) table from the drop-down list, and click the OK button (Figure 6-95).

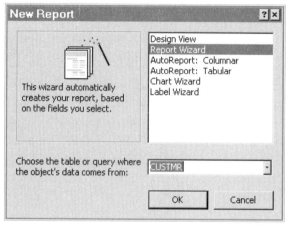

Figure 6-95: The NEW REPORT screen.

On the first REPORT WIZARD screen, Access asks which fields to put on the report (Figure 6-96). Select them all by clicking on the button with double arrows (>>) pointing to the right. Then click on the NEXT button.

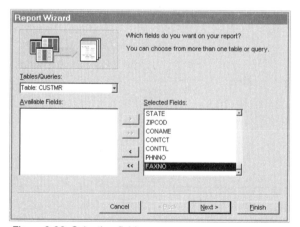

Figure 6-96: Selecting fields.

On the next screen, the wizard asks if you want to add any grouping levels (Figure 6-97). Because this is just a master-file listing, you don't need any groupings. Leave the screen as it is and click the NEXT button.

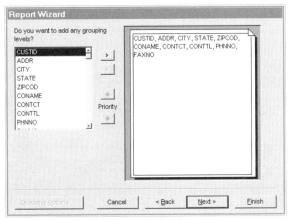

Figure 6-97: Selecting grouping levels.

Now you need to specify how you want the report sorted (Figure 6-98). Sort by customer name, in ascending order, by choosing the CONAME field in the first drop-down menu, and choose ascending order (A-Z) on the button to the right of the field. You can specify up to four sort fields on this screen. It is possible to sort by more than four

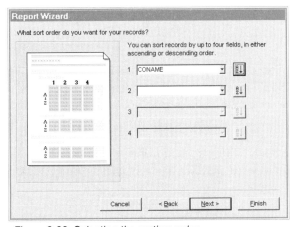

Figure 6-98: Selecting the sorting order.

fields using other methods, but four should be enough for most situations. In this instance, you will be sorting only by company name; click the NEXT button.

On the next screen, choose the type of report you want to create (Figure 6-99). The layout options include columnar, tabular, and justified reports. To get an idea of what each of these reports look like, you can select the option, by clicking on it, and the report preview window will show you the layout.

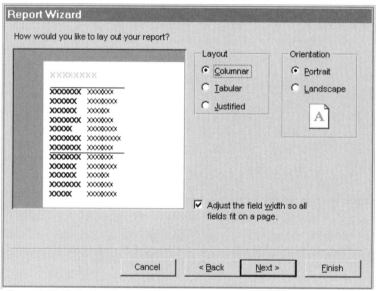

Figure 6-99: Selecting the layout for your report.

Because single-column reports are useful for producing master-file listings, choose the columnar option. Notice the option called ADJUST THE FIELD WIDTH SO ALL FIELDS FIT ON A PAGE. This option is very useful for helping you put maximum information on paper. Leave this box selected and click the NEXT button.

To specify the style options for your report (Figure 6-100), click on the different options to see what the various styles look like. For this example, select the CORPORATE style and press the NEXT button.

To name your report (Figure 6-101), change the report title to CUSTOMER MASTER LISTING and accept the defaults for the other options by pressing the FINISH button.

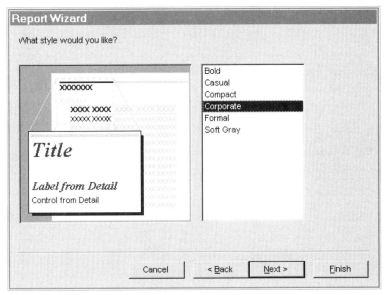

Figure 6-100: Selecting the report style.

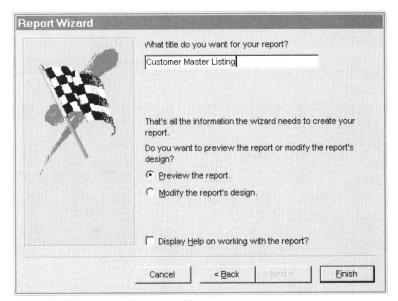

Figure 6-101: Selecting the report title.

Access creates the report and shows you a preview of what it looks like when printed (Figure 6-102).

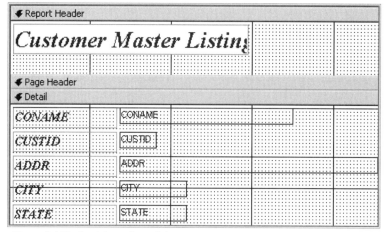

Figure 6-102: A print preview of the report.

To exit the print-preview mode and enter the report-design mode, click on the CLOSE button on the toolbar.

The Report Editor

Modifying the layout of the report is performed much like modifying the layout of a form. The report layout editor allows you to add and remove fields, create and change labels, and customize other features of the report to make it appear exactly the way you want it. If you haven't already done so yet, click the CLOSE button on the toolbar (Figure 6-103) to change from print preview to the report design mode.

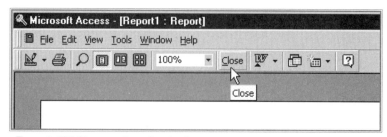

Figure 6-103: The report preview toolbar.

Notice the title bars on the report design window labeled REPORT HEADER, PAGE HEADER, and DETAIL. These bars separate the individual sections of the report (Figure 6-104).

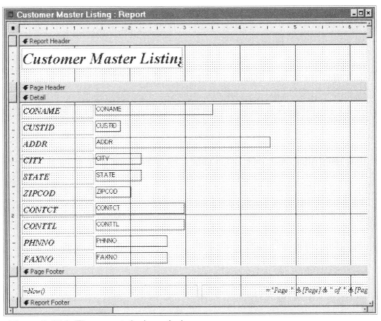

Figure 6-104: The report design window.

For example, if you place a field in the REPORT HEADER section of the report, it prints only on the first page of the report. If you place a field in the PAGE HEADER section, it prints before the detail on each page. A field in the DETAIL section prints for every record in the report.

Changing a field label is done in the same way as on the form editor. Simply click on the label, and then click again inside the label. Select the text and enter the label text you want as the replacement (see Figures 6-73 and 6-74).

Changing a field's position is easy using the report editor. To move a field within the editor, click on the right-hand textbox field to select the textbox and the label together. Then move the mouse pointer toward the top edge of the field until it becomes a hand. When the pointer becomes a hand, hold the left mouse button down and drag the field to where you want it (see Figure 6-75).

You also can change properties—such as the formatting and border style—of a field. To change the Date field on the report header to the short-date format, right-click on the Date field, which has the text "=Now()" in it. Next, select the PROPERTIES option (Figure 6-105).

Figure 6-105: The Date field pop-up menu.

This displays the PROPERTIES dialogue box (Figure 6-106). Change the FORMAT entry of this dialogue box to SHORT DATE. To do this, click on the ALL tab and click in the FORMAT text box. Now click on the arrow that has appeared on the right of the text box and select SHORT DATE from the drop-down list. Now close the window. The next time the report is run, the date will print with the short-date format.

Grouping and Totaling

Let's take a look at grouping and totaling reports. You can use wizards to create reports that group certain records together and display summary as well as grand totals for those groups.

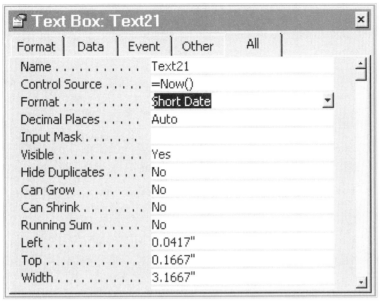

Figure 6-106: Changing the date format.

Before you can create a "groups and totals" report, you must create a query that shows what each customer has ordered by state. Create the query by clicking on the QUERY tab in the database window and clicking on the NEW button (see Figure 6-18). Then select DESIGN VIEW and click the OK button (see Figure 6-19).

Add the Customer (CUSTMR), Order Header (ORDHDR), and Order Detail (ORDDET) tables to the query (Figure 6-20). Make sure the Customer table is joined to the Order Header table with the CUSTID field, and that the Order Header table is joined to the Order Detail table with the ORDID field.

If not, drag the CUSTID field from the Customer table to the CUSTID field on the Order Header table. Then drag the ORDID field from the Order Header table to the ORDID field on the Order Detail table. Your screen should look like the example shown in Figure 6-39 when the tables are joined correctly.

Next, add all the fields from each table to the query by dragging the asterisk from each table to the QBE grid. While this shortcut is acceptable for this example, in most real-world situations, you wouldn't want to return more data than necessary to ensure maximum performance.

Add a calculated field to the query to give the extended price. In the right-most column in the QBE grid, enter the expression "Ext Price:QTY*UPRICE" (Figure 6-107). This creates a calculated field, like the one you created before, and gives it the name EXT PRICE.

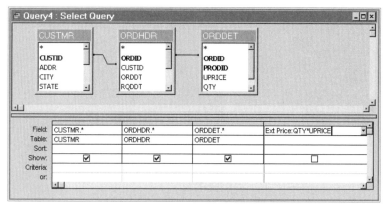

Figure 6-107: Adding an expression to the query.

Give this field the currency format by right-clicking in the column, selecting PROPERTIES from the menu, and choosing CURRENCY from the format field drop-down list (Figure 6-108).

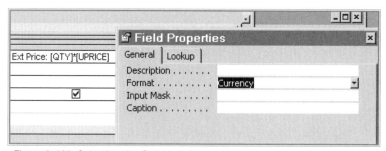

Figure 6-108: Selecting the CURRENCY format.

Close the properties dialogue and run the query by clicking on the Run button on the toolbar. Notice that there is one record for every order-line item for each customer, and the extended price field is in the query as well. Close the query window and save the query as the CUSTOMER SALES REPORT (Figure 6-109).

Now you can create a report from the customer sales query. Click on the REPORTS tab, and then click on the NEW button. Choose the CUSTOMER SALES REPORT query from the list, select the REPORT WIZARD, and click OK (Figure 6-110).

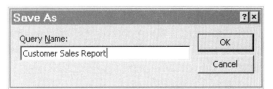

Figure 6-109: Saving a query as the CUSTOMER SALES REPORT.

On the REPORT WIZARD screen, choose the fields you want to include on the report (Figure 6-111). Select CONAME, ORDHDR:ORDID, RQDDT, SHPDT, QTY, UPRICE, and EXTPRICE. Move these fields one at a time to the right-hand list by highlighting each item and clicking on the single right-pointing arrow.

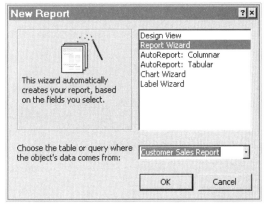

Figure 6-110: Creating a new report using a REPORT WIZARD.

Notice that because there are multiple-order identification fields in the query, Access prefixes the field with the name of the table where that field originates.

When you have your seven fields in the right-hand list, press the NEXT button. The next REPORT WIZARD screen is where you tell Access how to group the data on the report. You will group by company name and order to get totals for each of these groups.

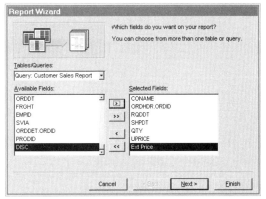

Figure 6-111: Choosing fields.

Choose the company name (CONAME) field and use the arrow button to move it to the right of the screen. Then choose the order identification (ORDHDR:ORDID) field and move that to the right of the screen (Figure 6-112). An image of the report breaks is built on the right side of the screen.

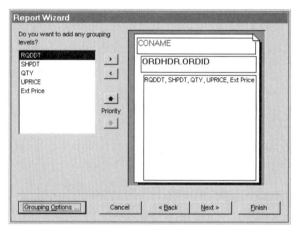

Figure 6-112: Selecting group identification.

Now click on the GROUPING OPTIONS button at the bottom left of your screen. On this screen, you can tell Access to group on partial field values (Figure 6-113). For this example, you want to group on the entire field. Therefore, leave the options set to NORMAL and press the OK button. Then press the NEXT button to continue.

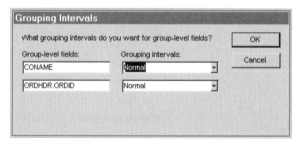

Figure 6-113: The REPORT WIZARD grouping options screen.

On the next screen, Access asks you which fields you want to sort by within the group (Figure 6-114). Because you don't need to sort by any of these fields, leave the list empty.

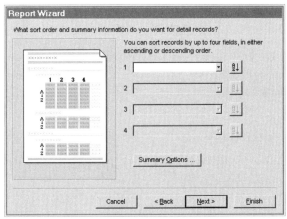

Figure 6-114: The REPORT WIZARD sort screen.

Click on the SUMMARY OPTIONS button. On this screen, you can select which types of summaries you want done for the report (Figure 6-115). Selecting a function for the field includes it in the report. For example, you could display the sum of the extended price, the average of the quantity, or any other combination. You can display the detail

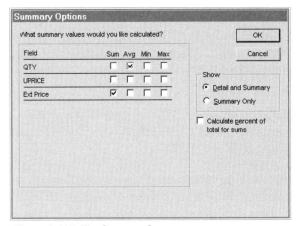

Figure 6-115: The SUMMARY OPTIONS screen.

and summary or just the summaries. And you can calculate a percentage of the total for sums. These powerful options can be invoked by the click of a mouse.

For this example, select the sum of the extended price and the average of the quantity by selecting the checkboxes. Set the display to DETAIL AND SUMMARY. Press the OK button to return to the previous screen and then select the NEXT button to continue.

On the "layout" screen, you choose how you want the report laid out (Figure 6-116). Clicking through the options displays the preview on the left of the screen. Choose the STEPPED layout and click the NEXT button.

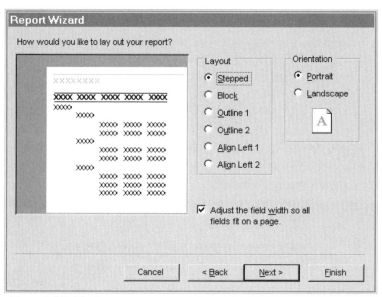

Figure 6-116: The layout screen.

The style screen is used to select what style you want for your report (Figure 6-117). Again, clicking through the options displays the preview on the left of the window. Choose the CORPORATE option and click NEXT.

You are now at the Report Wizard title screen (Figure 6-118). Here you set the report title and whether you want to preview your report or modify it. Keep your report titled "Customer Sales Report," accept the option to preview your report, and press the FINISH button.

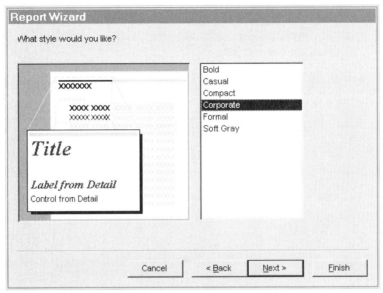

Figure 6-117: The style screen.

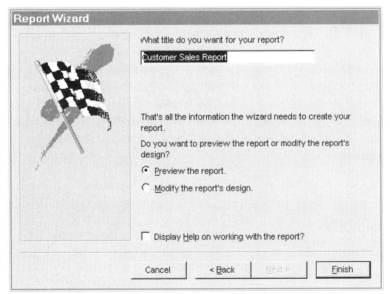

Figure 6-118: The title screen.

Access creates the report and displays it with data. As you can see from the preview, this report needs a little work to improve it's look (Figure 6-119).

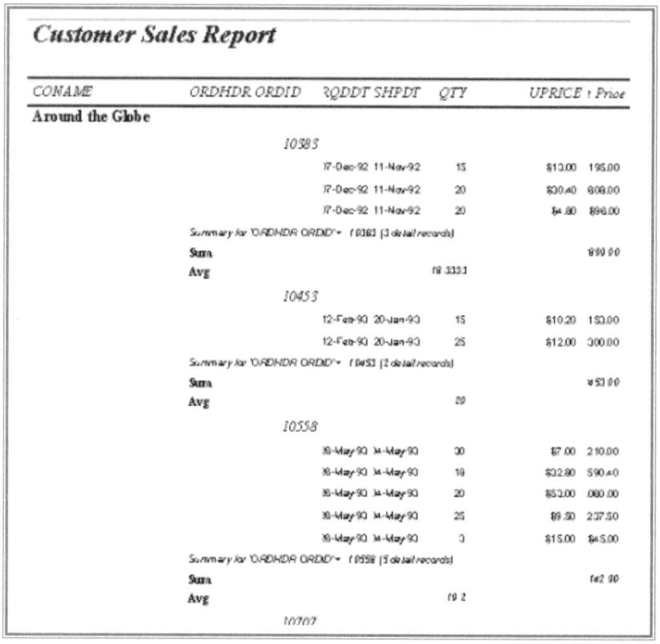

Figure 6-119: The print preview screen.

Switch to design mode by clicking the VIEW button on the toolbar. Notice that some additional sections appear on this report (Figure 6-120). In addition to the familiar report and page headers, there are some new header and footer sections. Fields in the CONAME header are printed when a new company is printed. Fields in the ORDID group are printed each time a new order is printed. Fields in the footer sections print before a section break.

In design mode, you can make some format changes, similar to those you made in the previous section, to make the appearance of this report more presentable. Experiment with those changes to see how it affects the look of your report. Figure 6-121 shows an example of how you could change the appearance of your report.

Mailing Labels

Access also can create mailing labels using report wizards. Using Access, you can create professional-style mailing labels directly from your AS/400 customer database. To create

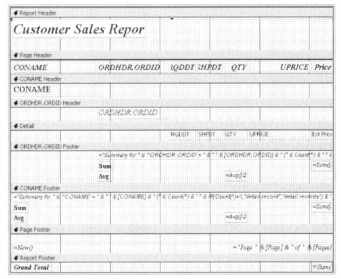

Figure 6-120: The design mode screen.

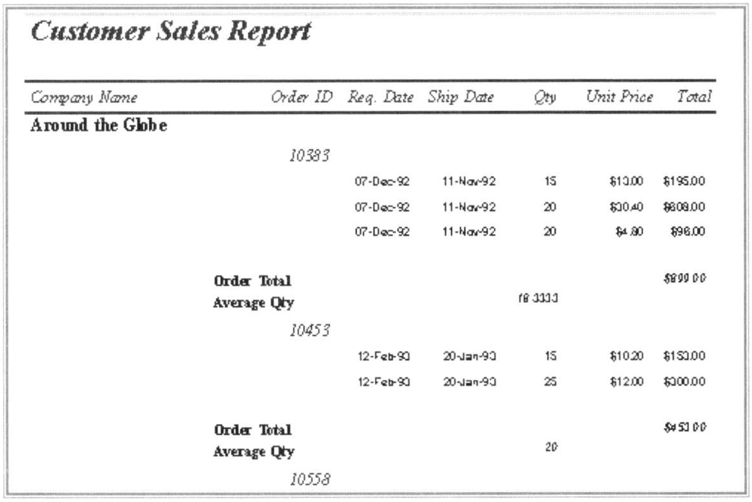

Figure 6-121: An amended report layout.

mailing labels, click on the REPORTS tab in the database window and click on the NEW button. Choose the Customer table (CUSTMR) from the drop-down list, select the LABEL WIZARD option, and click the OK button (Figure 6-122).

On the first LABEL WIZARD screen, tell Access what type of label you have (Figure 6-123). You can choose from the many predefined label formats.

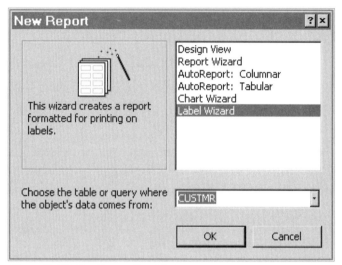

Figure 6-122: Creating mailing labels.

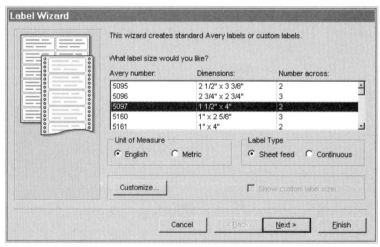

Figure 6-123: Selecting a label size.

If you don't see the label you prefer on this list, you can click on the CUSTOMIZE button to bring you to the NEW LABEL SIZE screen (Figure 6-124). Then click on NEW to create a new label specification from the new-label window.

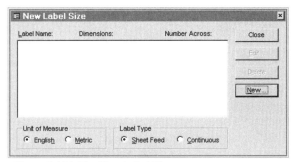

Figure 6-124: The New Label Size screen.

On the new-label screen, you can enter the dimensions of your label in the specified boxes, set options, and enter a name for your new labels (Figure 6-125). Click on CANCEL to exit without setting up a new label. Then click on the CLOSE button on the NEW LABEL SIZE screen.

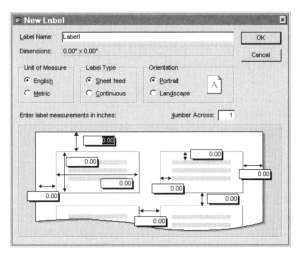

Figure 6-125: Naming the new labels.

Now you are back at the first LABEL WIZARD screen (Figure 6-123) where you must choose your label and set your measurement and feed options. For this example, choose the "5097" label. Choose "English" for the UNIT OF MEASURE and "Sheet feed" for the label type. When you are done entering your label information, click the NEXT button to continue.

The next screen is where you choose the font and color of the text for your labels (Figure 6-126). For this example, choose the "Comic Sans MS" font (or any other available font) and "10" for the font size. Set the font weight to "Light" and the font color to black. Then click on the NEXT button.

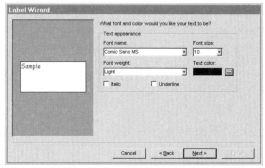

Figure 6-126: Selecting font and color options.

The next screen prompts you to create a prototype for the label (Figure 6-127). Do this by moving fields from the database to the prototype label. You also can type any text you want to appear on the label directly into the prototype. This is useful for such things as the standard comma between each city and state.

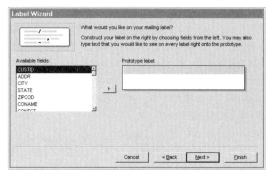

Figure 6-127: The prototype label.

First, select the CONAME field and move it to the prototype by clicking on the right-pointing arrow. Press the Enter key to move to the next line, add the CONTCT field followed by a hyphen (-), and then add the CONTTL field to the same line. Press the Enter key and add the ADDR field. Press the Enter key again and then add

Figure 6-128: Prototype details.

the CITY field, followed by a comma and a space, and then add the STATE and the ZIPCOD field to the same line. Your screen should look like the example shown in Figure 6-128. When you are done, click the NEXT button to proceed.

As shown in Figure 6-129, this screen is where you can specify a sort for the labels. Here you can sort by any combination of fields you like. Let's sort by ZIP code by selecting the ZIPCOD field and clicking the right-pointing arrow. Then click the NEXT button to proceed.

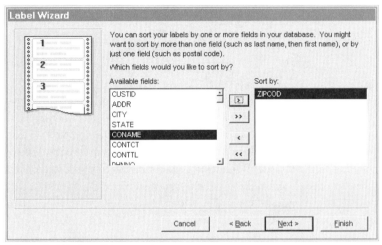

Figure 6-129: Specifying a sort.

As shown in Figure 6-130, you can specify a title for the label report as well as the action to be performed directly after the label report is created. In the title field, type "Customer Labels" and make sure the SEE THE LABELS option is selected. Click the FINISH button.

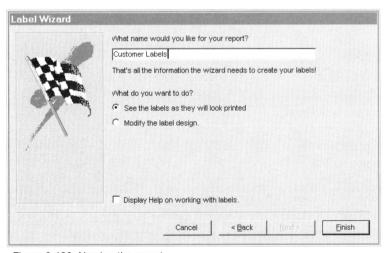

Figure 6-130: Naming the report.

When Access is finished creating the labels, it displays them in the print preview mode (Figure 6-131). Of course, if something doesn't look right, you can go back and adjust the label by clicking the VIEW button on the toolbar.

Best Bet Victoria Viscous-Sales Rep 123 Pickadilly Sq. Cleveland, OH56897	The Cracker Box Itsal Wong-Marketing Assistant 55 Doggy Peak Rd. Butte, MT59801
Big Gut Beer & Ale Art FulDodger-Sales Manager P.O. Box 555 Lander, WY82520	Midnight Markets Jose Luiz-Sales Rep 187 Wasup Ln. Boise, ID83720
Norte Emporium Simon Garfunkel-Sales Associate 300 Hackensack Rd. Albuquerque, NM87110	Snake Brand Juice Co. Paula Jones-Assistant Sales Representative 2817 George Dr. Albuquerque, NM87110

Figure 6-131: A label print-preview screen.

The report wizards and the report editor in Access are powerful aids in helping you manipulate raw data as information. The report editor can be used to make numerous modifications to your reports, including formatting fields, adjusting field size and position, and changing labels. Reports are easy to create with Access, and they provide many powerful options for presenting information in a format that is the most useful for your specific needs.

Exporting Data

Microsoft Access is a good tool for exporting data to the AS/400. Its capability to handle many different database types makes it an excellent candidate for moving data between systems. Access also can be used as a "go-between" to move data to other systems from the AS/400.

Exporting is the term used for getting data from Access to your AS/400. The first step in exporting data to the AS/400 is to be sure that you have the correct setup. Properly setting up is a two-step process designed to make sure that a library exists for the data (Figure 6-132).

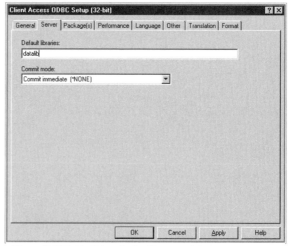

Figure 6-132: Verifying that a library exists.

The second step is to tell the ODBC driver, through the DSN, that this is the library to use for exports (Figure 6-133).

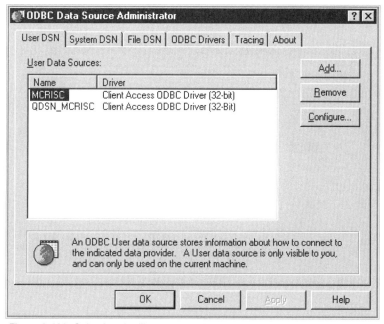

Figure 6-133: Selecting the library to use for exports.

If you already know the library exists, you can skip this step. To determine if the library does exist, enter the AS/400 command:

```
DSPOBJD <libname> *LIB
```

You should see a screen similar to Figure 6-132.

Once you know where you want the data stored, you need to configure the Client Access ODBC driver to use that library. Setting the DEFAULT LIBRARIES parameter does this. The first library in the parameter is where the data is placed on your AS/400.

To make sure that the library is correct, go into the ODBC DATA SOURCE ADMINISTRATOR (either from the Client Access folder or the Control Panel). Find your data source, select it, and click the CONFIGURE button.

Click the SERVER tab, and make sure that the first library in the DEFAULT LIBRARIES parameter is the library where you want the data placed. When you have this set correctly, click the OK button to exit the DATA SOURCE ADMINISTRATOR.

The next step in exporting your data is to find the table that you want to export. Open your Access database. In the TABLES tab, select the EXPORT SAMPLE table (Figure 6-134).

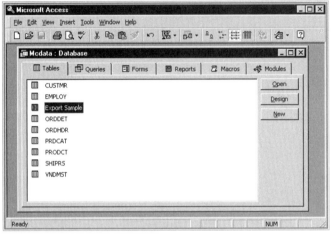

Figure 6-134: Selecting the EXPORT SAMPLE table.

To export this table, right-click on the table name and select SAVE AS/EXPORT from the menu (Figure 6-135). Alternatively, you can highlight the table and select the SAVE AS/EXPORT option from the FILE menu.

On the SAVE AS screen, select TO AN EXTERNAL FILE OR DATABASE, and click the OK button (Figure 6-136).

When the SAVE TABLE dialogue box appears, Access asks you to specify to which location you want the file exported. In the SAVE AS TYPE combo box, scroll down to select ODBC DATABASES at the bottom of the list (Figure 6-137).

Figure 6-135: Selecting the SAVE AS/EXPORT option.

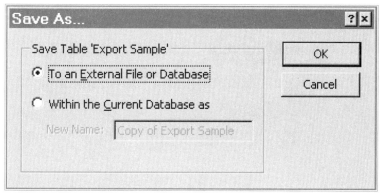

Figure 6-136: The SAVE AS screen.

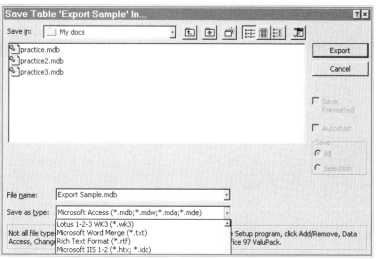

Figure 6-137: The SAVE TABLE dialogue box.

The EXPORT dialogue box prompts you for the name you want to use for the table on the AS/400. Because "Export Sample" is not a traditional AS/400 table name, change it to something closer to what might be found on the AS/400. Type "EXPSAM" (in all uppercase characters) in the textbox and click the OK button (Figure 6-138).

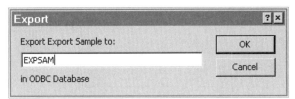

Figure 6-138: The Export dialogue box.

On the SELECT DATA SOURCE dialogue box, select the DSN for your AS/400 and click the OK button (Figure 6-139).

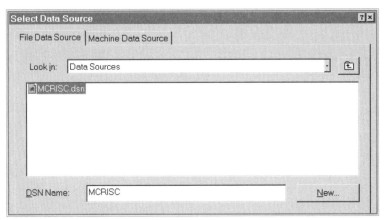

Figure 6-139: The Select Data Source screen.

At this point, Access exports the table to the AS/400. Depending upon your Client Access configuration, you might or might not be asked for your login information before the export begins.

The name you direct Access to assign the table on the AS/400 is important for a few reasons. First, it is common practice to assign AS/400 data tables names that are no more than six characters in length. While this isn't a requirement—and it does make sense to try to be more descriptive—if you stick to using the 6-character name, you will encounter fewer incompatibilities with existing AS/400 software.

Note that the table name, when entered in Access, must be typed in uppercase characters. The combination of six or fewer uppercase characters ensures that the new file name is created correctly for all AS/400 software to use.

Export Limitations

Be aware that the export function of Access does have some limitations when sending files to the AS/400. One such limitation is that you cannot append to existing files using the export function. Using this function, you can only create new files. One workaround for this is to link to the existing table on the AS/400, and then append the records from within Access. You could either append manually, using the Datasheet View, or you could create an "append" action query to add the records.

Another limitation of using the export function to export tables is that you cannot select which records to export. There is also a workaround to this limitation. You create a query within Access that selects the records you want, and then export the query to the AS/400. You can export the results of queries in the same manner you export tables.

One of the biggest limitations you will find, when exporting data from Access to the AS/400, is the amount of control you have over the types of fields that are created on the AS/400 when Access creates the table. For example, sometimes, Access creates floating-point numeric fields (which are not commonly used on the AS/400).

Of course, Access will not create any data types that the AS/400 does not understand. In fact, it cannot do this. But it will sometimes choose field types that are not widely used on the AS/400.

There are a couple of ways you can overcome this limitation. One way is to create the table on the AS/400, link it to the Access database, and append the records to it (thereby bypassing Access's export function). Another way would be to create a custom export utility using Visual Basic for Applications (VBA), which is the built-in programming language of Access.

SPEED TIPS

Sometimes, the performance of Access, when compared to the AS/400 database, leaves a little to be desired. This section provides some techniques to help you speed up your database operations. These techniques include using pass-through queries, offloading processing, and limiting library searching.

Before getting started with the examples, you should become familiar with the Access database engine. Access does all database processing through what is called the *JET database engine*. In this case, JET doesn't stand for speed. It stands for Joint Engine Technology.

The JET database engine is a very powerful and flexible relational database engine that is capable of many tasks. One such task is accessing data from ODBC-capable databases.

While the JET engine is very flexible, it is not optimized for connecting to external relational databases such as DB2/400. It can make the connection, but it will not necessarily be the most efficient means of connecting. However, the external database connectivity has improved with every new release of Access.

In many cases, the functionality provided by the JET engine overshadows the lack of optimization. For example, the JET database engine allows you to link to many different types of databases at the same time. You can even perform queries and generate reports using data from any of the supported database types in the same operation.

For instance, you could create an Access database with tables linked to your AS/400 data, a dBase database, and a SQL server database. Then you could create queries, reports, forms, and programs that use the data from all three databases at the same time.

The JET database engine has its own SQL compiler. A SQL compiler is a system function that takes English-like SQL statements and translates that into an optimized method to retrieve the data from the database. Because there are many different types of databases available that can be used with Access, the engineers who designed Access designed it for maximum flexibility across all database types rather than maximum performance on a single database. A real-world example of the flexibility provided by the Access SQL compiler is it's capability to use the same SQL statement to retrieve data from the AS/400, a SQL Server database, or a native Access database.

All AS/400s have a built-in SQL compiler that is highly optimized for accessing DB2/400 data. Your AS/400 has this SQL compiler regardless of whether or not you purchased any additional licensed programs from IBM. It's built in to OS/400.

Pass-Through Queries

Because all AS/400s have a built-in SQL compiler, it would be a good idea to use this highly optimized compiler to retrieve your AS/400 data. Fortunately, Access provides you with a means of doing just that. It's called the pass-through query. You can use pass-through queries in reports, forms, and other queries.

Pass-through queries are queries in Access that are written in the host database's native SQL language. When Access uses a pass-through query, it "passes" the SQL statement "through" to the AS/400 without trying to interpret it. This allows the AS/400 SQL compiler to generate an optimized access plan for the data. This translates into much faster data retrieval. The following sections explain how to create a passthrough query that will retrieve data from your Customer table.

From an open database, click on the QUERY tab, and then click the NEW button (see Figure 6-18). Select DESIGN VIEW and click the OK button (see Figure 6-19). Now Access asks you which tables to add to the query (see Figure 6-20). Because you're going to be creating this query manually with a SQL statement, you don't need to select any tables. Leave this blank and click the CLOSE button.

This brings up the Design View. For this example, click on the QUERY menu, choose SQL SPECIFIC from the list, and then select the PASS-THROUGH option (Figure 6-140).

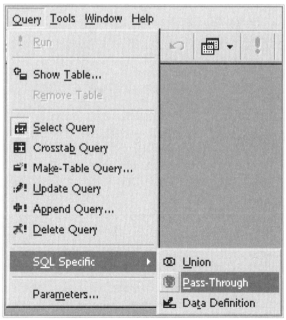

Figure 6-140: Selecting the PASS-THROUGH option.

The screen changes to a blank workspace where you can enter your SQL statements. Enter "select * from datalib.custmr" (Figure 6-141).

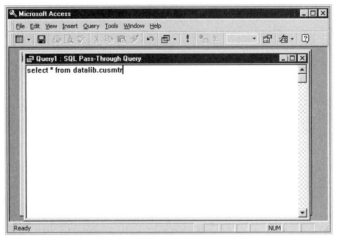

Figure 6-141: Entering the SQL statement.

To test the query, click the Run button on the toolbar. The Select Data Source screen prompts you to select which ODBC DSN to use. Select the one for your AS/400 and click the OK button (Figure 6-142).

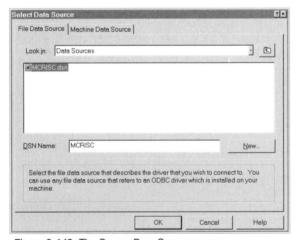

Figure 6-142: The SELECT DATA SOURCE screen.

The connection is made to the AS/400 and the data is returned. It might be hard to notice a speed difference on small tables, but on large tables or complex data retrievals, the difference is noticeable.

Go back to the SQL View by clicking on the VIEW button on the toolbar. Save the query by clicking on the SAVE icon on the toolbar or select SAVE from the FILE menu. Save this query as "Customer Pass-Through".

Now specify a data source for this query so it won't ask for one each time. From the QUERY tab in the database window, select your CUSTOMER PASS-THROUGH query and click the DESIGN button. This brings up the SQL PASS-THROUGH QUERY window as before.

Now, from the VIEW menu, select PROPERTIES. This brings up the property dialogue for this query. To avoid being asked for a DSN each time the query is run, change the ODBC CONNECTION STRING property (Figure 6-143).

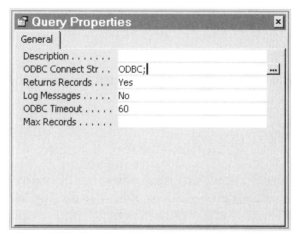

Figure 6-143: The QUERY PROPERTIES screen.

Note: To make use of the option not to be asked repeatedly for a DSN, be certain the Advanced Wizards were installed when Microsoft Office was installed. If you're not sure that the Advanced Wizards are installed, try to perform the following options. If the Advanced Wizards aren't installed, you'll get an error message saying so. Go back and install the Advanced Wizards using the Microsoft Office setup program.

To change the connection string, click in the ODBC CONNECTION STRING field and then click on the box with the three dots in it that appears to the right of the field. This will bring up the screen where you can choose your DSN. Choose your DSN and click the OK button.

Next, Access asks if you want to save the password in the connection string. With Client Access, this is not necessary. You can choose NO (Figure 6-144).

Saving the password in the connection string makes it easier for someone to determine passwords by reading the connection string, For this reason, it is suggested that you answer "No" to this question if you are concerned about security.

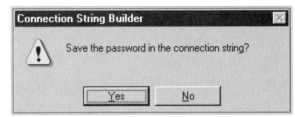

Figure 6-144: It's not necessary to save the password in the connection string.

Let's explore some of the other options on the screen shown in Figure 6-143. The RETURNS RECORDS parameter determines whether or not the query expects records to be returned. An example of a query that would not return records is a query that creates or modifies a file definition on the AS/400. Set the ODBC TIMEOUT parameter to a higher number if your AS/400 doesn't return records within the default value of 60 seconds. Preferably, you won't have to set this number higher, but you might need to if you have an extremely large query or a very busy AS/400.

The MAX RECORDS parameter is useful if you want to limit the number of records that are returned with the query. When you create a pass-through query, all records in the result are brought down to the PC. This could choke the PC if you ask for a huge number of records. Setting a limit here helps ensure that you won't have problems. Now you can close this dialogue box and close and save the query.

Run the query again by double-clicking on it. Notice that it does not ask you for either a DSN or a password. And it's fast!

Because pass-through queries use native AS/400 SQL, a good understanding of the techniques is essential to getting the results you need. You can learn more about SQL from the IBM manuals *DB2 for AS/400 SQL Programming* (SC41-5611-00) and *DB2 for AS/400 SQL Reference* (SC41-5612-00).

For more information about SQL, Midrange Computing offers a video called Harness The Power Of AS/400 SQL, by Brian Singleton, detailing the usage of AS/400 SQL. You can obtain the video by calling (800) 477-5665 or find out more information at

`http://www.midrangecomputing.com.`

Additional information on IBM manuals can be found at

`http://as400bks.rochester.ibm.com/.`

Pass-through Query Limitations

Pass-through queries do have some limitations. Aside from not being able to build them visually, you cannot use them to interactively update data on the AS/400 either. "Interactively update" means using the Datasheet View to directly type in data. However, you can use pass-through queries to update data with SQL.

Off-loading processing

Another way to speed up processing is to offload some of the work from the AS/400 to another database. This is best done with data such as item or customer master files that isn't updated frequently and isn't too large. While customer order-history might also work—if this has a tendency to be very large—it might be better handled by the AS/400.

Because Access uses the same methods to access data from many different sources, it makes no difference whether your query is from the AS/400, a SQL server database, or an Access table on your PC or network.

You should exercise caution when mixing offloading with AS/400 processing. The ideal situation is to have either everything copied to a local Access database or have every-thing existing on the AS/400. It's much harder for Access to join a local table and an AS/400 table than it is for it to join two tables at the same location. Therefore, joining two local tables or two AS/400 tables works best. Again, experiment to determine what works best for your specific situation.

Offloading can help you satisfy your users' demand for more information without putting an additional load on your AS/400. For example, if you have a user that needs to do extensive research on the data in your database, and you feel that the research would have an adverse affect on your AS/400's performance, you should consider offloading.

When you offload, you can copy the AS/400 data to a native Access file. This works well with a small data set and a limited number of users. It won't be the best solution for very large data sets or data sets that need to be accessed by multiple users. Other options include Microsoft SQL Server and IBM's DB/2 for Windows NT. Both of these databases are very good at handling ad hoc querying.

If you decide to offload the processing from your AS/400, you could easily create a VBA program that automatically transfers the data from the AS/400 to your secondary database.

Limiting Library Searching

The DEFAULT LIBRARIES parameter of the ODBC driver can be important to performance. The main thing to remember when entering the libraries in the default libraries list is that those libraries are searched to build information about the database. This can be a lengthy process if you have many libraries in this list. So, to keep performance to its maximum, you should only specify the library, or libraries, that you actually need. This will cut down on the work that has to be done by the AS/400, the PC, and the link through which they are attached.

Another way to speed things up is to put the most important libraries first on the list. Some ODBC applications stop searching when they find the table. The higher the table's library is on the list, the sooner it will be found and the quicker the response will be.

SECURITY WITH ACCESS, ODBC, AND AS/400 DATA

The power that can be achieved using Microsoft Access with your AS/400 data is a double-edged sword. The combination offers the capability to see your data in ways that make it easier to understand, but it also offers the capability to update sensitive data indiscriminately if your system is not properly secured.

The Client Access ODBC driver is part of the base support of Client Access 95/NT. Therefore, it's always installed when Client Access is installed. It can be deleted at a later time, but this is not a good security measure because it will be reinstalled the next time Client Access is installed.

As indicated in this chapter, it doesn't take too much knowledge for users to be able to point-and-click their way into trouble. The good news is that it is possible to prevent unwanted database updates from ever occurring. Before getting started on the following recommendations, please note that these are just suggestions for securing your data and are not intended as guidelines. Each installation has different requirements for security, and there are many more options for securing your data than it is possible to cover here. You must find a method for making your data secure that meets your specific requirements.

Client Access ODBC driver supports AS/400 object-level authority. This means that users are limited to the objects that they have access to under the user profile that they used to connect.

For example, if a user has read access to a file on the AS/400, but not update capability, that user won't be able to update the file using Access or any other ODBC-compliant product. Access prevents them from updating the data by simply not allowing them to type in the fields.

For more information on security and setting object level authorities, see the AS/400 reference manuals. These can be found on the Internet at http://as400bks.rochester.ibm.com/. Midrange Computing also has several products on security. See their Web site at http://www.midrangecomputing.com for a catalog.

Access can use SQL Views created on the AS/400 to access data on the AS/400 indirectly. This can be useful for a couple of different reasons. First, the view, much like a logical file, is an independent object based upon one or more AS/400 database files. Because they are separate objects, they can have their own security settings. You also can use them to subset data from the files on which they are based.

If you want your users to have access to only a certain set of records in a master file, you could create a view that includes only those records. Then you could secure the view as appropriate for your installation.

There are many more possibilities for sophisticated database access using SQL Views. The SQL command to create a view is simply CREATE VIEW. For more details, see the AS/400 SQL programming and SQL reference manuals.

SUMMARY

Having completed the examples in this chapter, you have gained valuable knowledge skills that help you how to combine the power of AS/400 databases with Microsoft Access data retrieval and presentation tools. You know how to configure the Client Access ODBC driver, and how to use that driver to link AS/400 tables to Access databases. You have learned how Access query provides you with many powerful options for retrieving your data in exactly the way you want it. You have created forms to

customize your AS/400 data displays, including displaying AS/400 information graphi-
cally. And you have used reports to turn AS/400 data into information to help you in
your daily data-processing needs. You should now have a good understanding of how
powerful the Access 97 and the IBM AS/400 combination is.

7

Retrieving E-Mail with Outlook

The focus of this chapter is on using your AS/400 as an e-mail server for Microsoft Outlook. One of my favorite programs in the Microsoft Office suite, Outlook is an e-mail client, a personal-information manager, and more. It can be the central point for managing all of your information.

> Note: Because the AS/400 and Microsoft Outlook both use standard Internet e-mail protocols, the procedures described in this chapter work for Internet e-mail clients other than Outlook (i.e., Eudora, Netscape, etc.)

BACKGROUND

Integrating Microsoft Outlook with the AS/400 involves setting up your AS/400 as a POP3/SMTP e-mail server and then configuring Outlook to use your AS/400's e-mail capabilities. SMTP and POP3 are e-mail protocols that enable e-mail exchange between computers. They are the standards used on the Internet. Whether you are connected to the Internet or not, you can use these standards to deliver mail within your organization.

See Figure 7-1. SMTP has been available on the AS/400 for some time. The e-mail equation was completed when POP3 support was added to V3R2 and V3R7. This support allows AS/400s running these OS/400 versions to serve as e-mail servers. Both of these protocols are part of OS/400 TCP/IP support. To use your AS/400 as an e-mail server, you must have TCP/IP configured on your AS/400.

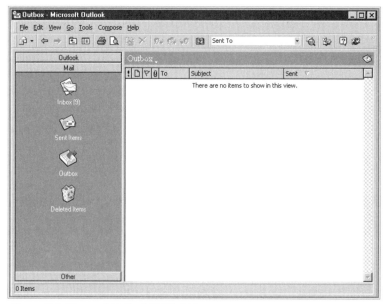

Figure 7-1: Microsoft Outlook 97 Mail View.

For more information on getting TCP/IP up and running on your AS/400, see the *OS/400 TCP/IP Configuration and Reference Manual* (SC41-5420-01). The manual is available online at http://as400bks.rochester.ibm.com/. Step-by-step instructions also are available in the video *Exploiting V3R1's Free TCP/IP* by Brian Singleton and Robin Klima and the book *TCP/IP Primer for the AS/400* by Jim Hoopes, Robin Klima, and Martin Pluth. The video and the book are published by Midrange Computing.

Setting up the AS/400 to be an e-mail server is a fairly straightforward process. The example described here shows the configuration of the e-mail server in an environment with one AS/400 acting as the only e-mail host. In this example, the e-mail clients communicate with the AS/400 to send and retrieve e-mail. All e-mail users access the AS/400 through TCP/IP.

It is possible to perform a lot of complex tasks using the combination of SMTP, POP3, and SNADS. However, in the interest of simplicity, we will take some shortcuts to enable you to get e-mail configured with the fewest number of steps required for most configurations. If you have a complex network, consisting of several AS/400s, connections to the Internet, or SNA and OfficeVision users, please consult the previously mentioned TCP/IP reference manual.

SETTING UP THE AS/400 AS A MAIL SERVER

There are seven steps to setting up a POP mail server. These steps presume that you are signed on to an AS/400 using a profile with sufficient authority. The steps are:

1. Making sure the mail server framework is running.

2. Configuring and starting the SMTP server.

3. Creating user profiles for e-mail users.

4. Adding system distribution directory entries.

5. Configuring and starting the POP3 server.

6. Configuring the e-mail clients (Outlook).

7. Reading your e-mail.

Step 1: Making Sure the Mail Server Framework is Running

The first step to setting up your e-mail server is to make sure the mail server framework is running. This is done by looking for a couple of jobs on the system. Key in WRKACTJOB SBS(QSNADS) on an AS/400 command line. If the subsystem has started, you'll see a list of jobs running in it (as shown in Figure 7-2).

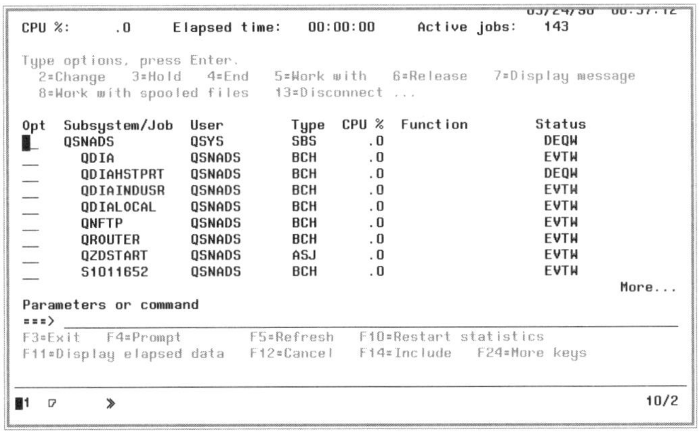

Figure 7-2: Verifying the QSNADS subsytem has started.

If the subsystem has not been started, start it now by typing STRSBS QSNADS and pressing the Enter key. Now you need to find the mail server framework job. This job runs in the QSYSWORK subsystem. Key in WRKACTJOB SBS(QSYSWRK) and press the Enter key. Look for a job called QMSF (see Figure 7-3). If you don't see the QMSF jobs, start the mail server framework by issuing the STRMSF command from an AS/400 command line.

```
                           Work with Active Jobs                  MCRISC
                                                    03/24/98    06:43:58
 CPU %:      .0      Elapsed time:    00:00:00   Active jobs:    143

 Type options, press Enter.
   2=Change   3=Hold   4=End    5=Work with   6=Release   7=Display message
   8=Work with spooled files   13=Disconnect ...

 Opt  Subsystem/Job  User       Type  CPU %  Function       Status
  __   QIJSSCD        QIJS       BCH    .0   PGM-QIJSCMON    DEQW
  __   QMSF           QMSF       BCH    .0                   DEQW
  __   QNPSERVD       QUSER      BCH    .0                   SELW
  __   QNSCRMON       QSYSM      BCH    .0   PGM-QNSCRMON    DEQW
  __   QPASVRP        QSYS       BCH    .0   PGM-QPASVRP     DEQW
  __   QPASVRS        QSYS       BCH    .0   PGM-QPASVRS     TIMW
  __   QPASVRS        QSYS       BCH    .0   PGM-QPASVRS     TIMW
  __   QPASVRS        QSYS       BCH    .0   PGM-QPASVRS     TIMW
  __   QPASVRS        QSYS       BCH    .0   PGM-QPASVRS     TIMW
                                                                More...
 Parameters or command
 ===>
 F3=Exit    F4=Prompt       F5=Refresh    F10=Restart statistics
 F11=Display elapsed data  F12=Cancel    F14=Include   F24=More keys

 1     ⏚     »                                                     10/2
```

Figure 7-3: Finding the mail server framework job.

Step 2: Configuring SMTP

The second step is to configure and start SMTP. Starting SMTP is very important because SMTP provides the transport mechanism for your e-mail. If SMTP doesn't start, your e-mail won't be delivered properly.

Before starting SMTP, you must be sure that SMTP was installed correctly when TCP/IP was installed on your AS/400. To do this, first make sure the distribution queues are set up correctly. From an AS/400 command line, type CFGTCPSMTP and press the Enter key to bring up the SMTP configuration menu (Figure 7-4).

Select option 12 from the menu to run the CONFIGURE DISTRIBUTION

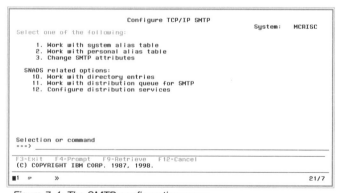

Figure 7-4: The SMTP configuration menu.

SERVICES command. On the next screen, select option 1 and press Enter to display the distribution queues (Figure 7-5).

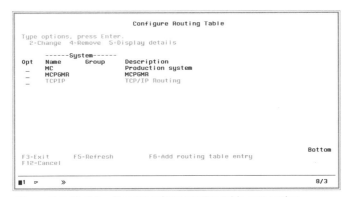

```
                        Configure Distribution Queues

    Position to . . . . .     _____

    Type options, press Enter.
      2=Change   4=Remove   5=Display details

                                        Remote                    Remote
    Opt   Queue Name      Queue Type    Location Name   Mode Name  Net ID
          MC              *SNADS        S1011652        *NETATR    *LOC
    _     MCPGMR          *SNADS        S1034786        *NETATR    *LOC
    _     QSMTPQ          *RPDS         TCPIP           *NETATR    *LOC




                                                                    Bottom
    F3=Exit        F5=Refresh          F6=Add distribution queue
    F10=Work with distribution queues                   F12=Cancel
  _____
  ▋1    ▭    »                                                    10/3
```

Figure 7-5: Verifying that the QSMTPQ entry exists.

Verify that an entry with the name QSMTPQ exists and that it has a remote location name of TCPIPLOC. This is the distribution queue SNADS uses to distribute mail to SMTP.

Press the F12 key to return to the previous screen. Select option 2 and press the Enter key to display the routing table (Figure 7-6). Look for the TCPIP entry. This entry is necessary for SNADS to route mail to SMTP. If the TCPIP entry is present, SMTP is installed correctly on your AS/400.

```
                        Configure Routing Table
    Type options, press Enter.
      2=Change   4=Remove   5=Display details

          ------System------
    Opt   Name       Group     Description
    _     MC                   Production system
    _     MCPGMR               MCPGMR
    _     TCPIP                TCP/IP Routing




                                                                    Bottom
    F3=Exit        F5=Refresh          F6=Add routing table entry
    F12=Cancel
  _____
  ▋1    ▭    »                                                     8/3
```

Figure 7-6: Verifying that the TCPIP routing table entry exists.

Press F12 twice to return to the SMTP configuration menu (Figure 7-4). While you are working with the SMTP configuration menu, this is a good time to set SMTP to start automatically. This way SMTP will start every time TCPIP starts.

Select option 3 to see the SMTP configuration screen (Figure 7-7). On this screen, make sure the AUTOSTART server parameter is set to *YES. Press the Enter key. You will need to do this procedure only once to have SMTP start each time TCP/IP starts.

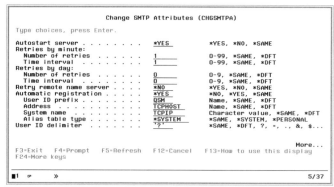

Figure 7-7: The SMTP configuration screen.

To start SMTP manually, from an AS/400 command line, key in STRTCPSVR and press the F4 key. This brings up a screen for you to specify starting the server TCP/IP (Figure 7-8). For the server, specify *SMTP and press the Enter key.

```
                     Start TCP/IP Server (STRTCPSVR)

 Type choices, press Enter.

 Server application . . . . . . . .    *SMTP        *ALL, *SNMP, *ROUTED...
                  + for more values    _____






                                                                  Bottom
 F3=Exit   F4=Prompt   F5=Refresh   F12=Cancel   F13=How to use this display
 F24=More keys

 ▮1    ⌐    »                                                       5/42
```

Figure 7-8: Starting the SMTP server.

To verify that SMTP has started, key in WRKSBSJOB QSYSWRK and press the Enter key. Look for a job called QTSMTPSRVR (Figure 7-9). If this job is active, SMTP has been started on your system.

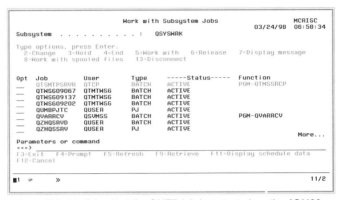

Figure 7-9: Verifying that the SMTP job has started on the AS/400.

STEP 3: CREATING USER PROFILES

The third step in setting up your e-mail server is to create user profiles for your e-mail users. Everyone who is to receive e-mail from your AS/400 must have a user profile.

If you are adding e-mail capability to users who already have an AS/400 sign-on, you can skip this step. If you want to provide new users access to the AS/400 POP3 e-mail system, you first need to create a new user account on the AS/400.

To set up a user account, from an AS/400 command line, key in CRTUSRPRF and press the F4 key. This will display a screen like the example shown in Figure 7-10.

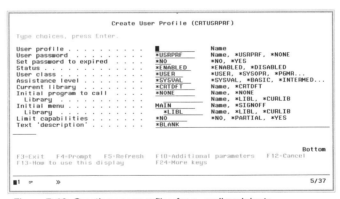

Figure 7-10: Creating user profiles for e -mail recipients.

Enter the user profile name. This name doesn't have to correspond to the e-mail address of the user, but it makes sense to use the same name when possible. Not using the same name is acceptable. In the following sections, you can find out how to create an e-mail alias for a user and map an e-mail name to a user profile when the names are different.

With the password parameter, you have a couple of options. If you set the parameter to the default value of *USRPRF, the password will be the same as the user-profile name. You also can enter a password by keying it here.

If you specify *YES to SET PASSWORD TO EXPIRED, new users will have to enter a new password the first time they sign on. This can be significant because, for the initial menu parameter, it is possible to specify a value of *SIGNOFF. If you set the INITIAL MENU parameter to *SIGNOFF, the user will not be allowed to log on using a terminal. However, the user will still be able to retrieve e-mail. This is an excellent way to help you get the level of security you need by not giving users unnecessary access to your system. Just remember that you will have to manually manage the passwords of the users who are not allowed to log on to the system.

Again, because each POP3 e-mail user has to have a user profile, you will have to do this setup for each user lacking an AS/400 profile.

STEP 4: ADDING SYSTEM-DISTRIBUTION DIRECTORY ENTRIES

The next step is to add system-distribution directory entries for your e-mail users. An entry must be made in the system-distribution directory for each user sending and receive e-mail using POP3. This is done from the WORK WITH DIRECTORY ENTRIES screen.

To get to this screen, key in WRKDIRE from an AS/400 command line and press the Enter key. This brings up the screen (Figure 7-11) that lists the existing directory entries on your system.

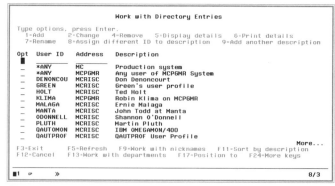

Figure 7-11: Creating or modifying directory entries for e-mail users.

If the e-mail user doesn't have a system-distribution directory entry, you must create one. If they do have an entry, it might need to be modified to use POP3/SMTP e-mail.

To create a new directory entry, put a "1" in the OPT column of the blank line at the top of the screen and press the Enter key. To edit an existing user profile, select an existing entry and put "2" in the OPT column and press the Enter key.

Either action brings up a screen like the example shown in Figure 7-12. On this screen, enter the user profile name for the user ID. For the system, enter the name of your AS/400 system. Enter a description of the user. Also, make sure the system name parameter is set to the name of your AS/400. For the user profile, enter the name of the user profile that will be used to sign on to get mail. In most cases, this will be the same as user ID at the top of the screen. This is the parameter that associates a specific directory entry with a user profile.

Now roll down until the screen with the MAIL SERVICE LEVEL parameter is showing (Figure 7-13). Enter a "2" for the mail service level. In the PREFERRED ADDRESS

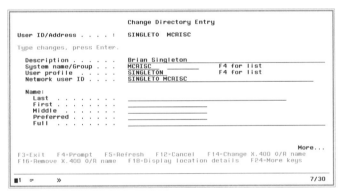

Figure 7-12: The CHANGE DIRECTORY ENTRY screen.

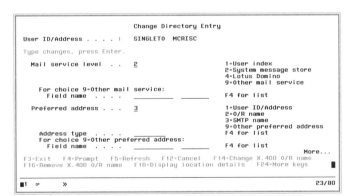

Figure 7-13: Setting the necessary system-distribution directory parameters.

parameter, enter a "3" to use the SMTP name. These are all the parameters that need to be filled out for POP3 e-mail. However, don't press the Enter key—yet.

Pressing F19 brings up a screen where you can change the actual SMTP user ID for this profile (Figure 7-14). This allows you to have an SMTP user ID that is separate from the system-distribution directory entry name. This also allows you to create an e-mail address, using the less restrictive SMTP address type, and still have the AS/400 recognize the e-mail address and be able to deliver the mail to the appropriate user profile.

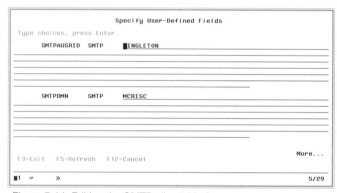

Figure 7-14: Editing the SMTP alias table for a user.

You do not have to have an SMTP user ID, but it could prove useful in certain circumstances. If you don't want to have an e-mail ID that is different from your user profile, press the F12 key to return to the system-distribution directory screen.

Now press the Enter key to create or modify the entry. Again, you will need to do this for each of your e-mail system users.

STEP 5: CONFIGURING POP3

This step explains how to configure and start the AS/400 POP3 server. To configure the server, key in CHGPOPA from an AS/400 command line and press F4. The CHANGE POP SERVER ATTRIBUTES screen appears (Figure 7-15).

There are a few parameters on this screen that need your attention. The first is the AUTOSTART SERVERS parameter. Set this parameter to *YES so that the POP3 server starts automatically each time TCP/IP starts. Then set the ALLOW STANDARD POP CONNECTIONS parameter to *YES. Once these parameters are both set, press the Enter key.

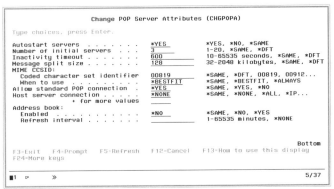

Figure 7-15: Configuring the AS/400's POP server.

Now you can start the POP server manually. Key in STRTCPSVR and press the F4 key. This brings up a screen for specifying the server TCP/IP to start (as shown in Figure 7-8). For the server, specify *POP and press the Enter key.

STEP 6: CONFIGURING YOUR E-MAIL CLIENTS

Now it's time to configure your e-mail clients. The many different POP/SMTP e-mail programs available for PCs all share some common configuration parameters. By knowing these parameters, you should be able to get any e-mail client to talk to the AS/400. The parameters that you need to know are:

❖ The POP3 server name.

❖ The SMTP server name.

❖ The user log-in name.

❖ The user log-in password.

For AS/400 e-mail servers, the POP3 server name and the SMTP server name are the same. They are the TCP/IP name of your AS/400. The user log-in name is the AS/400 user profile you created for the e-mail account, and the user log-in password is the password for that profile.

To configure Microsoft Outlook 97 as your e-mail client, I recommend that you use the Outlook Internet E-mail enhancements from Microsoft. Keep in mind that the AS/400 is configured as an Internet-type e-mail server whether or not your AS/400 is attached to the Internet.

> Note: This discussion and the screen captures are based upon Outlook 97. Outlook 98 is currently in beta, and should be available as you read this. The principles of setting up e-mail should still be the same, but the screens might look different. Also, the Internet e-mail enhancements required in Outlook 97 might be built into Outlook 98. In any case, the basic parameters will remain the same.

You can obtain the Outlook Internet e-mail enhancements from the Outlook page on the Microsoft Web site. The URL is http://www.microsoft.com/outlook. Once there, locate the "downloads" or "free stuff" area and you will find the Outlook enhancement patch. Download and apply this patch, according to the supplied instructions, before you configure Outlook to retrieve mail from your AS/400.

Once the patch is installed, you can configure Outlook. The basic goal is to add an Outlook "service" to retrieve the e-mail from the AS/400.

There are several ways to access the service configuration screen. For this example, begin by starting Outlook. Select SERVICES from the TOOLS menu and the SERVICES configuration screen appears (Figure 7-16). If you don't have all these entries on your screen, don't worry because the following information explains how to create the one screen necessary to communicate with the AS/400.

Figure 7-16: The Outlook SERVICES configuration screen.

On this screen, you can create, remove, and edit services. To create a new service to get mail from your AS/400, click the ADD button. When the ADD SERVICE TO PROFILE dialogue box appears (Figure 7-17), select INTERNET MAIL and click the OK button.

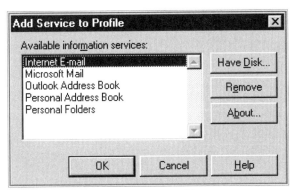

Figure 7-17: Selecting a service to add.

The MAIL ACCOUNT PROPERTIES screen appears (Figure 7-18). On this screen, the first parameter is the name you want to give this service. You can type anything you want here. For this example, type "AS/400 e-mail".

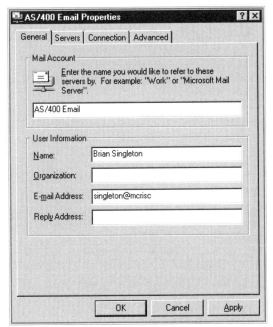

Figure 7-18: The Outlook service configuration window.

Next, enter your user information. After NAME, enter your name. For ORGANIZATION, you can either enter an organization or leave this space blank. For the E-MAIL ADDRESS parameter, enter your full AS/400 e-mail address here.

> Note: An SMTP e-mail address is composed of two main elements separated by the @ symbol. On the left side of the @ sign is your user name. This can be either your real AS/400 user profile name, as defined by the system-distribution directory entry, or an SMTP alias that is associated with that entry. On the right side of the @ symbol, enter your e-mail system name. If you're using TCP/IP, you should put the TCP/IP name of your AS/400. This most likely will be the same as your AS/400 system name.

The REPLY ADDRESS is the address where replies to your e-mail messages will arrive. If you leave this option blank, the e-mail address you have already entered will be used. This is the most common option.

Click the SERVERS tab at the top of the screen. As shown in Figure 7-19, this screen is where you enter information about your e-mail servers. In this case, both servers have the same name (which is the TCP/IP name of your AS/400). Again, this will usually be

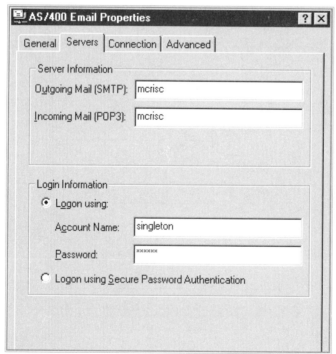

Figure 7-19: Configuring the server properties to point to the AS/400.

the same as your AS/400 system name. Type in your AS/400 TCP/IP name for the POP server and the SMTP server. For logon information, enter your AS/400 user ID and password.

There are a couple of other tabs at the top of the e-mail configuration screen. The CONNECTION tab (Figure 7-20) allows you to specify how you connect to the E-mail server. At your business or office location, you will most likely use a LAN connection, and you will want to use the network option. If you are using a dial-up connection or accessing e-mail remotely, you will want to use the modem option or the remote-mail option.

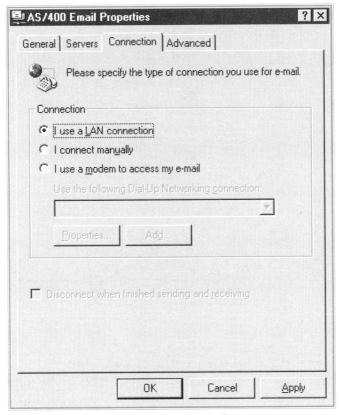

Figure 7-20: Specifying a connection method.

The screen displayed by clicking the ADVANCED tab (Figure 7-21) has some fine-tuning controls that you will probably not need if you are using a standard setup. You should be aware of these options and know where they are located if you ever need to change them in the future. For this example, you don't need to change these settings.

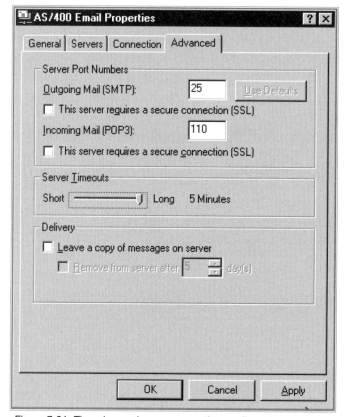

Figure 7-21: The advanced server properties configuration panel.

You now have entered all the information you need to set up your e-mail client. Click the OK button. Outlook displays a message telling you that the service will not be available until you restart Outlook. Restart Outlook and you will see that this service has now been added.

STEP 7: READING YOUR E-MAIL

You can control how often Outlook checks for new mail on the AS/400. To do this, select the TOOLS menu and then choose OPTIONS. This brings up a screen with several tabs across the top that control the configuration of many of Outlook's operations. Click on the INTERNET E-MAIL tab.

Note: In Outlook 97, if you haven't downloaded the Internet E-mail enhancements, you won't see this tab.

On the bottom of this panel (Figure 7-22), there is a parameter that specifies how often to check for mail. Set this to the value, in minutes, that you want. Clicking the OK button saves your settings.

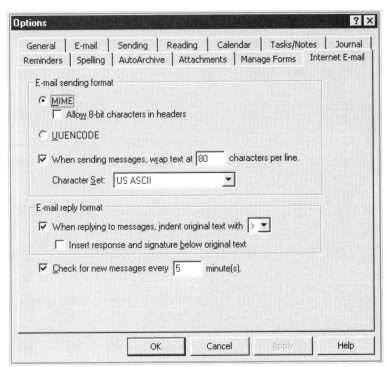

Figure 7-22: Specifying how often to check the AS/400 for .

If you don't want to wait for the predetermined mail check, press the F5 key from the Outlook main screen or select the CHECK FOR NEW MAIL option from the TOOLS menu. Outlook will perform an e-mail check for you immediately.

SUMMARY

Outlook is a very powerful program with many features that should prove to be very valuable to you. I use this program all day, every day. It's a very capable tool and a nice addition to the Microsoft Office suite. While it does take some time to get everything working properly, once you do you'll be glad you did.

The AS/400 in the
Network Neighborhood

Sometimes, to the point of getting in the way, IBM's Client Access 95/NT is well integrated with the Windows desktop. One of the more intrusive features of Client Access is the association of the AS/400's integrated file system (IFS) with the Windows Network Neighborhood (Figure 8-1). But this function also can be very useful for quick and easy-to-use (mostly the latter) AS/400 data transfers.

The AS/400's integration with the Windows Network Neighborhood allows you to access the AS/400's disk drive much the same way you access a local drive on your PC. It is very similar to the "shared folders" functionality of the past.

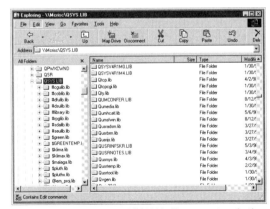

Figure 8-1: Viewing the AS/400's library system in the Windows Explorer.

This chapter describes some of the advantages network drives have over shared folders. You'll discover how to begin using network drives and what some of the configuration options are. I'll also show you some tricks you can use to access data stored in files on the AS/400 and examine the security implications of having AS/400 data just a point and a click away.

With V4R2, IBM simplified life for us somewhat by including Server Message Block (SMB) technology natively on the AS/400 through NetServer (which is part of OS/400). Therefore, the special drivers included with Client Access that enabled AS/400 network drive functionality no longer must be present for the AS/400 to show up in the AS/400's Network Neighborhood. (Unfortunately, at this point, Client Access loads those drivers anyway. Let's hope this redundancy is resolved soon.)

NETWORK NEIGHBORHOOD INTEGRATION ADVANTAGES

If you're familiar with the shared folders support in previous versions of Client Access, you'll find that the network drives support in Client Access for Windows 95 is a big improvement. The main difference is that you can access your AS/400's complete filing system through the Network Neighborhood without having to assign a drive letter by using a Client Access application (as was the case with shared folders).

Through the IFS, if you have the proper security, you have access to the entire AS/400 filing system. With shared folders, you were previously restricted to the QDLS file system. QDLS was designed to store OfficeVision documents and, as a result, had a lot of performance overhead associated with it. With network drive and Windows Network Neighborhood integration, you can access files in AS/400 libraries, documents in the shared folder area, other AS/400s that are sharing their filing systems, any UNIX systems sharing their files with the AS/400 through NFS, and more.

Copying files back and forth between the PC and the AS/400 becomes as simple as copying any other file within Windows 95/NT. You can cut files and paste them onto the AS/400, you can drag files from your desktop and drop them into a folder on the AS/400 (and vice-versa), and more.

When you copy files between the systems, they can automatically be translated from ASCII to EBCDIC or vice-versa as needed.

Using the Network Neighborhood functionality, you can map a drive (using standard Windows drive-mapping methods) to an area (folder, library, etc.) on your AS/400 so that, when you access that drive on your PC, the contents actually come from the

AS/400. See Figure 8-2 for an example. This is very similar to PC Support Shared Folders, but it allows you to map any valid AS/400 area instead of just the QDLS file system.

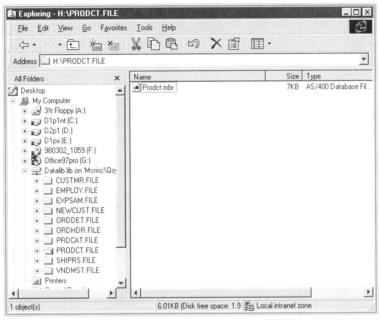

Figure 8-2: A drive mapped to the DATALIB *library on the AS/400.*

Client Access also will create Windows associations—which tell Windows which program to run when a file is opened or double-clicked—with AS/400 database files and the Client Access data-transfer function. Therefore, you can view database files on your PC just by double-clicking them.

Client Access even gives you the "convenience" of being able to delete any files that you have authority to by simply highlighting the files and—like any other Windows file (GULP)—pressing the Delete key. Yes, you read that right. You better have your AS/400 security up to snuff. See the section on security near the end of this chapter.

NETWORK NEIGHBORHOOD INTEGRATION DISADVANTAGES

Before I explain how to use AS/400 network drives, let's take a look at some of the disadvantages. In my opinion, there are three main disadvantages of AS/400 Network Neighborhood integration. They are:

❖ **Speed**. I'm connected to a AS/400 through a high-speed Internet link, and I could grow vegetables waiting for the screen to unfreeze when I try to perform a file operation. Local speed isn't much better. Speed is supposed to be improved with the implementation of SMB in V4R2, but I haven't tested it, yet.

❖ **Security**. As with other client-integration tools for the AS/400, the Network Neighborhood integration introduces no new security holes. It merely gives point-and-click access to existing ones (which has huge implications).

❖ **PC Overhead**. The Network Neighborhood integration is part of base support of Client Access. This means it will be installed when Client Access is installed. There is no option to not install it. Even if you don't use the functionality, it's always present (and consuming precious PC memory). You can shut the functionality off, but that involves editing the Windows registry (which is not convenient and not something end users should be doing).

To be fair, IBM is working on fixing these issues. Each new release of OS/400 improves the speed. The security issues introduced are the same ones—they're not isolated to this function—introduced in any distributed environment. I've spoken with the installation team at Rochester and they're strongly considering making the installation optional. If you decide that this functionality isn't for you right now, check back occasionally to see if it meets your current needs.

PREREQUISITES

Before you can use network drives to access your AS/400, you must install Client Access for Windows 95/NT and then, as discussed in Chapter 1, configure an AS/400 connection. Network drives work over all AS/400 connection types.

The network drive function is part of the base support. Therefore, it has to be installed when Client Access is installed. However, the Network Neighborhood integration function also has a hook into the data transfer facility that you might find advantageous.

When you install the data transfer component of Client Access, an association is made between files with a " .mbr" file extension and the data transfer facility. This file association allows you to view AS/400 file members on your PC by double-clicking them from within Network Neighborhood. See Figure 8-3 for an example.

If you don't install the data transfer component, you won't be able to take advantage of this capability. Be aware that the MINIMUM CLIENT ACCESS installation option doesn't include the data-transfer component.

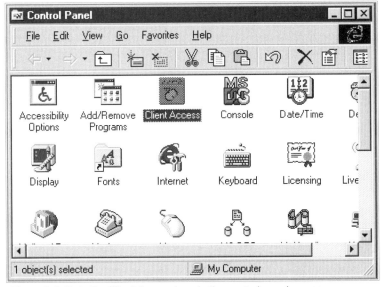

CUSTID	ADDR	CITY	STATE	ZIPCOD	CONAME
AROUT	5379 Paso Robl...	San Diego	CA	92013	Around the Glob...
BSBEV	123 Pickadilly S...	Cleveland	OH	56897	Best Bet
CONSH	4345 Gadman C...	San Francisco	CA	94118	Consolidated Ho...
EASTC	905 Jefferson C...	Portland	CA	97201	Eastern Connect..
GREAL	2732 Baker Blvd...	Portland	OR	97403	Great Falls Food..
ISLAT	123 Crowley Lan...	Orange	CA	92568	Inland Transport...
LAZYK	12 Symphony T...	Walla Walla	WA	99362	Square K Count...
LONEP	89 Chiaroscuro ...	Portland	OR	97219	Lonesome Dove..
NORTS	300 Hackensac...	Albuquerque	NM	87110	Norte Emporium...
OLDWO	2743 Rochester ...	Anchorage	AK	99508	Old Food Delicat...
RATTC	2817 George Dr...	Albuquerque	NM	87110	Snake Brand Jui...
SAVEA	187 Wasup Ln. ...	Boise	ID	83720	Midnight Market...
SEVES	90 Weatherby R...	Seattle	WA	98967	Seven Seas Imp...
SHALE	645 Corte Loren ...	San Marcos	CA	92069	Porcelain Desig...
SPLIR	P.O. Box 555　...	Lander	WY	82520	Big Gut Beer & A..
THECR	55 Doggy Peak ...	Butte	MT	59801	The Cracker Bo...
TRAIH	722 Lombard Bl...	Kirkland	WA	98034	Trail's Head Gou..

Retrieved record 17

Figure 8-3: Viewing a library database file on the PC.

When you create connections within Client Access, each AS/400 connection that you configure shows up when you select the Network Neighborhood icon on your desktop. If you don't have an active connection to the AS/400, one will be made when you select an AS/400 from within the Network Neighborhood.

There's one more setting you'll want to make before you begin using network drives. In the Windows 95 Control Panel, you'll find a Client Access icon (Figure 8-4).

Figure 8-4: Note the Client Access icon in the control-panel screen.

When you select it, you're presented with the Client Access properties window. Select the NETWORK DRIVES tab, and you'll see a window similar to the example shown in Figure 8-5. The top portion of the window lets you control the size of the network drive cache buffer.

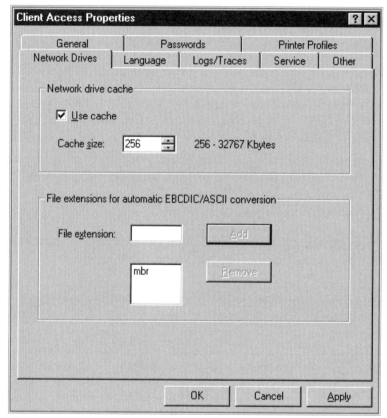

Figure 8-5: Changing the CA NETWORK DRIVES settings.

Specifying a cache buffer helps you get more apparent performance out of the AS/400 in the Network Neighborhood. If your PC has less than 12MB of memory, the cache buffer size should be 256KB. If your PC has more than 12MB of memory, you can increase the cache buffer size to get better performance.

The bottom portion of the window allows you to identify file extensions that you want to have automatically converted between ASCII and EBCDIC. You identify these files by entering their file extensions and selecting the ADD button. I recommend that you enter "mbr" because all file members in the QSYS.LIB file system have a "mbr" extension. Entering the extension here causes all AS/400 file members to be automatically converted between ASCII and EBCDIC.

Note: When you enter the extension, it's not necessary to type the leading period (.). To convert all files, enter an asterisk (*). To convert files without an extension, enter only the period (.).

USING THE NETWORK DRIVE FUNCTION

To begin using the network drives function, double-click the Network Neighborhood icon on the desktop. Next, double-click the computer icon for the AS/400 you want to access. As I mentioned earlier, if you haven't already established a connection to that AS/400, one will be started for you automatically.

Once the PC-AS/400 connection is established, you'll see a list of folders similar to the one shown in Figure 8-6. This is the highest level (known as the "root" level) of the AS/400 Integrated File System. This level represents the entire AS/400 system, and it allows you to navigate to each filing system by going to the appropriate folder.

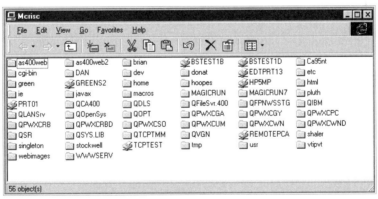

Figure 8-6: The AS/400 "root" file system.

The folders in the filing system represent different AS/400 filing systems. Here is an explanation of the filing systems from the *IBM OS/400 Server Concepts and Administration Manual* (SC41-3740-01):

- 'root' - The '/' file system. This file system is designed to take full advantage of the stream file support and hierarchical directory structure of the integrated file system. It has the characteristics of the DOS and OS/2 file systems.

- QFileSvr.400 - The OS/400 file server file system. This file system provides transparent access to the Integrated File System (IFS) of remote AS/400 systems.

- QOpenSys - The open systems file system. This file system is designed to be compatible with UNIX-based system standards, such as POSIX and XPG.

- QOPT - The optical support file system. This system provides access to the CD-ROM device and optical media library devices that are directly attached to AS/400.

- QSYS.LIB - The library file system. This file system supports the AS/400 library system. It provides access to database files and all of the other AS/400 object types that are managed by the library support.

- QDLS - The document library services file system. This file system supports the folders structure. It provides access to documents and folders. [DOS and OS/2 Clients can access only this system.]

- QLANSRV - The LAN Server/400 file system. This file system provides access to the same directories and files that are accessed through the LAN Server/400 licensed program.

As long as the user profile you made the connection with has the appropriate authority, you can venture down into any of the file systems you want.

> Note: The files and directories under the QOpenSys directory are case sensitive, and the Windows 95/NT FAT filing system isn't. This can cause unpredictable results if you access files in this directory using a network drive. For example, you might get a "File not found" message even though the file appears to exist. This problem applies only to the QOpenSys directory. The rest of the AS/400 file system is not case sensitive.

The standard AS/400 library filing system is called QSYS.LIB and it's likely to be where most of your data is located. Because of the large number of objects in this filing system, accessing QSYS.LIB can be rather slow. If you double-click QSYS.LIB, you'll see a folder for each library on your AS/400 (including all of the OS/400 libraries, as shown in Figure 8-7). Each folder name has a "lib" extension.

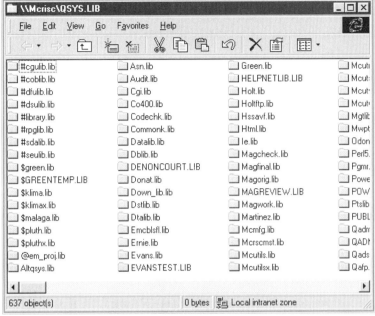

Figure 8-7: Libraries appear in the QSYS.LIB directory.

When you open one of these folders, you'll see all of the objects in an AS/400 library (Figure 8-8). AS/400 database files look like folders, and all other object types appear as files. With the exception that they have extensions corresponding to their AS/400 object types, the folders and files have the same names as the AS/400 objects. For example, files have a "file" extension and programs have a "pgm" extension.

You can drill down still deeper by selecting one of the folders

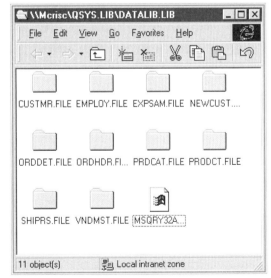

Figure 8-8: Looking at a library through the Windows Explorer.

with a ".file" extension. Here you'll find one or more AS/400 file members (Figure 8-9). These members appear as files with a "mbr" extension. As I mentioned earlier, if you installed the data transfer component of Client Access, you can double-click one of these files to view the data.

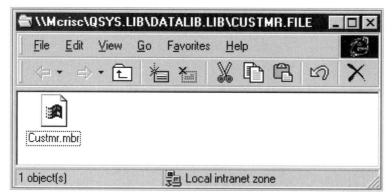

Figure 8-9: Looking inside an AS/400 database file with the Windows Explorer.

Another cool way to transfer the data to your PC is to send it to an application such as Notepad using the SEND TO function of Windows 95. An example is shown in Figure 8-10.

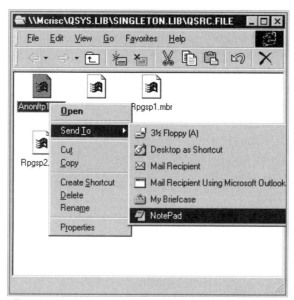

Figure 8-10: Sending an AS/400 file to Notepad.

As discussed previously, to implement this feature, you first must have configured Client Access to automatically translate files with a "mbr" extension between ASCII and EBCDIC.

If a shortcut doesn't already exist, you must put a Windows 95 shortcut in your SEND TO folder (which resides in your Windows directory).

> Note: If you're using user profiles in Windows, place the shortcut in the SEND TO folder of your profile directory (the directory with the name of your login ID) underneath \Windows\Profiles\.

The shortcut must point to the application—for example, Notepad—to which you want to send the data. Once you've done this, you can use your mouse to right-click on an AS/400 file member, select SEND TO from the pop-up menu, and select the shortcut for the application to which you want to send the data.

> Caution: Obviously, this will work best with source files. Because AS/400 database files can be very large, attempting to send them to Notepad could have a negative affect on performance.

> Note: This will work only against character and zoned data. Other data types, such as packed decimal, won't convert properly.

Another way to transfer members is to copy and paste them using one of the varieties of ways Windows lets you do that. For example, you can select COPY and then PASTE from the right mouse-button menu, use the Ctrl-C and Ctrl-V shortcut keys, or use the COPY and PASTE buttons on the Explorer toolbar. Using this method, you can, for example, copy a source member from the AS/400 to your Windows 95 desktop. You can then modify the source member on your PC and copy and paste the file back to the AS/400.

MAPPING A PC DRIVE TO THE AS/400

If you use network drives to access a certain area of the AS/400 often, you might want to consider mapping a drive to it. When you do that, the drive shows up under the MY COMPUTER icon on your desktop (Figure 8-2). When you select the drive, it takes you directly to the area on the AS/400 that you want.

You can map a drive by right-clicking the Network Neighborhood icon on the desktop and selecting MAP NETWORK DRIVE from the menu (Figure 8-11).

Figure 8-11: Selecting MAP NETWORK DRIVE.

When the MAP NETWORK DRIVE window appears (Figure 8-12), select the drive letter you want to assign in the DRIVE parameter. Then enter the path to the area you want to access in the PATH parameter.

The path name is composed of two back slashes (\\) followed by the AS/400 connection name, another back slash (\), and the AS/400 library name with the ".lib" extension. For example, if you want to map a drive to DATALIB on our AS/400 (called MCRISC), you would use the following path name: \\MCRISC\QSYS.LIB\DATALIB.LIB.

From then on, you could bring up the contents of DATALIB by selecting the mapped drive under the MY COMPUTER icon on the desktop (see Figure 8-2).

In addition to what you've seen so far, there are other types of operational tasks that you can perform against AS/400 files by using the Client Access network drive function.

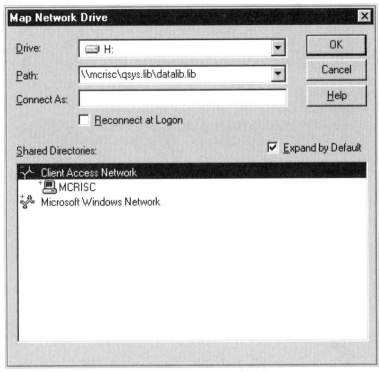

Figure 8-12: Mapping a drive to an area on the AS/400.

Presuming you have adequate authority, you can rename a source member, delete an object, or move an object from one library to another. You also can use network drives to explore other file systems, such as QDLS, QLANSrv, and QOPT. Basically, Client Access now lets you access your AS/400 the same way you would access most other systems on your network.

OH NO! WHAT ABOUT SECURITY?

If network drive capability—combined with the fact that it's currently automatically installed with Client Access—alarms those of you responsible for your AS/400's security, you are not alone. Gone are the days when you could secure your AS/400 fairly well by simply making sure users didn't have access to a command line. See Figure 8-13.

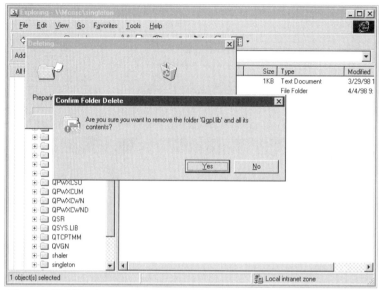

Figure 8-13: With the proper authority, click YES and QGPL is gone!

To ensure that your AS/400 is safe in a today's networked world, you must use AS/400 resource security. While a complete discussion of AS/400 security is beyond the scope of this tome, there are a couple of things to keep in mind:

❖ The authority to objects through all OS/400 client integration functions (network drives, ODBC, file transfer, etc.) is set by the profile used to make the connection. If that profile has the authority to delete a file, it can easily be done through the Windows Explorer. If the profile doesn't have that authority and the user attempts to perform the operation, the user will be denied.

❖ There is an authorization list with a specific name (QPWFSERVER) that can be used to secure access to the QSYS.LIB objects via the network drive function. If you create this authorization list on the AS/400, only the user profiles contained in the list will be able to access the objects in the QSYS.LIB filing system. However, this authorization list does not secure the other directories in the IFS. It also is an all-or-nothing proposition. It can't be used to secure portions of QSYS.LIB.

I hope you are sufficiently concerned about security to make certain your AS/400 settings are adequate. Numerous resources are available to those who are interested in security. Consult the IBM security manuals and the Midrange Computing product catalog (http://www.midrangecomputing.com) for more security-related materials.

SUMMARY

The network drive functionality is a perfect example of the power of the brave new networked world. It offers ease of use and convenience not possible previously, but with that power comes the responsibility to ensure that undesired actions don't take place. Make sure that your security is tight and, if it's fast enough for you, use the network drive function to give AS/400 data management yet another productivity boost.

9

The Client Access Data-Transfer Function

The data-transfer function has been around in the AS/400 world for some time. Its roots go back to the file-transfer function of PC support. Even though the interface has changed with the move to Client Access for Windows 95/NT, the underlying functionality is still basically the same. Lately, it seems the data-transfer function has been falling out of favor and is being replaced by other applications and methods such as FTP and ODBC. However, the data-transfer function is still a useful tool in many circumstances.

> Note: Although it might not be as flexible as ODBC, the data-transfer function easily handles AS/400 multimember database files natively.

In many cases, the data-transfer function can give you the best of both worlds. Unlike FTP, the data-transfer function allows record selection, and it doesn't require another package to be used to actually retrieve data (like ODBC does).

The data-transfer function is a stand-alone application because—as long as you use the predefined data transfer formats—it requires no extra software (other than Client Access, which it is a part of) to perform its function. Furthermore, the data-transfer function can be automated to perform transfers with a single click of the mouse and it even can be configured to perform file transfers automatically without user intervention. Read on to learn about this useful tool.

> Note: The descriptions and screen shots for this chapter were prepared using V3R1M3 of Client Access. This version contains many enhancements to the Data Transfer Function, including menus. If you have an older version of Client Access, the screens will vary slightly but the functionality is much the same.

BACKGROUND

The data-transfer function is a single program represented by two icons (Figure 9-1) in the Client Access program folder. The program determines whether you want to send data to the AS/400 or retrieve data from the AS/400 by looking at the command line that is passed in by the shortcut represented by the icon.

The program allows you to interactively build data-transfer requests by using your mouse to select the various options for the transfer. For example, when building a transfer, you can visually select the libraries, files, and members from which you want to obtain data.

Figure 9-1: The data-transfer function icons

The options you select for the transfer are stored in what is called a *transfer request*. These transfer requests are actually files stored on a PC. Depending on whether they are used to send data to the AS/400 or retrieve data from the AS/400, these files have different extensions. The extension TTO is used for requests that are to be sent to the AS/400 and the extension TFR is used for the requests to be sent from the AS/400.

These files can be used just like any other files. You can copy the files, create shortcuts to them, and perform other file operations on them. When you double- click on the file-transfer request, the data transfer-function is started and the request is loaded.

The file description file (using the extension FDF) is another type of file used by the data-transfer function. An FDF stores information about the data that is to be transferred, and it holds the layout of the data—such as the field names, field types, and field lengths. FDFs are important for transferring data to the AS/400.

PC FILE FORMATS

The data-transfer function supports several different file types that you can use when translating DB2/400 data to PC file formats. Different formats are better suited for certain PC applications than others. The following is a list of the formats supported by V3R1M3 (beta) of Client Access, their descriptions (in quotes) as provided by the help text in Client Access, and my comments.

❖ **ASCII Text**. "PC Code character data used for editing, displaying, and printing." This is straight text with no delimiters between fields. ASCII test is useful for importing into many types of programs, but you'll usually have to separate the fields in the records manually.

❖ **BASIC Random**. "Character, numeric, single precision, and double-precision data for random-processing by BASIC programs." BASIC random can still be used in Visual Basic. Refer to the Visual Basic open command for more information.

❖ **Basic Sequential**. "Character and numeric data forconsecutive processing by BASIC programs." Can still be used in Visual Basic. Refer to the VB OPEN command for more information.

❖ **BIFF3**. "Binary Interchange File Format that Microsoft Excel 3 uses to save data."

❖ **BIFF4**. "Binary Interchange File Format that Microsoft Excel 4 uses to save data."

❖ **BIFF5**. "Binary Interchange File Format that Microsoft Excel 5 uses to save data."

❖ **CSV**. "Comma separated variables format that is used to save data." CSV also is a very common format to move data back and forth between databases. However, the data contains no descriptions of itself. Therefore, you will have to manually describe the fields to the target program. Because the comma is used as a delimiter, it also doesn't properly handle fields where data contains commas.

❖ **DIF**. "Data format that is used by spreadsheet applications." DIF is a common format that is used to transfer data between many types of applications, including spreadsheets and some databases.

❖ **DOS Random**. "A standard PC format that is used with many database applications. This PC format is identical to the DOS random type 2 format except that the internal sign representation for packed decimal and zoned decimal data types are different."

❖ **DOS Random Type 2.** "A standard PC format used with many database applications. This PC file type is identical to the DOS Random file type except that the internal sign representation for packed decimal and zoned decimal data types follow Systems Application Architecture (SAA) standards. Some PC applications, such as applications written in IBM COBOL/2, need to have the signs for packed decimal and zoned decimal data types represented this way. Use this file type for those PC applications." IBM COBOL/2? SAA standards? On a PC? <shrug>

❖ **No Conversion**. "Data is transferred exactly as it was on the host system." If you're transferring database files, you'll most likely get a bunch of junk that is the actual EBCDIC data that resides on the AS/400.

❖ **HTML**. This format is found under the "Output Device" section on the main screen.

The preceding list should describe a format you can use to transfer the data you want. Notice anything missing? What about dBase? Once a very popular PC database file format, still in wide use today, dBase is also one of the most common formats used to transfer data between PC programs. However, dBase has been missing from the data-transfer function since the days of PC Support. Fortunately, if you have Microsoft Access, you can use it to bring AS/400 data in and then export it from Access to dBase format. For more information about Access, see chapter 6.

TRANSFERRING DATA FROM AN AS/400 TO YOUR PC

Let's walk through the steps of transferring data from the AS/400 to the PC. These screen shots you see in this section are from V3R1M3 Beta of Client Access. If you have a different version of Client Access, the screens might differ slightly, but the majority of the functionality should be the same. Begin with the Client Access program folder open. Then perform the following steps:

1. Double-click the DATA TRANSFER FROM AS/400 icon to start the program.

⇨ You should see a screen like the example shown in Figure 9-2. This is the main screen where you design the file-transfer request. Here, you tell the data-transfer function program which data you want to transfer and how you want it converted during the transfer.

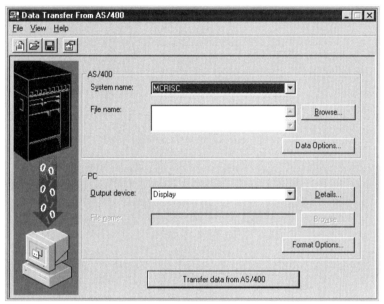

Figure 9-2: The data-transfer function screen for building transfers from the AS/400.

⇨ You will be building a transfer request interactively, using the visual aids of the file transfer function. The next step is to determine from which AS/400 to transfer the data.

2. Select the AS/400 to transfer data from by using the AS/400 SYSTEM NAME drop-down list.

⇨ All your previously defined AS/400 systems should be on the drop-down list. If you don't see a list, configure a connection to your AS/400 as discussed in chapter 1.

3. Click the BROWSE button next to the FILE NAME input box.

⇨ This brings up a screen with a list of libraries like the example shown in Figure 9-3. Clicking the "+" next to the library name shows a list of files within that library. Clicking the "+" next to the file shows a list of members within that file.

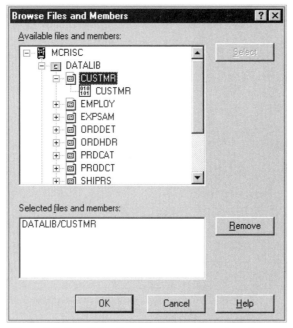

Figure 9-3: Specifying libraries, files, and members from which to retrieve data.

⇨ If you don't see a library on the list, you can go back to the previous screen (Figure 9-2), enter the name of a library to view, and then press the BROWSE button again to have that library displayed.

4. Select the files you want to retrieve data from by highlighting them with the mouse and clicking SELECT.

⇨ The files you select will be listed in the SELECTED FILES AND MEMBERS box. You can select multiple files on this list. If you do so, you must join the files using common fields (as in a query or SQL statement).

5. Once you have the desired file(s) selected, click the ok button.

    ➪ This brings back the screen shown in Figure 9-2. If you want to transfer the entire file, skip to step 9. If you want to specify which records are returned or if you need to join two or more files, continue with the following steps.

6. Click the DATA OPTIONS button (Figure 9-2).

    ➪ This brings up a screen, like the example shown in Figure 9-4, where you can determine which records are transferred from the AS/400. This screen allows you to select records using familiar SQL (or SQL-like) syntax.

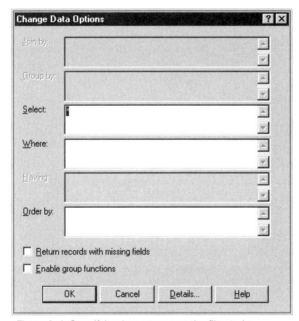

Figure 9-4: Specifying how you want the files to be retrieved from the AS/400.

➪ You can build the retrieval specifications either manually or with assistance.

➪ In the SELECT parameter, specify the fields you want. Separate multiple fields by commas.

⇨ In the WHERE parameter, build the filter that determines which fields you want. For example, you could filter for all customers from the state of California by entering "state=CA" in this field.

⇨ In the ORDER BY parameter, you determine which fields the data is to be sorted by, as well as the order of the sort (ascending or descending).

⇨ If you select ENABLE GROUP FUNCTIONS, the gray boxes—representing operations that can be performed on group data— that are disabled on this screen will become input capable.

⇨ Continue with step 7 to proceed with building the specifications visually.

7. Click the DETAILS button (Figure 9-4).

⇨ A screen like the example shown in Figure 9-5 is displayed. The tabs across the top of this screen allow you to choose areas on which to work.

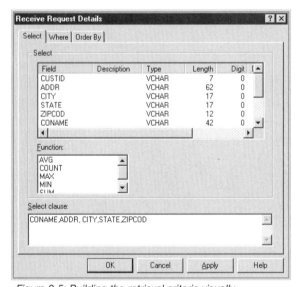

Figure 9-5: Building the retrieval criteria visually.

⇨ Under the SELECT tab (Figure 9-5), the fields in the files that you have chosen are displayed. Double-click the fields in the top list to select them for retrieval.

➪ Under the WHERE tab (Figure 9-6), specify how you want your data filtered as it is transferred to the PC. For example, entering "state=CA" filters for all customers from the state of California.

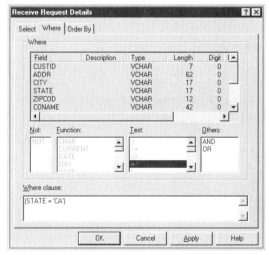

Figure 9-6: Specifying which records to retrieve.

➪ Under the ORDER BY tab (Figure 9-7), you have the option of determining the order in which the data is retrieved. For example, if you wanted to sort by city, you simply double-click the city field in the list of fields displayed on this panel. It will be copied to the ORDER BY CLAUSE box, and the data will be sorted by this field when it is transferred.

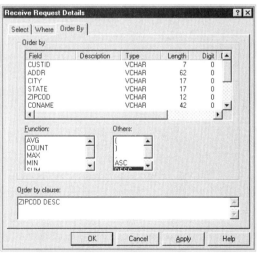

➪ If you have the ENABLE GROUP FUNCTIONS option selected

Figure 9-7: Specifying the sort order for the retrieved

from the previous step, some additional panels will be displayed that allow you to visually build the specifications for the group functions.

➪ The HAVING tab (Figure 9-8) allows you to perform record selection based upon the results of a summary function. This is typical, for example, if you want to see sales by state and you want to limit the results to states that had over $1000 of sales. The WHERE section won't work using similar limits because it works at the detail level. The HAVING section works after the summary has been performed.

Figure 9-8: Specifying a filter on summary records.

➪ The GROUP BY tab (Figure 9-9) is where the grouping level is set. For example, if you had a retrieval set up to total customer sales, and you wanted to see what the total sales were for each state, you could select the STATE field as a GROUP BY field and you would get a total record for each state.

8. Once you have completed building the transfer specification, click the OK button.

➪ A screen with some of the options filled in, like the example shown in Figure 9-6, is displayed. This screen shows the options chosen that will be applied to your transfer request.

9. If everything looks correct, click the OK button again.

➪ You are returned to the main screen (shown in Figure 9-2). This time, the name or names of the files you want transferred are shown in the FILE NAME box.

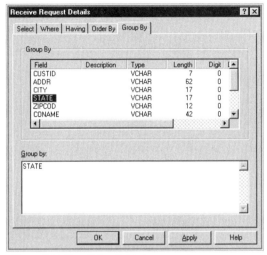

Figure 9-9: Specifying fields to group by.

⇨ You now have completed telling the data-transfer function which data you want to retrieve. The next steps are used to determine in which format you want to retrieve the data. This example describes how to save data to a BIFF5 file for import into Excel.

10. In the OUTPUT DEVICE drop-down list, select FILE.

⇨ This tells the data-transfer function that you want the data written to a file on the PC (Figure 9-10).

11. Click the DETAILS button.

⇨ This brings up the screen shown in

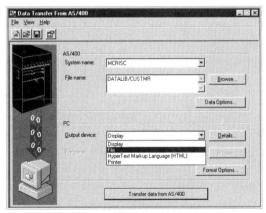

Figure 9-10: Selecting the output device for the AS/400 file.

Figure 9-11. On this screen, there are several settings that you can use to control the details of the process of saving the files to the PC. For example, in a OUTPUT PC file frame, you can specify what to do when the file already exists on a PC. The options you have available are to create a new file, overwrite an existing file, or append to an existing file. The "append" option became available in V3R1M3 of Client Access.

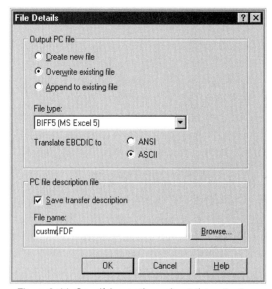

Figure 9-11: Specifying options about the output device.

⇨ You also specify which file type you want to save the data as. In the FILE TYPE drop-down list, you can choose to save the file as ASCII, DIF, BIF, or any of the other data-transfer function supported file types. You also can control whether not the EBCDIC is translated to ANSI or ASCII.

⇨ If you are going to send this file back to the AS/400 for any reason, you must save the transfer description. To do this, check the SAVE TRANSFER DESCRIPTION option and enter a file name for the file description file. The file description file contains information about the structure of the file that was transferred to the PC. This information is used to reconstruct the file on the AS/400 when you want to send it back. If you want to import data to an AS/400 database file, you have to download the file from the AS/400 before you can send it back (which means that you have to create the file on the AS/400).

12. Once you have completed specifying the PC file details, click the OK button.

13. In the PC FILE NAME box, enter the name you want to use for the file on the PC (Figure 9-12).

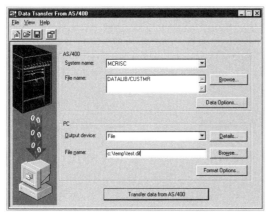

Figure 9-12: The completed transfer specification screen.

⇨   Click the BROWSE button if you want an easy way to specify a directory where the file is to be saved.

14. Save the transfer request by selecting SAVE from the FILE menu (Figure 9-13).

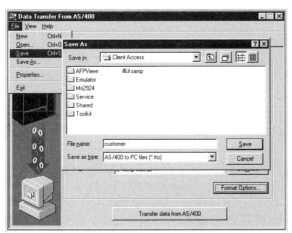

Figure 9-13: Save the transfer request before running it.

⇨ Saving a file transfer request before running it ensures that you won't have to recreate everything from scratch should something go wrong while the transfer is running. It also allows you to recall the transfer request so you don't have to recreate it when you want to run it again.

15. Click the TRANSFER DATA FROM AS/400 button to begin the transfer.

⇨ When the transfer is complete, the screen shown in Figure 9-14 is shown and the file is placed where you specified.

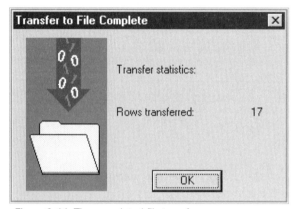

Figure 9-14: The completed file transfer.

That's how you create a file-transfer request to bring data from your AS/400 to your PC. Now that you know how to import files into Office programs, keep in mind that you can perform complex operations such as multiple file joins and grouping functions. There are many ways to get at your AS/400 data.

TRANSFERRING DATA FROM A PC TO AN AS/400

The following sections outline the steps for transferring data from a PC to an AS/400. Remember, if you want to transfer database data to the AS/400, you must have previously created a file description file (.FDF). Refer to the steps on transferring data to a PC from an AS/400 for information on how the FDF file is created. If you don't have an FDF file, you can still send data—but only in source format, which basically treats the data in the file as one big field—to an AS/400.

To transfer files to the AS/400, you also must have a field reference file that exists on the AS/400 before the transfer can be performed. This file is a compiled database file that is created from DDS or any other method. You can use the same file that you used to build the FDF file. The file transfer function uses this file to determine the layout of the file when it gets to the AS/400.

Yes, you read that right. To transfer a new file to the AS/400, a file must exist on the AS/400 that can be used as a reference. And it requires an FDF file, which is created when a file is downloaded using the Data Transfer Function. This makes the data-transfer function less than ideal for putting new data on the AS/400.

If you have no field reference file to use, you must create it and download it (to create the FDF) before you can send it to the AS/400. If you have an FDF and a field reference file, then the data-transfer function is adequate for putting data on the AS/400. If you don't have these things, you might want to look at other products such as Microsoft Access (which can more easily create files on the AS/400).

To transfer data from a PC to an AS/400, begin with the Client Access program folder open. Then perform the following steps:

1. Double-click the DATA TRANSFER TO AS/400 icon (Figure 9-1) to start the program.

   ➭ You should see a screen like the example shown in Figure 9-15 (except the parameters won't be filled in, yet).

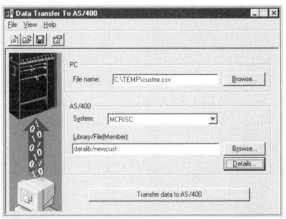

Figure 9-15: The data-transfer function screen for building transfers from the PC to the AS/400.

⇨ This is the main screen where you design the file-transfer request for sending data to the AS/400. Here, you tell the data-transfer function program which data you want to send to the AS/400 and how you want it handled during the transfer.

⇨ For this example, you will be building a transfer request interactively, using the visual aids of the file-transfer function. The next step is to determine from which AS/400 to transfer the data.

2. Select the PC file to transfer.

⇨ You can quickly select a file that you want to transfer by clicking the BROWSE button. This displays a standard file-open dialogue box (Figure 9-16) that you can use to navigate your system to find the correct file. Once you've found a file, select it and proceed with the next step.

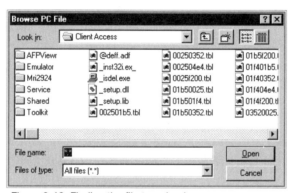

Figure 9-16: Finding the file to upload.

3. Select the AS/400 to transfer data from using the SYSTEM drop-down list.

⇨ All your previously defined AS/400 systems should be listed in the drop-down list. If you don't see the list, configure a connection to your AS/400 as discussed in Chapter 1.

4. Enter the name of the AS/400 library, file, and member to which you want to transfer.

⇨ You must tell the AS/400 which file is being sent to it. Do this by placing the library name of the file first, followed by a backslash (/), followed by the name of the file. If you want to send your data to a specific member in that file, put the member name in parentheses following the file name. The format is: LIBRARY/FILE(MEMBER).

⇨ You can get a list of files that are ready exist on the AS/400 by clicking the BROWSE button.

5. Click the DETAILS button to specify the AS/400 file details.

⇨ This brings up a screen like the example shown in Figure 9-17. On this screen, you specify many options about how the AS/400 is to handle the file.

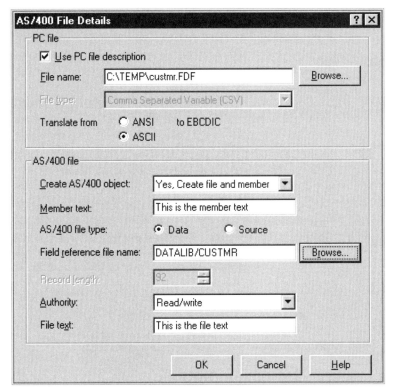

Figure 9-17: Setting upload options.

➪ If you are sending a database file to the AS/400, you must select the USE PC FILE DESCRIPTION option. Then you specify an FDF file name by either entering it in the File name box or clicking the browse button to find the file.

➪ Under the CREATE AS/400 OBJECT parameter, you can specify whether not to create the file and member, replace an existing member, or create a new member.

➪ If you are adding a new member, place the description of the new member in the MEMBER TEXT parameter. The AS/400 FILE TYPE parameter allows you to choose whether you're sending a data file or source file to the AS/400. If you don't select USE PC FILE DESCRIPTION, the data-transfer function will always assume that you are sending source data and not database data.

➪ If you are sending database data, put the name of the pre-existing field reference file in the FIELD REFERENCE FILE NAME parameter. You can click the BROWSE button to view the files on your AS/400 that can be used. The fields in this file must match the fields in the file that is to be uploaded to the AS/400.

➪ If you're transferring source data, the RECORD LENGTH parameter will be enabled and you will be able to specify a record length for the file on the AS/400. Standard source files are usually 92 by bytes in length. You can, of course, specify different lengths here if you're transferring different types of data.

➪ The AUTHORITY parameter determines the initial public authority for the file after it is created on the AS/400.

➪ The FILE TEXT parameter is used as a text description of the file on the AS/400.

6. Click the OK button.

➪ This returns you to the main screen (Figure 9-15).

7. Select SAVE from the FILE menu.

⇨ This will save the file transfer request for later recall. This is an optional step, but it is recommended so that you don't have to recreate the transfer request again if you want to redo it or if something goes wrong.

That's how you transfer files from the PC to the AS/400. Because the data-transfer function requires so many "needless" steps to get the data on the AS/400, it's not my first choice when it comes to uploading data. However, once you get it set up, the transfer can be performed over and over, and even automated, with relative ease. Therefore, it might just fit the bill for you.

AUTOMATING WITH BATCH FILES

If you frequently perform the same data transfer over and over, you can simplify the process with batch files and Client Access commands. Using these commands and a PC job scheduler, you could even perform data transfers in an unattended mode.

There are two commands provided by Client Access that allow you to initiate a data transfer from a DOS command line. These commands are RFROMPCB (receive from PC batch) and rtopcb (receive to PC batch).

The RFROMPCB command transfers data to the AS/400 using a file transfer request that you previously set up. The extension of the file transfer-requests used to send data to the AS/400 is ".TFR" (transfer from). To initiate a transfer to the AS/400 from the command line, the basic syntax is:

```
RFROMPCB XXXX.TFR
```

This will run the xxxx transfer request. There are a number of command line options that you can use to further customize the transfer.

One of the new features of V3R1M3 is that you can specify more than one request to run at a time. If you list more than one file-transfer request on the command line, separate each entry by a space. Running multiple transfers at once is more efficient because the process of initiating the request only has to be done once. If you transfer lots of files, this can add up to significant savings.

Other command-line options for the RFROMPCB command are the / s parameter, which will display the file-transfer statistics, the /c parameter, which processes the subsequent transfer request independently of the others, and the /F parameter, which will read a list of transfer request file names from a file that you specify. The /F parameter could be useful in cases where there are more transfer requests than can easily be fit on a DOS command line or if the request list needs to be frequently maintained.

The RTOPCB command transfers data from the AS/400 to the PC. It uses a transfer request with a .TTO extension. The basic syntax of the RTOPCB command is:

```
RTOPCB YYYY.TTO
```

This will run the transfer request YYYY. As with the RFROMPCB command, there are a number of command-line options you can use to modify the transfer.

As with the RFROMPCB command (as of V3R1M3), you can specify multiple file transfer requests on a single command line. This makes the processing of multiple requests more efficient by eliminating the startup time for each individual request.

The other command-line options for the RTOPCB command are the /S parameter, which will display the file-transfer statistics, the /C parameter, which processes the subsequent transfer request independently of the others, and the /F parameter, which will read a list of transfer request file names from a file that you specify. The /F parameter would be useful in cases where there are more transfer requests than easily can be fit on a DOS command line or if the request list needs to be frequently maintained.

If you frequently transfer the same data back and forth between a PC and an AS/400, the batch commands of the data-transfer function might be just the ticket to automate this process.

WHY DOES MY DATA LOOK LIKE GARBAGE?

One of the biggest complaints I here about the file-transfer function is: "When my data came down to the PC, it looked like garbage." This is a common complaint and it stems from the AS/400's Coded Character Set Identifier (CCSID) setting. The following describes CCSIDs from the perspective of transferring data between the AS/400 and other systems. Just keep in mind that, in the big picture, CCSIDs are related to more than just data files. Nevertheless, that's what I'll concentrate on here.

Files on the AS/400 have an attribute called the CCSID that determines the character set that is used to represent the data. This enables the AS/400 to correctly handle the translations between multiple languages, character sets, text data, and binary data. The CCSID is a number between 0 and 65535. One of the values, 65535, is used to indicate that the file stores binary data that is not to be translated. The idea is that binary data, for example a GIF file, can't be translated like character data is translated. Therefore, the AS/400 should just leave it alone instead of translating it.

The problem transferring data to the PC stems from when files are incorrectly coded with CCSID 65535. On the AS/400, the data will not be translated. Because data in AS/400 files is usually in EBCDIC anyway, this works just fine—as long as it stays on that AS/400.

When the data is moved to another system, the AS/400 looks at the CCSID and, upon finding that it's 65535, determines that no translation is necessary and ships the data merrily along its way. When it gets to the PC, users see the EBCDIC code, which looks like garbage because the PCs don't use EBCDIC – they use ASCII, ANSI, and/or UNICODE.

There are two methods to get the data down correctly without changing the AS/400 database file's CCSID. Which one is available to you depends upon the version of Client Access you have.

CURING CCSID PROBLEMS WITH V3R1M3

As of Client Access V3R1M3, curing the CCSID problem is as simple as checking an option on the file-transfer properties screen. This screen is accessed by clicking the Properties button on the toolbar (Figure 9-18) or selecting Properties from the File menu.

Doing so brings up the screen shown in Figure 9-19.

Check the CONVERT CCSID 65535 option and the AS/400's CCSID setting will be ignored and the data is translated.

Figure 9-19: Setting for translation of CCSID 65535.

Figure 9-18: The Properties button.

CURING CCSID PROBLEMS WITH V3R1M2 AND PRIOR

Prior to V3R1M3, fixing a problem is a little more involved. You need to put an .INI (CWBTFR.INI) file in the \WINDOWS directory to tell the Client Access data-transfer function to translate the data. To do so, perform the following steps:

1. Start Windows Notepad.

   ➭ Notepad is usually found by going to START: PROGRAMS: ACCESSORIES MENUS.

2. Enter the following text and see Figure 9-20:

   [CLIENT ACCESS DATA TRANSFER]
   ```
   ForceTranslation=1;
   ```

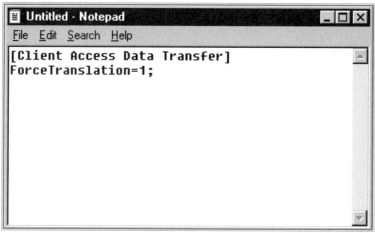

Figure 9-20: Setting for translation of CCSID 65535.

3. Save the file as CWBTFR.INI in the /WINDOWS directory and see Figure 9-21.

   Note: I'm using Windows NT, and my Windows directory is actually \WINNT. Other variations I've seen include the most common (\WINDOWS) and \WIN95.

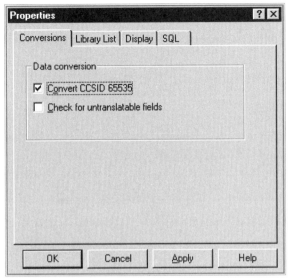

Figure 9-21: Setting for translation of CCSID 65535.

Setting the file-transfer function to translate CCSID 65535 will eliminate any errors caused by the incorrect setting of the CCSID on data files. To change the default value on your AS/400 (which isn't necessary for this function, and should only be done with a full understanding of the implications) is accomplished by changing the QCCSID system value to the correct one for your country.

SUMMARY

That's a tour of the Client Access data-transfer function. It is an adequate method of getting data to and from your AS/400. It might or might not offer you all the flexibility you need, but it is still a useful tool that will get the job done.

10

Transferring Data with FTP

Ever since there were two computers in the world, there has been a need to transfer files between systems. In the past, IBM met that need with a product called PC Support (now known as Client Access/400) to provide a link between the personal computer and the AS/400.

Systems using TCP/IP as their main communications protocol have another method for transferring files between systems. This method is called FTP, and it's a good weapon to add to your arsenal of problem-solving tools.

WHAT IS FTP?

FTP is an acronym for file-transfer protocol, and it is a primary means of transferring files between two systems running TCP/IP. Every AS/400 running V3R1 and higher has TCP/IP built right into the operating system. This also is true for most other popular computer systems today, including Windows PCs.

TCP/IP has become the widespread standard for networking computers from multiple vendors. TCP/IP has a common set of basic applications that allow you to communicate in various ways with other systems on a network. FTP is an application that allows you to send and receive copies of files to or from one computer system to another. One advantage of using FTP is that it is supported on a wide variety of platforms. For example, if you need to transfer files from an AS/400 to a UNIX or PC system, FTP will get the job done.

On the AS/400, file transfers traditionally have been accomplished either with the Send Network File (sndnetf) command over a SNADS network or by using a PC application such as the Client Access data-transfer function. However, many non-IBM systems do not speak SNADS or Client Access. FTP can be used in place of either of these two methods to accomplish a similar task with a multitude of other systems. You also can use FTP to transfer files between two AS/400s. Let's briefly take a look at the pros and cons of using FTP on the AS/400.

FTP PROS

People have long relied on Client Access/400's download function to transfer files from the AS/400 to a PC. However, with TCP/IP's rapid spread, FTP has garnered increased attention. FTP has several advantages over the Client Access/ 400 data-transfer function.

One main advantage of FTP is speed. There is little overhead associated with the protocol; it's primarily pedal-to-the-metal data transfer without the burden of unneeded functionality.

Another advantage is its cross-platform interoperability. Files can be transferred to DOS, Windows, Macintosh, Unix, OS/2, or even other AS/400 systems. Because the commands on these systems are very similar, there's nothing new to learn for specific platforms.

In my opinion, another big advantage is that it's native. No router programs are needed. On the other hand, Client Access/400 downloads require a router program to be loaded. Examples of routers include the Client Access connections program and the Netsoft Router. Because FTP only needs the TCP/IP protocol to be running on both machines, the requirements of specialized software and its associated overhead are eliminated.

You can use FTP to transfer almost all AS/400 object types. For types other than files, save them into an AS/400 save file prior to transferring them. If the other system is an AS/400, you can restore the objects in the save file after the file transfer. Just be sure to create the save file on the target system first. Create it first and then overwrite it with the file you want to copy.

Even if the other system is not an AS/400, you still can transfer save files. This is not possible with Client Access (not directly anyway). For example, you could save an AS/400 program into a save file and use FTP to send the contents of the save file to a PC file. You could then give that PC file to someone who could use FTP to send it back to a save file on another AS/400. The second operator would be able to restore the program to that system. No special programming is required to accomplish this. In addition to supporting save-file data, FTP supports transferring documents as well as files stored on optical drives.

FTP CONS

The primary disadvantage of FTP is that it supports only minimal data-type translation capabilities when sending files to a system other than an AS/400. For example, while it will translate data from EBCDIC to ASCII, it will not translate packed decimal fields to character data. If you must transfer this type of data to anything except another AS/400, be sure the data is in a format that the other system can recognize.

Another disadvantage of FTP is that it won't allow you to perform any type of record selection (as is possible with Client Access data-file transfer). You either have to transfer the entire file or nothing at all. If you do want to transfer only certain records, you'll have to write them to a separate file that can be transferred in its entirety.

FTP BASICS

Now that you're familiar with some of FTP' s capabilities and limitations, you're ready to take a closer look at the AS/400 implementation. There are two sides to the AS/400 FTP application. The FTP server handles requests from other systems and the FTP client allows you to access files on other systems. The AS/400 can either be a client, a server, or both.

When you use FTP to request file transfers, you're running an FTP client component. The FTP client component communicates with an FTP server component on a remote system. Although a remote system is usually another computer attached through a TCP/IP connection, it can be the same system. FTP automatically translates characters when one system uses EBCDIC characters and the other uses ASCII characters.

FTP is controlled by subcommands. There are many subcommands, but the most commonly used are PUT and GET. On some platforms, FTP subcommands are case sensitive, but on the AS/400 they are not (e.g., PUT or "put" is interpreted as the same subcommand). The client system sends a file to the server system with PUT, and the client system retrieves a file from the server system with get. FTP supports three types of file transfers:

- ❖ ASCII.

- ❖ EBCDIC.

- ❖ IMAGE (or BINARY).

ASCII and EBCDIC are normally used to transfer files containing only displayable characters (often referred to as text files). For example, transferring an AS/400 source member to a PC requires an ASCII transfer; transferring an AS/400 source member to another AS/400 requires an EBCDIC transfer. ASCII is the default transfer type. However, when both the client and the server use EBCDIC data representation, as with two AS/400s, EBCDIC automatically becomes the default. Therefore, with text files, you don't need to be concerned with data translations handled automatically.

The image transfer type is used to transfer binary data (data that contains nondisplayable characters). With a binary transfer, no character translation takes place. For example, if you want to transfer an AS/400 source member to a PC but did not want the characters to be translated to ASCII (which by default would happen), you perform an image transfer. To perform an image transfer, execute the BINARY subcommand prior to executing the PUT or GET subcommand.

As you will see when working through the examples that follow, the FTP command has only one required parameter. The REMOTE SYSTEM parameter is where you enter the host name or IP address of the system to which you want to connect. Once FTP connects with the remote system, you will be placed into an interactive FTP session. The remote system will prompt you for your user ID and password. Once those are validated, you can begin using FTP subcommands. There are a number of standard FTP subcommands. Read on to find out what they are.

FTP ON THE AS/400

Before using FTP on the AS/400 for the first time, you will need a basic AS/400 TCP/IP configuration. The TCP/IP Connectivity Utilities/400 licensed program ships with FTP servers configured. You can view or change the FTP server configuration by prompting the Change FTP Attributes (CHGFTPA) command (see Figure 10-1).

You will probably want to leave most of the FTP attributes set to their default configurations. However, you might want to consider changing a couple of them.

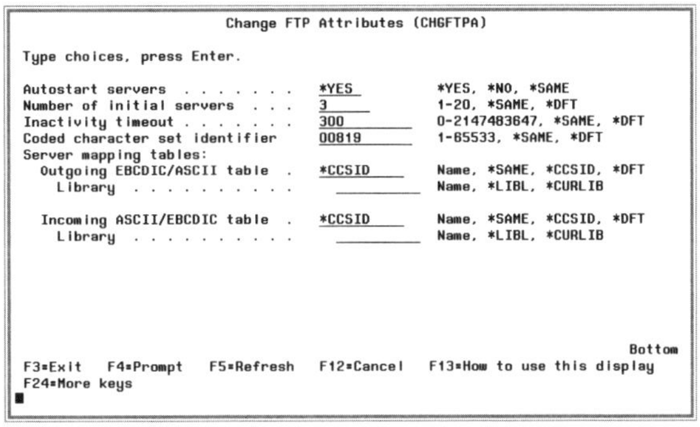

```
                      Change FTP Attributes (CHGFTPA)

 Type choices, press Enter.

 Autostart servers . . . . . . .    *YES        *YES, *NO, *SAME
 Number of initial servers . . .    3           1-20, *SAME, *DFT
 Inactivity timeout . . . . . . .   300         0-2147483647, *SAME, *DFT
 Coded character set identifier     00819       1-65533, *SAME, *DFT
 Server mapping tables:
   Outgoing EBCDIC/ASCII table  .    *CCSID      Name, *SAME, *CCSID, *DFT
     Library . . . . . . . . . .                 Name, *LIBL, *CURLIB

   Incoming ASCII/EBCDIC table  .    *CCSID      Name, *SAME, *CCSID, *DFT
     Library . . . . . . . . . .                 Name, *LIBL, *CURLIB




                                                               Bottom
 F3=Exit   F4=Prompt    F5=Refresh   F12=Cancel  F13=How to use this display
 F24=More keys
```

Figure 10-1: Setting the AS/400 FTP server attributes.

The NUMBER OF INITIAL SERVERS parameter defaults to 3. This is the number of FTP servers that start when TCP/IP is started. Having multiple FTP server jobs running improves the performance of initiating an FTP session when multiple users attempt to connect at the same time. If you think you are going to be serving many FTP users, increase this value.

The other parameter to consider changing is INACTIVITY TIMEOUT. This is the number of seconds the system allows an FTP connection to be inactive before it is automatically ended. The default value is 300 (which represents five minutes). If you are accessing your AS/400 through FTP and find that you are constantly receiving timeout error messages telling you that the remote host closed your connection, consider increasing this value.

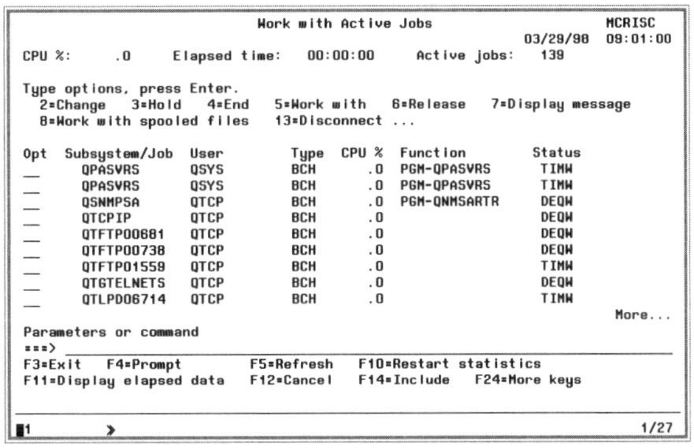

```
                          Work with Active Jobs             MCRISC
                                                    03/29/98  09:01:00
 CPU %:      .0   Elapsed time:   00:00:00    Active jobs:   139

 Type options, press Enter.
   2=Change   3=Hold    4=End     5=Work with   6=Release    7=Display message
   8=Work with spooled files   13=Disconnect ...

 Opt  Subsystem/Job  User     Type  CPU %  Function       Status
  _     QPASVRS      QSYS     BCH    .0    PGM-QPASVRS     TIMW
  _     QPASVRS      QSYS     BCH    .0    PGM-QPASVRS     TIMW
  _     QSNMPSA      QTCP     BCH    .0    PGM-QNMSARTR    DEQW
  _     QTCPIP       QTCP     BCH    .0                    DEQW
  _     QTFTP00681   QTCP     BCH    .0                    DEQW
  _     QTFTP00738   QTCP     BCH    .0                    DEQW
  _     QTFTP01559   QTCP     BCH    .0                    TIMW
  _     QTGTELNETS   QTCP     BCH    .0                    DEQW
  _     QTLPD06714   QTCP     BCH    .0                    TIMW
                                                           More...
 Parameters or command
 ===>
 F3=Exit   F4=Prompt      F5=Refresh   F10=Restart statistics
 F11=Display elapsed data  F12=Cancel  F14=Include   F24=More keys

 1     >                                                       1/27
```

Figure 10-2: The FTP server jobs is ready to receive client requests.

The FTP servers must be started before any other systems can make FTP requests. This will usually happen automatically when you run the STRTCP command. You can verify that the FTP servers are active by looking for job names, starting with QTFTP in subsystem QSYSWRK. Issue the command WRKACTJOB SBS(QSYSWRK). If you see these jobs, your system should be ready to accept FTP requests from an FTP client. See Figure 10-2.

TRANSFERRING FILES WITH FTP

Before you can transfer files with an FTP server, you must first know the host name or IP address of the server and a user ID and password (if required).

The following steps take you through a simple example of transferring a database file to a PC. FTP on Windows 95/NT can be done either with a graphical client or from the DOS command prompt. Work through the examples using the DOS commands to get a feel for how FTP works. To start a TCP/IP transfer, begin at the Windows command prompt.

1. Type "FTP" followed by a space and the TCP/IP name of your AS/400. Press the Enter key.

   ⇨ As you can see in Figure 10-3, FTP will be started on the PC, the AS/400 will be contacted, and you will be prompted for a user ID and password from the AS/400.

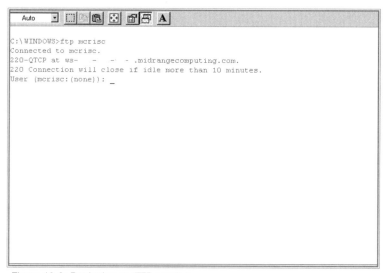

Figure 10-3: Beginning an FTP session.

2. Enter your AS/400 user ID and password when prompted.

   ⇨ You will be logged on the AS/400's FTP server.

⇨ You can use the same user ID and password as you use to sign on to the AS/400. Keep in mind that this ID and password could flow over the network in clear text unless you take security measures beyond the scope of this book. A sinister person running a network sniffer might be able to detect your user ID and password.

3. Enter the following command:

```
GET LIB/FILE.MEMBER <localfile>
```

⇨ Where lib is the library you want to retrieve data from, FILE is the name of the file to get, and MEMBER is the member name from which to retrieve data, you can leave the MEMBER parameter off if the member has the same name as the file. The <LOCALFILE> parameter is the full path and name of the file to be transferred. In Figure 10-4, you can see that I used c:\temp\testa.txt.

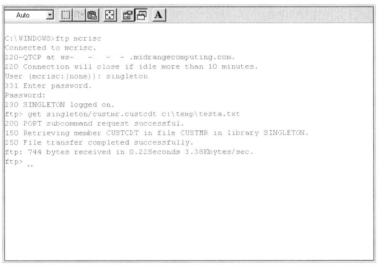

```
C:\WINDOWS>ftp mcrisc
Connected to mcrisc.
220-QTCP at ws- - - - .midrangecomputing.com.
220 Connection will close if idle more than 10 minutes.
User (mcrisc:(none)): singleton
331 Enter password.
Password:
230 SINGLETON logged on.
ftp> get singleton/custmr.custcdt c:\temp\testa.txt
200 PORT subcommand request successful.
150 Retrieving member CUSTCDT in file CUSTMR in library SINGLETON.
250 File transfer completed successfully.
ftp: 744 bytes received in 0.22Seconds 3.38Kbytes/sec.
ftp> ..
```

Figure 10-4: Retrieving a file with the get command.

4. To end the FTP session, type QUIT at the FTP command line.

⇨ By looking at the file you just transferred with something like NotePad, you'll see that, if it was a database file, the data comes through in columnar text. See Figure 10-5.

```
┌─────────────────────────────────────────────────────────────┐
│ ▤ testa.txt - Notepad                              _ □ ×      │
├─────────────────────────────────────────────────────────────┤
│ File  Edit  Search  Help                                      │
│ 938472Henning G K4859 Elm Ave  DallasTX752175000300370000000▲│
│ 839283Jones   B D21B NW 135 StClay   NY130410400101000000000 │
│ 392859Vine    S SPO Box 79     BrotonVT050460700104390000000 │
│ 938485Johnson J A3 Alpine Way Helen GA3054599992398750003350 │
│ 397267Tyron   W E13 Myrtle Dr HectorNY148411000100000000000  │
│ 389572Stevens K L208 Snow PassDenverCO802260400100587500015  │
│ 846283Alison  J S787 Lake Dr  Isle  MN563425000300100000000  │
│ 475938Doe     J W59 Archer Rd SutterCA956850700202500001000  │
│ 693829Thomas  A N3 Dove CircleCasperWY826099992000000000000  │
│ 593029WilliamsE D485 SE 2 Ave DallasTX752180200100250000000  │
│ 192837Lee     F L5963 Oak St  HectorNY148410700204895000005  │
│ 583990Abraham M T392 Mill St  Isle  MN563429999305000000000  │
│                                                             ▼│
│ ◄                                                          ► │
└─────────────────────────────────────────────────────────────┘
```

Figure 10-5: Viewing a file transferred by FTP.

FTP COMMANDS

FTP has a small number of commands that you'll use to get things accomplished. Table 10-1 lists the more commonly used FTP subcommands and their meanings.

A complete list of FTP subcommands can be viewed by keying "HELP" on the FTP command line. Help text for a specific subcommand can be viewed by typing a question mark (?) followed by the subcommand on the FTP command line.

FTP takes care of all character translation for the transferred files. AS/400 files transferred to a remote PC are translated to nondelimited ASCII files.

NAMEFMT—GETTING YOU TO YOUR AS/400 DATA

The AS/400 has several filing systems that can all be accessed through FTP. Normally, AS/400 data files and programs are stored in the library system. But objects also can be stored in the AS/400's IFS.

Some of FTP's syntax is similar to MS-DOS based file syntax. For example, the CD command will change directories, the DIR command will list the contents of a directory, etc.

In order to allow access to the AS/400's standard library system and the IFS within the context of FTP's commands, IBM had to use some "tricks" to allow us to specify the files we want. Within AS/400 FTP, there is a setting called the name format (NAMEFMT). The name format setting helps determine file references. There are two settings to the NAMEFMT parameter.

Table 10-1: Some Basic FTP Commands	
FTP COMMAND	**PURPOSE**
OPEN	Connect to an FTP server from an FTP client.
CLOSE	Disconnect from an FTP server from within an FTP CLIENT session. Does not end the client session.
QUIT	Disconnect from all connected FTP servers and end the FTP session.
PUT	Transfer a file from the AS/400 client to the FTP server. The syntax is: PUT library/file.member target_file_name.
GET	Retrieve a file from the remote server to the AS/400 client.
CD	Change the current directory of the remote FTP server.
DIR	List the files in the current directory of the remote FTP server.
USER	Send your user ID (logon) to the remote FTP server.
PWD	Send your password to the remote FTP server.
ASCII	Changes the default transfer type to ASCII. Use this before transferring data files. Syntax: ASCII <enter>
DIR	List the files in the current directory of the remote FTP server.
USER	Send your user ID (logon) to the remote FTP server.
PWD	Send your password to the remote FTP server.
ASCII	Changes the default transfer type to ASCII. Use this before transferring data files. Syntax: ASCII <enter>
BINARY	Set the transfer mode to IMAGE. Use this to transfer binary objects such as save files. Syntax: BINARY >enter>

❖ NAMEFMT 0 sets all subsequent FTP commands to operate on the AS/400's standard library system.

❖ NAMEFMT 1 sets subsequent FTP commands to work within the context of the IFS system.

❖ In order to set the name format on the AS/400, you must be able to pass a command to set the state of the AS/400 FTP server. This is done with the QUOTE SITE command.

❖ QUOTE SITE NAMEFMT 1 is the full syntax to set all subsequent file commands to act upon IFS data. See Figure 10-6.

Figure 10-6: Setting the name format to 1.

❖ QUOTE SITE NAMEFMT 0 is the full syntax to set all subsequent file commands to act upon standard AS/400 library system data.

While it's good to know about the preceding list of tricks, what if you want to use an FTP client that doesn't know about the AS/400-specific NAMEFMT command? Fortunately, the clever people at Rochester thought of a method to implicitly set the NAMEFMT.

By default, the AS/400 FTP server uses NAMEFMT 0, which accesses things in the standard library system. You can change the NAMEFMT without using the QUOTE SITE method by being careful about the way you specify your file name.

To set the NAMEFMT to 1, begin the first file name of your session with a / or a ~ character.

Example 1. After logging on, entering "DIR /SINGLETON" sets NAMEFMT to 1, and the contents of the directory named SINGLETON are listed. See Figure 10-7. Note that typing "DIR ~SINGLETON" would have the same effect.

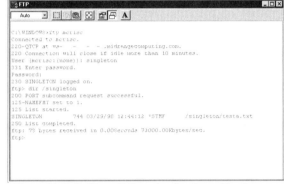

Figure 10-7: Getting a listing of a directory without setting namefmt.

Example 2. After logging on and entering DIR SINGLETON, the NAMEFMT is set to 1, and the contents of the library named SINGLETON are listed. See Figure 10-8.

As you can see, the NAMEFMT parameter of the AS/400 is a clever way to allow you to get to all the data on the AS/400 no matter which filing system it resides in.

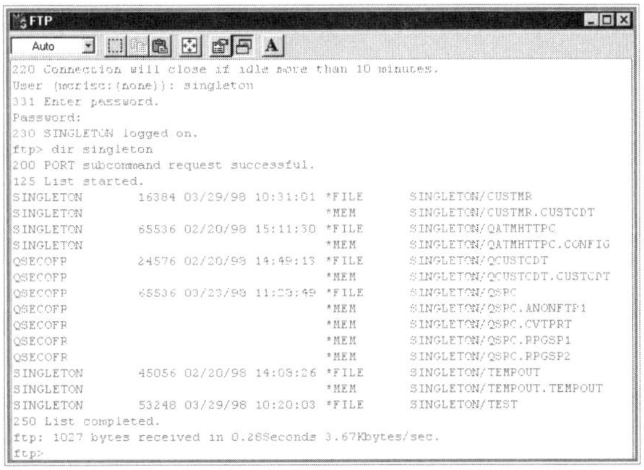

TO FTP OR NOT TO FTP?

In today's world, the need to communicate and transfer files between diverse systems is steadily growing.

Figure 10-8: Getting a listing of a library without setting namefmt.

The FTP file transfer application—that venerable building block of TCP/IP—provides an easy, fast, dependable method for filling that need. The strengths of FTP lie in its flexibility. FTP is a versatile tool that has some limitations. While it won't be the best choice in every situation, it has capabilities that shouldn't be overlooked when transferring data. Sometimes old and reliable is fancy and flexible. Armed with the information in this chapter, you'll know when each is appropriate.

Appendix A
Installing the Sample Data

Many of the samples and exercises throughout this book are performed with sample data. Having a separate library with some sample data that you can play with ensures that you are free to learn and experiment with the Microsoft Office products and AS/400 data without worrying about somehow causing a problem with production data.

Installing the sample data allows you to follow along with the exercises in each chapter. This is the same data used to create the examples and screen images for this book. However, If you aren't able to install the sample data for some reason, you should be able to apply the examples you've seen to your own data. The sample data is provided for illustration purposes only.

The sample data comes in the form of an Access database that can be obtained from Midrange Computing over the Internet. Point your browser to http://www. midrange-computing.com/ftp/prog/officebook to find out how to download the data to your PC. Once the data has been copied to your PC, you can upload it to your AS/400 using Microsoft Access and the following procedures. Note that any revised instructions will be provided on the Web page mentioned above and, if present, they supercede the instructions printed here.

To upload the sample data using this procedure, you must have Microsoft Access. If you don't have Access, check the above-mentioned Web site for more information.

LOADING THE SAMPLE DATA

There are several steps to loading the sample data on your AS/400.

1. Retrieve the data from the Midrange Computing Web site. The URL is

   `http://www.midrangecomputing.com/ftp/prog/officebook`.

   Save the data to your hard drive using the procedures outlined on the page. Once you have completed those procedures, you should have a Microsoft Access database called MCDATA.MDB on your system.

2. Make sure you have an ODBC DSN configured for your AS/400 database.

   ➪ For detailed information see chapter 3. Make sure that you set the first entry in the DSN's DEFAULT LIBRARIES parameter to the library where you want the data to be placed. This is because Access will not ask you to specify in which library to place the data. The data automatically goes in the default library.

3. Double-click on MCDATA.MDB.

   ➪ This will load Microsoft Access and the MCDATA database (Figure A-1).

4. Create a library or collection for the data on the AS/400.

   ➪ To create a library from an AS/400 command line, enter the following command:

   CRTLIB LIBNAME TEXT(MS OFFICE SAMPLE DATA)

   ➪ A library also can be created by creating a pass-through query in Access and issuing the CREATE COLLECTION SQL statement. See chapter 6 for more information on creating pass-through queries.

5. From the Access TABLES panel, right-click on the table you want to export and select SAVE AS/EXPORT from the menu (Figure A-2).

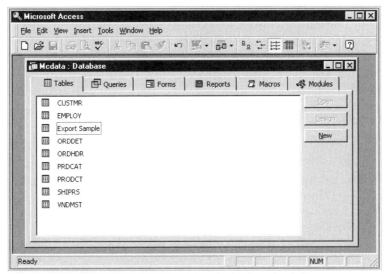

Figure A-1: Microsoft Access with the sample database loaded.

Figure A-2: Selecting SAVE AS/EXPORT.

6. Select TO AN EXTERNAL FILE OR DATABASE on the SAVE AS screen.

⇨ This will allow you to save the data to an ODBC data source and it brings
     up a screen like the example shown in Figure A-3.

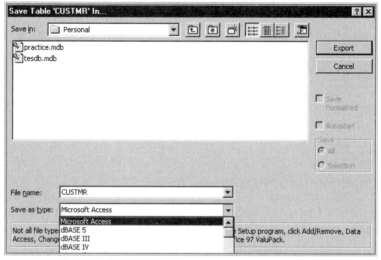

Figure A-3: Selecting ODBC Databases.

7. In the FILES OF TYPE parameter, select ODBC DATABASES.

⇨ The destination name screen will immediately appear.

8. Enter a name (or leave it as the default) and click the ok button.

⇨ I used the default name because it's short and will work well on the
     AS/400.

9. Choose your ODBC DSN from the screen shown in Figure A-4.

⇨ Once you choose your DSN, Access will immediately begin exporting your
     table. Remember, the table will be created in the default library (see step
     2). When Access is done, you'll be returned to the main database window
     (Figure A-1).

⇨ Repeat steps 5 through 9 for each table sent to your AS/400.

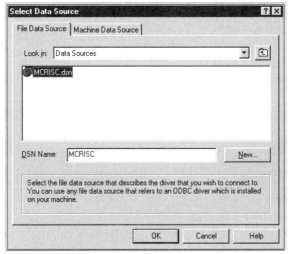

Figure A-4: Choose your ODBC DSN.

CREATING UNIQUE INDEXES

When you export a table from Microsoft Access to the AS/400, no index or key information is created for the new file on the AS/400. If you want to be able to update the data through Access, you must create a unique index for the file. While this is detailed in chapter 6, here are the steps to create a unique index on the sample tables.

1. Begin with the sample database loaded. Click the QUERIES tab.

   ➪ You want to create a pass-through query that builds a unique index over the sample data file on the AS/400.

2. Click the NEW button.

The screen shown in Figure A-5 will be displayed.

3. Select DESIGN VIEW and click the OK button.

   ➪ Access shows a screen with a list of the tables in the database.

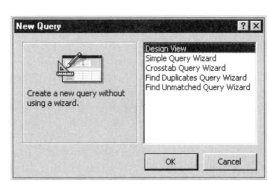

Figure A-5: Creating a new query.

4. Click the CLOSE button without selecting any tables.

⇨ You will be building a pass-through query.

5. From the QUERY menu, choose SQL SPECIFIC and then PASS-THROUGH. See Figure A-6.

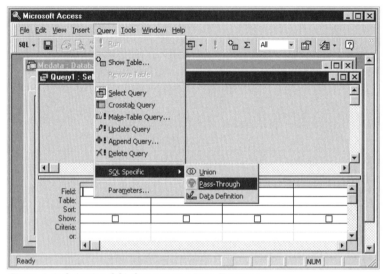

Figure A-6: Selecting SQL SPECIFIC and PASS-THROUGH.

⇨ The screen changes to where you can enter the SQL statements that are to be executed on the AS/400.

6. As shown in Figure A-7, enter the following SQL statement:

CREATE UNIQUE INDEX DATALIB.CUSTM1 ON DATALIB.CUSTMR (CUSTID)

⇨ This will create a unique index named CUSTM1 in DATALIB. The index will be keyed on the CUSTID field of the CUSTMR file.

⇨ For each occurrence of DATALIB in the above SQL statement, you should substitute the name of the library where your test data resides.

7. Click the RUN button on the toolbar (the exclamation point).

⇨ You will be asked to choose an ODBC data source.

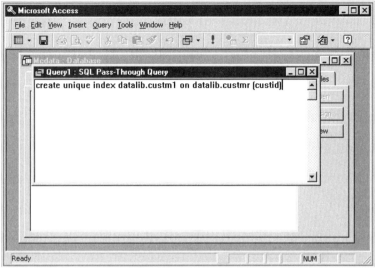

Figure A-7: Using SQL to create a unique index on the AS/400.

8. Choose your ODBC data source and press OK.

⇨   The SQL statement will be passed through to the AS/400 and executed
    there. When the query is completed, you'll get a message saying that the
    query didn't return any records. This is normal for this type of query. If
    you want to turn off this message in future queries of this type, edit the
    query properties to set the RETURNS RECORDS parameter to NO. See chapter
    6 for more information.

Repeat the index creation process for each sample table that you want to be able to
update. A list of the sample tables and their key fields is shown in Table A-1.

Table A-1: Sample Database Tables and Key Fields.	
SAMPLE TABLE NAME	KEY FIELDS
CUSTMR	CUSTID
EMPLOY	EMPID
ORDDET	ORDID, PRODID
ORDHDR	ORDID
PRDCAT	CATID
PRODCT	PRODID
SHIPRS	SHIPID
VNDMST	SUPID
EXPORT SAMPLE	N/A

Appendix B
Support and Troubleshooting

S ometimes, despite our best efforts, things don't work the way we want them to. This seems specially true in computers. When problems happen, it's good to have resources to rely on to help diagnose problems and find solutions. In this appendix, I also will show you some resources available that you can turn to when you can't figure the problem out on your own.

WEB RESOURCES

Probably the best location you turn to for troubleshooting and support is the World Wide Web. IBM has a very large Web site dedicated to the AS/400 and there are numerous other Web resources available.

IBM's Web site includes reams of technical information about many different aspects of the AS/400. On the IBM Web site, it's sometimes difficult to find things because the site tries to be all things to all people in regards to the AS/400. Don't worry, however, because I've got some URLs that will lead you to the type of information you can use to solve problems related to Client Access and Microsoft Office.

The place to start is the Client Access home page (Figure B-1) in Rochester. The URL is

`http://www.as400.ibm.com/.`

On this page, you'll find links to the latest Client Access news, downloads, and troubleshooting information. Begin by checking the Client Access Informational APARs.

Figure B-1: The IBM Client Access home page.

For issues related to the Microsoft Office programs, the place to begin is http://www.microsoft.com/office. This is the Microsoft Office home page (Figure B-2). From here, you should be able to get product and support information.

For this book, a home page is located on Midrange Computing's Web site (Figure B-3). The Midrange Computing Web site home page is at http://www.midrangecomputing.com and the direct URL to the book page is http://www.midrangecomputing.com/ftp/prog/officebook.

Figure B-2: The Microsoft Office home page.

Figure B-3: The Midrange Computing home page.

For general AS/400 related technical information, IBM has a great Web site at http://www.as400.ibm.com/techstudio. This is their TechStudio Web site, and it contains a wealth of technical information for the AS/400.

NEWSGROUP RESOURCES

Another Internet resource that can be very valuable for getting general support from other AS/400 professionals from around the world is the Usenet newsgroup comp.sys.ibm.as400.misc.

Newsgroups are message-based discussion groups. Messages entered on one server are replicated to other servers throughout the world. When you ask a question or give an answer, the message will be seen by most people who view the newsgroup. The reason I say "most people" is that the process isn't 100 percent guaranteed. Some articles could get lost on some servers and your server might not get all articles everyone sends. For the most part, it is a reliable means of communication.

A news reader program is required to view newsgroups. Newsreaders are provided with both Microsoft's Internet Explorer and Netscape's Communicator (most users should have one or the other). The configuration varies depending upon the program used, but the general configuration information to supply is the name of your news server, which you can usually get from your ISP, and the name of the newsgroup, which is: COMP.SYS.IBM.AS400.MISC.

Another way to access the newsgroups using only a Web browser is to go to http://www.dejanews.com/. DejaNews is a Web site that archives the Usenet newsgroups. It has excellent searching capabilities and long message retention. Therefore, you should be able to determine if someone has asked the same question before by searching the COMP.SYS.IBM.AS400.MISC newsgroup using DejaNews. If you can't find the answer, you can always use DejaNews to post your question to the newsgroup.

As you can see, there are many resources available to help in the troubleshooting process. Each of the resources mentioned above has links to other resources. I've shown you just the tip of the iceberg. I encourage you to explore these links to mine the wealth of information available online.

INDEX

Note: Boldface numbers indicate illustrations

E

e-mail with Microsoft Outlook, 213-230
  addresses in e-mail, 226
  advanced settings, configuration, 228, **228**
  AS/400 set up as mail server, 213, 215-230
  check for e-mail, 229, **229**
  client configuration, 223-228, **224-228**
  connections, 227, **227**
  post office protocol 3 (POP3), 213-215, 222-223, **223**
  properties configuration, 225-226, **226**
  QSNADS subsystem up and running, 215-216, **215, 216**
  reading e-mail, 229-230
  routing tables in TCP/IP, 217-218
  server properties configuration, 226-227
  SERVICES configuration, 224-225, **224, 225**
  simple mail transfer protocol (SMTP), 213-215, 216-218, **216-219**
  system-distribution directory entries, 220-222, **220-222**
  TCP/IP configuration, 214, 217-218, **217**
  user profile creation, 219-220, **219, 220**
envelopes (*See* addressed envelopes)
Excel (*See* Microsoft Excel)
exit programs, exit points, 25
exporting data in Access, 198-203
  configuring ODBC driver for library, 199
  library selection, 198-199, **198, 199**
  limitations to exporting, 203
  location for export, 200, 201, **201**
  name of table, 202-203
  Save As/Export, 200, **201**
  table selection, 200
expression fields, in Access, 146, **147**
expressions in calculated fields, 55-56

F

file description files (FDF), data-transfer function, 248
File DSNs, 14-15
file formats supported by data-transfer function, 249-250
file transfer protocol (FTP) (*See also* data-transfer function), 271-282
  ASCII files, 274
  commands, 278-281
  configuring AS/400 TCP/IP, 274-275, **275**
  cross-platform interoperability, 272
  disadvantages of use, 273

EBCDIC files, 274
  formats supported by FTC, 274
  FTP client component use, 273
  host names and addresses, 276
  image or binary files, 274
  NAMEFMT (Name Format) for AS/400 data, 278-281
  QSYSWRK subsystem location, 275
  REMOTE SYSTEM parameter setting, 274
  router programs unnecessary, 272
  save files, 272-273
  speed of transfers, 272
  step-by-step file transfer process, 276-278, **276-278**
  subcommands, 273-274
  TCP/IP and, 271-272
  timeouts, INACTIVITY TIMEOUT setting, 275
filters, in Access, 134, 138, **139**, 140
filters, in Query, 44-45, **44**, 50-52, **50, 51**
form letters, 69-73, **73**
  creating the letter document, 69
  getting source data, 69-72, 69
  merge fields added to letter, 70-71, **71**
  merging letter and source data, 72-73, **72**
forms in Access, 159-176
  calculated fields, 172
  chart wizard, 160
  columnar autoforms, 159
  creating a form, 160-164, **160, 161, 162**
  customizing a form, 164-169, **165-168**
  datasheet autoforms, 160
  fields in form, 160, **161**, 162
  graph forms, 171-176, **171-176**
  labeling fields, 166, **166**
  layout (design) of form, 162, **162**
  moving fields, 167, **167**
  PivotTable wizard, 160
  properties for fields, 168-169, **168, 169**
  sizing fields, 168
  style (design) of form, 162-163, **163**
  tabular autoforms, 159, 169-171, **170**
  title for form, 163, **163**
  viewing a form, 164

G

garbage data, data-transfer function, 266-267
graphs with Access, 171-176, **171-176**
grouping data, in Query, 56-57, **57**

H

header tables, 52